THE INTERNATIONAL LIBRARY OF PSYCHOLOGY,
PHILOSOPHY AND SCIENTIFIC METHOD

Edited by C. K. OGDEN

THE CHILD'S CONCEPTION OF PHYSICAL CAUSALITY

By JEAN PIAGET

About the Series

THE PURPOSE of *The International Library* is to give expression, in a convenient form and at a moderate price, to the remarkable developments which have recently occurred in Psychology and its allied sciences. The older philosophers were preoccupied by metaphysical interests which, for the most part, have ceased to attract the younger investigators, and their forbidding terminology too often acted as a deterrent for the general reader. The attempt to deal in clear language with current tendencies, has met with a very encouraging reception, and not only have accepted authorities been invited to explain the newer theories, but it has been found possible to include a number of original contributions of high merit.

INTERNATIONAL LIBRARY OF PSYCHOLOGY, PHILOSOPHY AND SCIENTIFIC METHOD

Edited by C. K. OGDEN

Many other titles to be published soon

The Child's Conception of Physical Causality

By

JEAN PIAGET

Doctor of Science, Professor at the University of Geneva, Director of the International Bureau of Education, Co-Director of the Institut J. J. Rousseau, Geneva; Author of "Language and Thought of the Child," "Judgment and Reasoning in the Child," "The Psychology of Intelligence"

Translated by

MARJORIE GABAIN

1969

LITTLEFIELD, ADAMS & CO.
Totowa, New Jersey

INTERNATIONAL LIBRARY OF PSYCHOLOGY,
PHILOSOPHY AND SCIENTIFIC METHOD

Edited by C. K. OGDEN

Reprinted, 1969

PUBLISHED BY LITTLEFIELD, ADAMS & CO.

Reprinted by arrangement with Humanities Press, Inc.

For sale only in the U.S.A., its possessions, and territories.

•

•

First published in the English language by Routledge and Kegan Paul, Ltd., London, in 1930 and reprinted in 1951. Cloth editions available from Humanities Press, Inc., New York, in the United States of America.

Students and former students of the Institut J. J. Rousseau who have collaborated in this work.

M. G. BIELER (Chaps. I and II).
Mlle. A. BODOURIAN (Chap. VIII).
Mlle. DAIBER (Chap. VI.)
Mlle. G. GUEX (Chaps. II, III and IV).
Mlle. L. HAHNLOSER (Chaps. VI and VII).
Mlle. R. HEPNER (Chaps. III and IV).
Mlle. HERZOG (Chap. VI).
Mlle. H. KRAFFT (Chaps. III and IV).
Mlle. J. LEBHERZ (Chaps. X and XI).
Mlle. E. MARGAIRAZ (Chaps. III and IV).
Mme. V. J. PIAGET (Chaps. II, III, IV and V).
Mlle. H. REHFOUS (Chaps. X and XI).
Mlle. M. RODRIGO (Chaps. III and IV).
Mlle. M. ROUD (Chaps. III and IV).
Mlle. N. SVETLOVA (Chap. VIII).
Dr VERSTEEG (Chaps. I and II).
Mlle. ZWICKHARDT (Chaps. I and II).

CONTENTS

SECTION I

EXPLANATION OF MOVEMENT

CONTENTS

SECTION I

EXPLANATION OF MOVEMENT

IN an earlier volume [1] we have tried to establish what
are the outstanding features of the child's conception of
the world. Intellectualism, animism, and artificialism
were what we found to be its prevailing notes. We
shall now proceed to make a more detailed analysis, and
to see whether, connected with mental realism, with
animism, and with artificialism, there is not a corresponding
conception of material force and a system of physics
peculiar to the child.

Three methods present themselves for this purpose ;
they are of unequal value, but must be used in con-
junction if nothing of interest is to be allowed to escape.
The first is the purely verbal method, and consists in
asking the children whether bodies (or a series of bodies
named in a given order) have weight, and if so, why.
In this way we obtain the definition of the verbal idea
of material force. The second method is half verbal,
half practical : a certain number of movements (those of
clouds, of rivers, of the parts of a machine, etc.) are
enumerated to the child who is then questioned as to
why and how these movements are performed. This
method gives a more direct view of child dynamics, but
one that is still tainted with verbalism, since no mani-
pulation is possible. Finally comes the third method
which is, as far as possible, direct : little experiments in
physics are carried out before the child, and he is questioned
as to " how " each event takes place. This gives first-
hand information about the mental orientation of children.

[1] J. Piaget, *The Child's Conception of the World* (this Library), 1928.

1

In the present section these three methods will be used in turn. Our procedure may seem unusual, but it is the fruit of earlier experimentation rather than of any pre-conceived ideas. We shall begin with the study of children's ideas about air, its movement and its origin. As will appear later, a large number of natural move-ments, such as those of the heavenly bodies, of rivers, of clouds, etc., are believed by the child to be produced by wind. Only, this statement is incomprehensible—we failed ourselves to understand it for many years—so long as no exact information has been collected about the explana-tions which children give of the wind itself ; for, strange to say, the wind is often believed to be produced by the actual clouds or waves that are in movement. One or more vicious circles would therefore seem to exist within the mind of the child, and we must beware of letting adult logic mislead us as to their nature. Above all, care must be taken to avoid distortion of meaning or, as the physicists call it, "systematic error", by which they mean mistakes that are the outcome of the very way in which the experiments are set, for these mistakes vitiate every result, and always in the same sense. It is in order to steer clear of this danger that we have begun our enquiry with an analysis of children's ideas about air. Once this analysis has been completed, we shall be able to examine the explanations given by the child concerning natural movements, and then pass on to a description of the idea of physical force.

CHAPTER I

EXPERIMENTS CONCERNING THE
NATURE OF AIR

THE problem of air is highly interesting to children and a large number of spontaneous questions bear witness to their natural curiosity about wind and air in general. Sully [1] mentions children, some of whom believed that wind was caused by a large fan waved by an unseen being, and others that it was produced by the movement of trees. Stanley Hall [2] quotes the following questions of a boy of six : " *What makes the wind blow ? Is someone pushing it ? I thought it would have to stop when it went against a house or a big tree. Does it know that it is making our pages blow over ?* " Miss Morse Nice [3] took down these questions of a child of four : " *What is air ? How do people make air ? What makes air ?* " These questions show that there exists in very young children a spontaneous interest in air and wind, together with a spontaneous tendency to think of wind as both alive and produced by human beings (animism and artificialism combined).

How can one get at children's real ideas about these matters ? The enquiry has been carried out here in a very concrete and direct manner, and is one in which no effort must be spared in the attempt to avoid verbalism and to capture the child's immediate reactions. This, after much tentative groping, is the method we adopted. First experiment : we show the child the lid of a box attached to a piece of string. We then put a penny in

[1] *Studies of Childhood*, pp. 98 and 99.
[2] *Pedag. Semin.*, 1903 (Vol. X), " Curiosity and Interest."
[3] *Ibid.*, 1921, p. 23.

the lid, swing the string round on a vertical plane, and ask the child why the penny does not fall out of the box. This preliminary experiment does not seem to have any connection with air. But, as will be seen later, it is by referring to the movement of the air that (at least in the succeeding stage) the child explains why the penny does not drop. Second experiment : we clasp our two hands together, and, by repeated pressure of the palms, produce a small current of air which the child generally becomes aware of with extreme surprise. We then ask the child where this air comes from, etc. Third experiment : we give the child an india-rubber ball punctured at a point which is clearly visible. We deflate the ball, taking care to direct the jet of air against the child's hand or cheek. The ball is thus completely deflated, and the child is made to observe that it is flat and contains no more air. We then let it fill itself with air and begin the experiment over again. We ask the child where the air comes from that is in the ball, where the air comes from that has gone into the ball, and so on. Later on, the same game is played with a small tube, or with a bicycle pump, etc. Fourth experiment : the lid is again swung round, but without the penny, and horizontally. The child is asked where the air comes from which this movement produces. A fan may also be used, but this is not necessary. Fifth experiment : the child is told to blow on his hand and is asked where this air comes from, where the air comes from that is in his mouth, etc. This leads to a series of questions on breathing. Finally, the sixth point which is purely verbal : the child is asked where the wind comes from, how it began, etc. It is naturally a good thing to add to these six questions other complementary enquiries as to the consciousness or life of the air.[1]

The order of succession given to these six groups of questions is intended to avoid as far as possible any suggestion " by perseveration ". The questions about the

[1] We also asked some of the children two sets of additional questions of which the results will be given in § 3 and § 4.

wind should only come at the end, otherwise the child will bring in the wind at every point. Finally, it goes without saying that as an indispensable precaution the room in which the experiments are carried out should be entirely shut in, even in summer. The windows should even be closed before the child arrives on the scene, otherwise he will not fail to say (at least if he is under 7–8) that the air of the hands or of the ball, etc., has just come in through the window, the room being ordinarily thought of as empty of air.

In the following exposition we shall pay no attention to the order in which the experiments have been carried out. The questions about wind and breathing, moreover, will be kept for the next chapter.

§ 1. PRESSURE OF THE HANDS.—The answers given by the children to the questions we asked in the second of our experiments, that of the pressure of hands, may roughly be divided into four stages. During the first stage, which extends on the average up to the age of six (average age of this stage : 5 years and 4 months), the child admits that the air issuing from the hands is due to the actual pressure, the room being considered as empty of air ; but in addition, and this is what characterises this particular stage, the hands, in producing air, attract, so to speak, a supplementary quantity of air which comes in from outside (air passing through the closed windows). Thus what characterises this first stage is an immediate participation between the air produced by the hands and a reservoir of wind out of doors. During a second stage, in which the average age is 7, the air is conceived as being produced by the pressure of the hands (the room being thought of as empty) but this pressure causes air to come out of the skin and the interior of the body. During a third stage (average age 8), the air is simply produced by the hands without any additional factor. Finally, when at about the age of 9 the fourth stage is reached, the mechanism is understood : the room is full of air and the hands simply collect and then send out again the air that surrounds them.

Here are some examples from the first stage, which is very interesting from the point of view of the child's conception of physical causality : the air from outside comes in obedience, as it were, to a call, and comes through the closed window.

BAT (4) tells us that the sound he hears is due to the air: "Where does it come from? . . ." [1] "Where does the air come from ?—*Through the window.*—Is it open ?—*No, shut.*—And yet the air could get through ?—*Yes.*—Where ?— . . . Look at my hands [they are open before him]. Is there any air in them ?—*No.*—And now [pressing them one against the other] ?—*Yes.*—Where does it come from ?—*From the window.*—Is there any in the room ? —*No.*"

ZEL (4½) : " Look, do you hear ? What is it ?—*Wind.* —Where does it come from ?—*From the window.*—Is there any wind in my hands ?—*No.*—And in the room ? —*No.*—And now [hand pressing] ?—*Yes.*—Where does it come from ?—*From the hands.*—And where does the wind in the hands come from ?—*From the window.*—And the wind in the window ?—*From the sky.*—How did it get in ?—*By the window, and then it went into the hands.*— When did it come ?—*When you did that* [when the hands are pressed together].—How did it come ?—*I don't know.* —How ?—*In between the window.* [The window is, of course, closed. Zel is supposing that the wind comes through the chink between the two sides of the French-window.] "

TAQ (7 ; 4. G.) [2] : " What am I doing ?—*You are shutting your fingers and then clapping.*" " It is blowing.— What is it ?—*Like the wind.*—Where does it come from ? —*From your hands.*—What is it that blows ?—*Wind.*— What is it called ? Air ?—*Yes.*" " Where does it come from ?—*It's the wind that comes from your hands.*—And where does the wind in my hands come from ?—*From outside.* (Taq points to the closed window.)—The air comes from outside, does it ? How ?—*Through the window.*—Is it open ?—*No. Through your open hand.*— [The experiment is repeated.] Is the wind coming now ?— *No . . . yes.*—How does it get in ?—*It comes into the*

---

[1] Throughout, only the children's words are in *italics*.
[2] 7 ; 4 = 7 years and 4 months completed. G = girl.

room, then it goes into your hand.—Is the window open ?—
It was open just a minute ago.—And the wind came in ?—
No. It is outside.—Is there any wind in here ?—*No.*"
" Is there any air on this table ?—*No.*—Here [pointing
up] ?—*No.*—Here ?—*No.*—On the floor ?—*No.*"   " How
does the wind manage to get in when I do this with my
hands ?— . . . —Could a butterfly get in ?—*No.*—And
could the wind ?—*Yes.*—What way ?--*By the window.*"
" Does the air get in through the window even when it is
shut ?—*Yes.*"

MONT (7 ; 2) The experiment is done and Mont exclaims : " *There is air !*—Where does it come from ?—
From outside. [He points to the street].—Is there any
outside ?—*Yes.*—And in the room ?—*No.*—Here [in the
hands] ?—*Yes.*—How is that ?   Where does it come
from ?--*From outside.*— . . . —What makes the air ?—
The hand makes the air.—How ?— . . ." We then try to
help Mont by showing him the displacement of air due
to the rotation of the box. " Where does this air come
from ?—*From inside there.*—And the air inside there ?—
From outside."   " Where does it come from ?—*From
inside there.*—How is that ?—*When you turn it round, it
makes air.*—Why ?—*Because it is cold* [the rotating lid
does produce a cold current].—Where does this air come
from ?—*From inside there.*—Then it doesn't come from
outside ?   Or does it come from outside ?—*From outside.*
—Show me where outside is [he points towards the street].
—[We return to the experiment of the hands.]   Where
does this air come from ?—*From outside.*"   The con-
versation is continued, but the answer is always the
same.   The case, then, is quite clear.   The rotation of
the box and the pressing together of the hands produce
air which immediately attracts the air from outside.

RE (8) : " What's happening ?—*It's blowing.*—Why ?—
Because you're clapping your hands.—What is blowing ?—
The air.—Where does it come from ?—*From outside.*—
Where from ?—*From the street.*—Is there any air in the
room ?—*There is in our room.*—Where ?—*Not here, at
home.*—Why is there at home ?—*'Cos it's cold.*   [It is
winter, and poor little Re does not look very well off].—
Is there air in here ?—*No.*—Why is there not any in this
room ?—*Because everything is shut.*—Is there some in my
hand ?—*No.*—And now [hands half closed] ?—*No.*—And
now ?—*Yes. When you clap your hands it makes air.*—
Where does the air come from ?—*From outside.*—Where ?

—From the street.—Did it come from the street into my hands ? — *No . . . yes . . . because you clapped your hands.*" Here again it is definitely asserted that the air is produced both by the pressure of the hands and by an irruption of external air which has been attracted precisely by the current of air made by the hands.

We need not multiply these examples of the first stage, of which we shall find the equivalent in connection with the experiments of the ball, the little tube, the box, etc. It will now be clear wherein the phenomenon consists. The child maintains that it is sufficient to squeeze one's hands together to make air, even though there is none in the room. But he adds that as soon as the hands are pressed together, the air comes rushing in from the street. In all the cases quoted this duality of origin is unmistakable : it is the hand that " makes air " (Taq, Mont, Re), but at the same time, the air comes " from outside " (same cases). This fact is of the utmost significance, and is no isolated feature. We shall meet with a large number of explanations by " agglomeration of causes "; in particular, we shall come across children who maintain that the shadow cast by an object on a table comes both from the object, from the night, and from under the trees. Are we dealing in the question of air with a case of action at a distance ? There is no need in the child's mind for such a concept as this. Air may easily be thought of as a fluid sufficiently subtle to pass through a closed window. Is it a case, then, of " attraction " ? But this is a grown-up way of speaking. The child does not go into details as to the " how " of things. The only adequate way of putting it is to say that there is " participation " between the outside air and that produced by the hands : there is wind out of doors, and the hands make wind, and these two kinds of wind are directly and concretely assimilated one to the other, regardless of " how " the relation effected. Such is the process which we designate under the name of participation. In a sense, this participation is rational, since it is an attempt to get at the origin of the wind produced by the hands. In another sense, it is not rational, since on the one hand, no concern is felt as to the " how " of such an explanation, and on the other, the origin of the wind in the hands is conceived as dual, without this duality in any way worrying the child. The hands make wind, but this wind is at the same time air from outside.

This childish conception would seem to admit of the following explanation. For lack of having subsumed particular cases under a general law, the child identifies one case with the other, not only logically but materially. He creates participations owing to his failure to establish comparisons. For, after all, why is it that when we identify the current of air made by the hands with the air out of doors, our identification applies, not to reality, but only to logic ? It is, in the first place, because we compare these two kinds of air currents so as to find what is common to both, and secondly, because we look upon this *quid commune*, not as the direct action of one current upon another, but as a general abstract law of the form : " All movement produces a current of air, etc." Like the child, we say : " The current of air produced by the movements of the hands is identical with the wind outside", but "identical" here means "comparable with", or "forming part of the same genus", or "actuated by the same law". The child, on the contrary, through deficient power of abstraction and synthesis, does not look for a law common to both kinds of air currents, and if by comparison we mean the search for the abstract common element, he does not compare. He actually identifies the two, which is the first stage of comparison. Analogy is felt as identity of being, and identity of being implies real participation.

It may be objected that the whole matter is much simpler, and that the child is merely looking for the origin of the air that has been displaced by the hands, just because he has failed to see that the movements made by the hands are sufficient to create the air. In this case, the child would be admitting, like ourselves, that the hands merely displace air without actually forming any, but as he is ignorant of the fact that the room is full of air, he has recourse to the air from outside in order to explain the phenomenon. Unfortunately, this interpretation is contradicted by the following facts. It is only in the later stages that the child discovers that air is a substance that can exist in an immobile state. Before that, the child knows only of " wind ", or air in movement. Moreover, even in the third stage the child still believes that the hands create air by moving, and would do so in an empty room. In the first stage, therefore, the child really does think that the hands create wind (air in movement) and that this wind, or the action of the hands, draws in the air from the street. There is genuine participation. The authenticity of the fact itself, however, will perhaps be called in question, and doubt thrown upon its claim to being based on observation. But we shall meet with this same fact in many forms in connection with other experiments, and above all, we shall find unmistakable traces of it in children capable of reaching the second, the third, and even the fourth stage.

In the meantime, let us turn to the answers of the second stage. They show a marked advance upon those of the first stage, in that the child tries to imagine an immobile supply of air, and places it in the body. The current of air made by pressing the hands together now becomes intelligible. When we squeeze our hands, air comes out of the skin, because we are " full of air ".

GAVA (6½) : " What am I doing ?—*You are clapping.*— What do you hear ?—*A slap.*—What is it ?—*The hands.*— What are the hands doing ?—*They are clapping and that makes it blow.*—What is blowing ?—*Wind.*—Where does the wind come from ?—*From the hands.*—And the wind of the hands ?—*From inside the skin.*—Where from ?— *From the meat inside.*—Where is this wind ?—*All through the body.*"

GEH (7) : " *It makes a breath.*—Where does it come

from ?—*From the hand.*—How ?—*Because you are doing that* [gesture].—Is there any air in the room ?—*No.*—Any breath ?—*No.*—Then where does it come from ?—*From the hand.*—And the air in the hand ?—*From inside there* [the skin].—And the air inside there ?—*When you do this* (he breathes), *it goes from there* [points to his mouth] *and goes to there* (points to his arm)." Naturally, for Geh, to breathe is to produce air, and not to take it in, the room being considered empty of air.

LUG (8) : " *It's the breath going away* [going out of the hands].—Where does this breath come from ?—*From the hands.*" " Does it come from the hands or from the room ?—*From the hands.*—How ?—'*Cos there are little holes in your hands, only you can't see them.*"

COM (10 ; 4) : " *Because you are leaning on your hand.*—What is it doing ?—*It's whistling and blowing.*—Where does the blowing come from ?—*It's the blood blowing.*—Why ?—*Because you pressed much too hard.*—And then ? —*Because you are hitting on it. That makes it scream if you press too hard.*—How does the blood blow ?—*Because it stops.*—What does this do ?—*It blows.*—Why ?—*Because the blood is more squeezed.*" In other words, the pressure of the hands stops the blood flowing ; it is then confined and blows when it is set free !

It is, of course, not on their own merits that these answers constitute a more advanced stage than the preceding. It is because the average age of the children of this type is 7 years and 3 months, whereas that of the first type was 5 years and 4 months. The explanation of the second stage will be seen to be rational in spite of its puerility. It is very much superior to the conception of wind that comes rushing in through closed windows. Nevertheless, we shall still find some of the children making the hypothesis that is characteristic of the first stage, while giving, in addition, the explanation of the second. Here is an example of those mixed cases which are, however, rare.

ROC (6½. G.) : " What is it ?—*Wind.*—Where does it come from ?—*From outside.*—Where from ?—*Through the window* (First stage)." " Where does it come from ?—*From our hands. . . .*—Where from ?—*From our bodies*

(Second stage)." The rest of the interrogatory shows a continuous oscillation between the two hypotheses.

The third stage is at the first glance more difficult to define than the two earlier ones, but it can easily be distinguished from them. By this time, most of the children have discovered that there is already some air in the room, so that the current produced by the hands is due in part to the fact that the hands are moving air that is already there. Others, however, have not yet made this discovery, and even those who have made it are of opinion that if there were no air in the room, some would be produced by the movements of the hands. What characterises this third stage is therefore the idea that the air made by the hands is produced only by the movements of the hands, or could have this as its sole origin. The idea that the hands created air was already present in the earlier stages, but always with an additional appeal to some reservoir of "winds" either outside the room or inside the body. This appeal is the only thing that disappears during the third stage, but the idea remains that the hands create wind. Again we must remind our readers that it is not "on its merits" that we designate this stage as superior to those preceding it ; it is simply because the average age of the children at this stage is 8 instead of being 7 or 5.

Here are some examples of this third stage :

KENN (8) : " What is it ?—*Wind.*—Where does it come from ?—*From the hands.*—Where does this wind in the hands come from ?—*From the hands.*—Is there any air in the room ?—*Yes . . . no.*" The experiment is renewed : " Where does this wind come from ?—*From the hands.*— Is there any there [hands opened] ?—*No.*—And there [hands shut] ?—*No.*—Does it come from the hands, or from the room ?—*From the hands.*"

ROY (7) : " What am I doing ?—*Clapping your hands.*— What is happening ?—*It makes air.*—Why ?—*Because you are clapping your hands.*—Where does the air come from ? —*From here.*—From where ?—*From where we are.*— Where ?—*From here.*—Show me where ?—*From the room.*

—Look ; when my hands are open is there any air round them ?—*No.*—Why ?—*'Cos you are not doing like what you was doing before."*

DUSS (10) : " What am I doing ?—*Making air.*—Where does it come from ?—*From the room.*—How is that ?—*Because the air goes in* [to the hands] *and it goes out. There is air all round* [the hands].—Would it make any in a room without air ?—*Yes.*—How ?—*Because when you move there's always a little air and then when you move, it stirs up the air.*—But if there were no air in the room at all, would it make some ?—*Yes."*

BUS (10 ; 7) : The air of the hands comes into the room, " *because there is always air about.*—Would it make any in a room without air ?—*Yes.*—Why ?—*Because it would be as if you pumped.*—Would the pump make air in a room without any air ?—*Yes, it would make air.*—Why ?—*It would come from the pump."*

The general tenor of these answers will now be clear. Some of the children (Kenn) still deny that there is any air in the room, others (Duss and Bus) admit that there is, while others again (Roy) hesitate between the two hypotheses. It may be objected that there is an ambiguity of vocabulary here, and that by " air " the child simply means air in movement. Thus Roy maintains at one time that there is air in the room, at another that there is none around the hands at rest. Is this not because in the one case he is thinking of air at rest and in the other of " wind " or air in movement ? This may be, but the important point is that for these children " making air " means " creating air ". Thus air at rest is not clearly distinguished from air in movement, or rather it is conceived as the residue or the product of air in movement, which is the more fundamental conception of the two.

This third stage is therefore the genuine outcome of the preceding stages, and throws light upon their true significance. In the first stage, the child knows only of air in movement, wind. But all winds participate with each other, and that issuing from the hands calls to that out of doors. During the second stage, wind is still the only thing that exists, but the body is full of it, and the air produced by the hands may come from the body's breath. Finally, in the third stage, the discovery is made of air as a substance at rest, but it is conceived as the result of "wind" or of air in action, so that the hands are still thought of as capable by their sheer movement of creating air in an airless room.

We now give the answers of the fourth stage, *i.e.* the correct answers. It is on an average from the age of 9 onwards that these explanations make their appearance :

DELESD (8) : "What is happening ?—*There is air.*—Where does it come from ?—*From the hands.*—Where does the air in the hands come from ?—[Delesd tries the movement.] *It doesn't blow when I do it.*—Have you got an idea ?—*No Sir, it comes from the room.*—Are you sure ?—*Not quite sure.*—Is there air in the room ?—*Yes.*—Where does it come from ?—*From outside.*—Is there any air in my hands [open hands] ?—*Yes.*—Where does it come from ?—*From the room.*—Did you know that ?—*Now, I've got it ! If there wasn't any, you couldn't blow !*—Why were you not sure before ?—*'Cos I didn't know.*—If I were in a room where there wasn't any air would this make some ?—*No, it would make nothing.*—Why ?—*Because there isn't* [= there would not be] *any air.*"

ARB (9) : " *It's air.*—How is it done ?—*Because you take it* [the air].—Where ?—*Here.*—Is there any air in the room ?—*Of course !*—Where does it come from ?—*From outside.*—In a room without any air would it make any to do this with my hands ?—*No, it wouldn't make any.*"

Such replies are excellent, and show sufficiently by contrast what those of the earlier stages amounted to.

§ 2. THE AIR OF THE PUNCTURED BALL, OF THE TUBE, AND OF THE PUMP.—The results that follow are put forward only as counter evidence of what has already been suggested. The hypothesis of air issuing from the body by the skin being unable to explain the presence of air in the ball as it did the current of air produced by the hands, it may be of interest to see what are the stages of explanation in relation to this new phenomenon. Actually, the stages are exactly analogous to those we have just been observing in connection with the pressure of hands. During a first stage, of which the average age is 5, the child declares that the air that is produced comes both from the ball and from outside (through the closed window). During a second stage (average age 6), the child answers that the ball is full of air because it was filled at the shop where it was bought, and that the air goes out of it and then in again when it is squeezed and then allowed to fill itself again. During a third stage, the child realises that the air of the ball comes from the room, but still claims that in an airless room squeezing out the ball would produce air. During a fourth and final stage (average age 9), the correct explanation is found. It will be seen that the stages follow the same sequence as they did in the case of the current of air produced by the hands.

Here are examples of the first stage :

SCHNEI (4½) : " Look what I'm doing [the ball is squeezed out, the current of air being directed on to Zel's cheek]. What is it ?—*The wind that comes when the ball is broken.*—Where does it come from ?—*From outside.* —Is there any now [the ball is completely deflated and flat] ?—*No.*—Where has it gone ?—*It has gone away.*— Where ?—*Out at the window.*—How ?—*When it is open.*— Is it open now ?—*No.*" The ball is allowed to fill up again before Schnei's eyes. " Where does this air come from ?—*From outside . . .*" etc.

ZEL (4) : " *It is a current of air.*—Where does it come from ?—*From the sky.*—How did it come ?—*Through the window* [which is shut] *and through the little hole* [in the ball].—When did it come in at the window ?—*When you did that* [when the ball is squeezed] *it comes at once.*" Like Schnei, Zel naturally maintains that there is no air in the room.

SUT (6) : " *It's because it* [the ball] *swells itself up with air.*—Where does this air come from ?—*From outside.*— Is there any air in the room ?—*No.*"

ANT (8) : " *It comes in by the window* [which is shut] *then it goes into the ball by the little hole. If you squeeze, it comes out, then it goes in again.*"

DE (8) : " *It makes air.*" This air comes from the ball being squeezed, and from outside.

It is easy enough to see how similar these answers are to those that we examined in connection with the pressure of hands. In the case of the ball, analysis can be carried even a step further. The older children of this stage dispense with the incessant stream of air coming through the closed window, and say that when the flattened out ball is allowed to fill again it is the same air that goes back into it after having wandered about the room. Thus the air comes in from outside at the beginning of the experiment, goes into the ball, comes out into the room, and then goes back into the ball according as the latter is squeezed or not. The younger children of this group, on the contrary, claim that at each squeeze the air comes into the ball from outside, or issues from the ball and goes out again through the closed window !

During the second stage, the child gives up the idea that the air passes through closed windows. He then appeals to an air forming part of the ball itself, and imagines that this air, which has been put in on purpose by the man in the shop, can go in and out at will. The air is like an animal which returns intelligently to its lair after venturing abroad.

Roy (6) : " *It makes air !*—Where does it come from ? —*From something where there is air.*—What is it ?—*It's something like when you pump up a bicycle* [in other words, the ball has been filled with a bicycle pump].—Is there any more air [the ball is flattened out] ?—*No.*—Is there some again now ?—*Yes.*—Where did it come from ?— *It's the air that went away and that's come back* [the same]." " Is it the same air come back again ?—*Yes.*—How did it come back ?—*Because the air pushes itself along.*—What does that mean ?—*Because it moves along.*—Why does it move along ?—*Because there is air, and behind there is a lot more air that pushes ; because there is some air that has pushed the other air along.*—How far did the air go that came out of the ball ?—*So far* " [Roy points to a place a few millimetres from the hole on the actual surface of the ball].

Re (8½) : " What is happening ?—*There is air. Because there is a hole, then it comes out.*—Where does the air come from ?—*They put it in.*—Who ?—*The man.*" "*The man who took the ball and put air into it.*" The ball is deflated and allowed to fill itself again: "*It is coming back.*—How ?—*By the hole.*—But where from ?—*It is going in.*—Is it the air of the room that is going in, or the air that I took away ?—*The air that you took away.*"

GEH (6) : "*It* (the ball) *makes a breath. . . .*" "*Because inside there it is full of breath.*—Where does it come from ?—*From the ball. They put a little thing, and they put breath in* [blow it out], *and then they stick on the same colour where the hole was.*" The ball is deflated : "*I see ! You've flatted it out. The breath is flat too.*—And now where does the breath come from ?—*From the ball.*—But there was none left !—*The breath flats itself out, and then when you put it* [the ball] *back, it* [the breath] *goes back where it was before.*"

It will be seen that according to these children, air is capable of remaining fixed to the place where it has been put. The air has been put into the ball by the shop-man, and will therefore return thither as soon as it has the chance. Note too that for all these children the air is conscious and alive. It " knows " that it has come out of the ball and it " knows " that it must go back again, etc. The air is " *alive* ", as Com tells us ; it " knows " that it is moving forward, says Geh, " *because it runs* ". Interesting also is Roy's explanation of how the air moves : the air pushes itself along, that is to say it moves spontaneously and pushes the air ahead of it. We shall return to these facts later on.

We shall now give examples of the third stage, during which the children generally admit that there is air in the room. This is the air which goes into the punctured ball and comes out again when the ball is being deflated. But at the same time, the mere action of squeezing the ball produces air, and even if there were no air in the room the ball would create some in this way.

KENN (8) : " Is there any wind in there [deflated ball] ?—*No.*—And now ?—*It has gone in by the hole.*—Where does it come from ?—*From the room.*—Is it the same or another ?—*It has come back ; the same that went*

out.—Is there any wind in the room ?—*Yes.*—Where ?—
Everywhere." " Could the ball make any wind if there
were none ?—*Yes.*—Where would it come from ?—*From
inside there* [inside the ball]."

BUSS (10) : " Would it make any air in a room without
any ?—*It would make a little.*"

Children of the fourth stage, finally, reason like adults :

BURD (9) : " What has happened ?—*There is air.*—
Where does it come from ?—*From the ball.*—And where
does the air in the ball come from ?—*From the room.*—
How ?—*Because there is air in the room.*—[The ball is
deflated.] Is there still any air in it ?—*No.*—And now ?
—*Yes.*—Where does it come from ?—*From the room.*"
" In a room without air would the ball make any air ?—
No.—And would the little tube ?—*No.*—Why not ?—
Because there wouldn't be any air."

The reader will see how closely the evolution of these
answers follows that of those obtained by means of the
experiment with the hands. Not only this, but the
experiments of the pump and the tube produced exactly
the same results, so much so, that there is no need to
put them on record here.

§ 3. THE MAKING OF AIR AND THE MOVEMENT OF
PROJECTILES.—One definite result seems to emerge from
the foregoing paragraphs, namely, that one has only to
make a movement to produce air, and even to draw in
the wind from outside by means, as it were, of an immediate participation. We must now give final confirmation to this fact by means of a more elementary
movement than those which we have made use of up till
now, and we must try to follow to their conclusion the
conceptions of the child with regard to the explanation
of movement.

Let us simply show the child the box tied with string
which we have already spoken of ; let us swing the box
round and ask the child where the air comes from which
he sees to be produced in this way. The answers reveal
three stages of development.

During the first stage (average age 5½), the child states

that the box makes wind, and that in so doing, it attracts air from the outside.

REC (6) : " What is happening ?—*The box is making air.*—Where does it come from ?—*From outside.*—How ?— *Through the window* [which is shut]."

TAQ (7 ; 5) : " What is happening ?—*The wind is blowing.*—Where does it come from ?—*From the box.*— Where does the wind in the box come from ?—*It's from outside. It's the box. . . .*"

During the second stage (average age 7), the box makes wind in a room thought of as airless, or could do so if there were no air in the room.

GEH (6) : " What is happening ?—*It's making wind, it's blowing.*—Where does it come from ?—*When you swing it, it makes wind, just a little wind.*" Geh assures us that there is no air in the room.

DELES (8½) : " *It makes air when you make it go round.* —Why ?—*Because it goes round.*—In a room without air [Deles has just assured us that there is air in the room] would it make any, or would it not ?—*It would make air.*— Why ?—*Because it goes round,*" etc.

At a third stage, finally (average 9 years), the box displaces the air in the room but does not produce any air.

CHAR (11 ; 8) : " *If you swing it round quickly, it makes a lot of air.*—Where does this air come from ?— *Round the box. You take all the air of the room.*—If you were to do the same thing in a room without air would it make any ?—*No.*"

Thus we are faced with the usual schema of stages, *minus* the complications arising from the hands and the ball in the second stage of the previous series. It is very interesting to note that this succession of stages remains the same in the special case of an object in movement. This circumstance has led us to raise the question whether the same thing would not hold good for movements of translation such as that of a ball thrown across a room. Now, the remarkable thing is this : not only did we find the process of evolution to be the same, but we discovered quite unexpectedly that children give of the movement of projectiles an explanation which very closely recalls the ἀντιπερίστασις of the Greeks.

Let us take two entirely spontaneous facts as our starting point. A child of 6, of whom we have asked whether the wind is strong, answers immediately : " *Yes, because if I am walking it makes me run, it pushes me along.*" To which we object : " But where does the wind come from when we run ? ", and the child answers that we make it ourselves by running. Another child gives the same explanation of his top.

CAR (4½), taking a top from his pocket during the interrogatory : " *When it makes wind it makes it go round.*—Does it make wind ?—*Yes.*—Where does it come from ?—*From that* [the top]."

Facts like these have led us to put to the children the very question which Aristotle asked himself : why does a projectile left to itself continue to move, instead of immediately falling to the ground ? In other words, why does this ball which we have thrown across the room move along instead of dropping ? It may be objected that this is a very artificial question to put to a child. We quite agree, but we shall meet, in the course of this work, with so many spontaneous explanations by ἀντιπερίστασις that we have thought it worth while to submit this phenomenon to experimental control by questioning the children on the problem of projectiles. And since this problem is naturally allied to that of the production of air by moving objects, we shall give an account of our results now, at the risk of leaving a certain impression of doubt in the reader's mind.

The question as to why the ball moves gives rise to five types of answers, which, in view of the age average, may be regarded as characteristic of five successive stages.

During the first stage, the child fails to understand the problem, and simply declares that the ball moves because "it has been thrown". During the second stage (average 7 years), the child says that the ball moves "because it makes air", and that, in addition to this, the air from outside comes in and sustains it. We naturally chose children for this experiment who had not already been questioned on the punctured ball, the hands, the tube, etc. In these conditions there could be no danger of perseveration. Here is an example of the second stage :

VEL (7) is of opinion that there is no air in the room. " Why does the ball go on, when I have thrown it and let go of it ?—*When it goes, it goes fast, and it can't fall.*—Why does it not fall down when it goes fast ?—*The air holds it up.*—What air ?—*The air of the sky.*" Vel, on the other hand, says that "*there is always some air*" when it goes fast, because the projectile "*makes air*". In other words the ball, as it advances, attracts the air of heaven which prevents it from falling down.

During the third stage (average 9 years), the child says that the ball makes air and that this air pushes it. Children at this stage think that there is no air in the room, or that if there were none, the ball would create some. It should be noted that the average age of this stage is 9 and not 8, as was the case in the corresponding stages examined in § 1 and § 2. This is because the illusion that movement creates air of itself is stronger in the case of a projectile than it was in that of the hands or of the punctured ball. Here are examples of this stage :

GAL (10 ; 2) : " Why does the ball go on . . ., etc. ?—*It's been given a push* [Fr. *élan*].—But how does it go so far ?—*By the air.*—Where does the air come from ?—*From us, because we are moving.*—Why is there air right down to the floor ?—*Because it makes air.*—Was there some air in the room already ?—*Yes.*—And in a room without air, would the ball fall down if I were to let it go ?—*It wouldn't fall down because it's a movement. . . . The ball makes a movement and that makes air.*"

TAC (9) : " *You throw hard, it goes a long way.*—How ? —*It's the wind.*—What wind ?—*It's the air.*—How ? What air ?—*Because you throw hard . . . because it* (the wind)

pushes it.—How does the wind push it ?—*It's the force.*—
What force ?—*Of the wind."* Tac says that there is no
air in the room, so the wind he speaks of is that of
the ball.

During the fourth stage (average 10 years), the child
says that the ball displaces the air of the room, which,
blowing behind it, pushes it along. In an airless room
the ball would not move, and could not of itself produce
any air. Here is a good example :

MART (10). We place a match on the table and send it
across the room by flicking it with the nail of our fore-
finger. We ask why it goes so far : *" Because it's been
given a start* [Fr. *élan*], *it's gone off ever so quick.*—
What happens when it has been given a start ?—*It
pushes it.*—How ?—*It went hard. That helped it.*—What
helped it ?—*The wind.*—What wind ?—*The air.*—How
does it help the match ?—*The match went off, and the air
went* [after it] *all the time and that pushed it along.*—
What would happen in a room without any air ?—*It
would fall down at once* [= the match could not be thrown].
—Why ?—*Because the air pushes it."*

When, finally, the fifth stage is reached, the child
declares that the impetus (*l'élan*) is sufficient to explain
the advance of the match, and that the air hinders rather
than helps the movement. In an airless room the phenomenon would occur all the more easily. Here is an
example :

DESP (12 ; 1) : *" It's the force, the impetus* (Fr. *élan*).—
How does the force make it stay in the air ?—*If there is
any wind it stops it.*—How ?—*When you throw* [the ball]
*the wind can't make it come back if there is too much force
in the throw."* " But my hand does not touch it when it
is in the air !—*It's what is left of the force:*—How is it
that there is any force left ?—*Because there is still some
of the impetus left.*—In a room without any air could I do
this with the ball ?—*Just the same."*

We see, therefore, that the conception of an impetus
sufficient to itself is later, genetically speaking, than the
hypothesis of a reflux of air which comes and pushes the
object before it. It is true that all the younger children

began by appealing to an impetus, but when pressed, they very soon introduced the idea of air ; whereas the children of the fifth stage refused to make this hypothesis. This is probably due to the industrial setting of modern life in which the presence of machines accustoms the mind to the principle of inertia, and enables the children of 11–12 to rise above the level of commonsense which formed the basis of Greek physics.

In conclusion, without touching upon the very subtle problems which would have to be solved before any comparison could be made between the physics of the child and that of the ancient Greeks, it will suffice to say that the explanations given by our children of the third and fourth stages bear a close (or distant) resemblance to the two famous explanations of projectiles which Aristotle has discussed in his *Physics*. The first of these explanations is that of ἀντιπερίστασις, which Aristotle seems to accept in some passages while he rejects it in others. ". . . It is the air that plays the part of motor. Shaken by the projectile issuing from the sling of the catapult it flows after it and drives it along." [1] But, says M. Carteron, Aristotle regards this phenomenon " as an effect rather than a cause. . . . We have therefore to believe that the projectile confers not only movement but motive force to a surrounding medium, which has the power both to move and to be moved." [2] In other words, " the continued movement of the projectile after it has lost contact with the motor is to be explained by a transference . . . of the original impulse to the medium traversed by the projectile." By means of a phenomenon comparable to magnetism the intervening medium acquires the power to move objects. If, then, this faculty decreases at a distance it must be because of the resistance in the actual mass of the projectile, that is, in its natural weight.

[1] Arnold Reymond, *Histoire des Sciences exactes et naturelles dans l'Antiquité gréco-romaine.* Paris, 1924, p. 183.
[2] H. Carteron, *La notion de force dans le système d'Aristote.* Paris, 1924, p. 23.

Thus Aristotle is still a long way off from the principle of inertia." [1]

We may regard these two explanations—that of the reflux of air behind the projectile, and that of movement transferred to the air by the projector—either as closely allied (M. Reymond's view) or as completely distinct (M. Carteron's view). The fact remains, however, that stripped of their elaborate setting and taken apart from their relations with the sum of physical ideas propounded by the Peripatetics, they are both to be found among the spontaneous conceptions of children thus showing themselves to form part of the commonsense belonging to a definite mental level or to a definite degree of information. In the examples quoted above, Mart tells us that when the projectile is launched, "the air . . . went all the time and pushed it along." He adds that without air the projectile would fall to the ground, and that "the air pushes it." This is a typical case of ἀντιπερίστασις. On the other hand, Gal tells us that the air pushes the projectile, but that this air "comes from us because we are moving." This is the idea that the projector transfers its movement to the surrounding medium. In both cases, there is a striking analogy with the physics of the Peripatetic school. Of course, the child generally conceives projectile and projector as producing (and not merely as displacing) the air (third stage) ; but the schema of interpretation remains the same in passing from the third to the fourth stage, and this is the important point to bear in mind.

It is true that the problem of projectiles is a very artificial one for children. But we repeat that the sequel will show the schema of explanation of movement by reflux of air to be a very general one ; the movements of clouds, of rivers, of waves, and sometimes even of the heavenly bodies are explained in this way. We shall have occasion, moreover, from the next paragraph onwards to see a new application of the same principles.

[1] Léon Robin, *Greek Thought*, p. 279.

§ 4. CENTRIFUGAL FORCE.—We are now going to show that the effects of centrifugal force itself are explained by the child through the idea of a reflux of air. This is why we are introducing at this point of our exposition the account of an experiment which at first sight seems to bear no relation to the problem of air.

Two experiments may be carried out on centrifugal force. The first consists in putting a penny in the box already described, in swinging the box round on a vertical plane, and in asking the child why the penny does not drop out. The second consists in swinging the empty box round on an horizontal plane, very slowly at first, then faster and faster, and in asking the child why the box rises higher and higher the faster one goes (though the child must be left to find out this relation for himself).

The first of these experiments has yielded four types of explanation, characteristic of four stages of development in the child. During the first stage (average age 6), the child answers that the penny does not drop because the box has sides ; the child takes no account of the position of the box during rotation. During a second stage, the child answers that the penny does not drop because the box is swinging round very fast and the penny has no time to drop. During a third stage, the child declares that in swinging round the box produces air (whether or not there is any air in the room), and that this air flowing back into the box is what keeps the penny in position. Finally, during a fourth stage (average 9–10 years), the child says that in moving round, the box displaces the air of the room and thus produces a current of air which holds up the penny.

The children we questioned were naturally not the same as those who were discussed in § 3, so that the hypothesis of perseveration is ruled out.

Here are some examples of the first stage :

GEH (6) foresees before the experiment begins that the penny will not drop : " *I've tried doing that at home with water*.—[The experiment is carried out.] Why did it not

fall down ?—*Because it is in the box.*—Why does it stay?
—*Because there are sides so the penny doesn't fall.*—Why
do the sides hold it back ?—*Because the penny was there*
(he points to the sides). *Of course it doesn't fall out !*—
Yes, but why does it not fall out ? When the box is up
there it is upside down. The penny is underneath, do
you see, and it ought to drop out. Why doesn't it drop
out ?—*Because there is that* [the side].—But how is it that
the penny does not drop out ?—*Because there is that*
(the side) *to hold in the penny.*"

GAV (6) also foresees that the penny will remain :
" *I often put onions in the basket and swing it round.*—
[The experiment is made.] Why does it stay ?—*Because
it wasn't swinging* [= because the box has remained in
the same position !]—What do you mean by that ?—
(Gav makes the experiment himself, but too slowly and
the penny falls out).—Why did it drop ?—*The sides were
holding it back.*—Will it fall if I swing it slowly ?—*No.*—
[Gav has not noticed the part played by speed].—(A
demonstration is made). *It fell because you were going
slowly.*—Why does it not fall out when I go fast ?—
Because of the sides.—Why do the sides not stop the
penny from falling out when I go slowly ?— . . . —Do
you think so ?— . . . —[Fresh demonstration : the
penny drops out].—*It's the sides that hold it back.*"

The answers at this stage are remarkable, but more
from a geometrical than from a physical point of view.
Either the child does not realise that the box is upside
down when it is passing through the highest point of the
trajectory, or else he bases his argument on the sides,
without taking the position of the box into account.
Thus in both cases the child fails to understand that the
sides cannot hold in the penny when the box is upside
down, and this failure is due to an absence of spatial
representation of the successive positions of the box.

Here are two examples intermediate between the first
and the second stage : the sides still hold back the penny,
but only when the box is going fast enough.

DELES (8) foresees that the penny will " stay.—Why ?—
Because it is going round.—[The experiment is made].—
Why does the penny stay when I swing it round ?—
Because the sides are there.—[The box is swung round

slowly]. It has fallen out. Why ?—*Because you weren't swinging it round fast enough.*" "Why does it stay when it is swinging round fast ?—*Because the sides are there.*—And when it goes slowly ?—*It drops out because you are not going fast enough.*"

BURD (9) : "What will happen ?—*It won't fall out.*—Why not ?—*Because it goes fast.*—Then why ?—*Because it has not time to drop out.*—Why ?—*Because the sides of the box stop it.*"

The idea here seems quite clear : when the box travels quickly, the penny is thrown against the side and held in by it. It has not the time to drop out. This leads us to the second stage, when the child gives up the notion that the sides play any part, and attributes only to the speed of the rotation the fact that the penny does not fall out of the box. Here is an example of this second stage :

LUG (8) : "*It won't fall out.*—Why not ?—*Because it is going round fast.*" "If I go slowly will it fall out ?—*Yes.*—Why does it fall out when I don't make it go round fast ?—*Because it* [the penny] *doesn't have time to drop out.*—Why not ?—*Because you are going too fast.*—Does something hold it back ?—*No, no one.*—No, but does something ?—*No.*"

PAT (10) : "*The penny won't fall out.*—Have you already seen this ?—*Yes, with milk.*—Why does it not fall out ?—*Because it hasn't time to fall out.*—How does it do it ?—*Because it is turning round fast.*—Why does it stay when you turn it round quickly and not stay when you do it slowly ?—*The penny hasn't time to fall out, and then when you go slowly it has time.*"

This stage looks more advanced than those that come after it. But the children's ages show that this is not the case. With the exception of Pat, no child of this second stage is more than 8, and the average age is 7. The average age of the third stage, on the contrary, is 8, which means that a large proportion of the children are 9 or 10 years old. During this third stage, the child says that the penny remains in place because the box, in swinging round, produces air which flows back towards the inside of the box and keeps the penny there. Here are examples :

ROY (7) : " What will the penny do when we swing it round ?—*It'll fall out.*—[The experiment is made.]—Why has it stayed ?—*Because it has gone round fast.*—Why does it not fall out when you swing it round fast ?—*Because it stops it falling out.*—Why does it stop it ?—*Because of the air.*—Where does the air come from ?—*Because it's going round.*—Is there air in the room ?—*Yes.*—Is there any now ?—*No.*—When I swing the box round, where does the air come from ?—*Because when you swing it round it makes air.*—Is there any air here [near the box] ? —*No.*—Is there any in the room ?—*No.*"

ACK (8½) : " What will happen ?—*It'll fall out.*—Look [experiment done]. Has it fallen ?—*You're making it go round too fast* [for it to fall out].—How is that ?—*The air does it.*—How ?—*The air pushes* [the penny]. *The air makes a push.*—Why does the air not make the penny fall out ?—*You're making it go round too fast.*—And then ? —*It's the current.*—Where is the current ?—*In the box.*— What is the current ?—*Air.*" " Where does this air come from ?—*When you swing it round it makes air.*" " Is there air in the room ?—. . . . *Yes . . . no! Because everything is shut.*"

BOR (9½) : " What will happen ?—*It* [the penny] *will not fall out.*—Why not ?—*Because it stays in the middle. The air pushes it in the box.*—Where does this air come from ?—*It's the draught made by the box when it goes round.*—Is there any air in the room ?—*No.*—Is there any air in the box ?—*No.*—And now [making the box swing round] ?—*Yes, because the box is going round.*"

These are very definite cases, and closely recall the schema of explanation given for the movement of projectiles (third stage).

Here are some examples of the fourth stage. The air is still supposed to keep the penny in place, but this time the air is thought of as coming from the room, and not as produced by the box itself. Between the third stage and the fourth there are naturally many intermediate cases.

CAM (10 ; 4) : " Will the penny fall out or not ?— *It'll fall.*—[Experiment].—Why did it not fall out ?—

Because you swung round too hard.—Why does it not fall out when you swing it hard ?—*The box keeps in the air.*—Why does it not keep in the penny when we go slowly ?—*If you go fast the penny stays, if you go slowly it falls out.*—Why does it stay ?—*The air keeps in the air.*—What air ?—*The air that is here."* " Where does this air come from ?—*From the room . . ."*

CHAI (11 ; 8) : " What will happen ?—*It* [the penny] *will fall out.*—[Experiment]. — Why has it not fallen out ?—*It can't fall out going round."*—" Why not ?—*Because the air goes against the penny.*—And when I go slowly why does it fall out ?—*Because you don't go fast enough ; and then when you make it go round quickly it gives a lot of air.*—Where does this air come from ?—*Round the box. It takes* [swinging the box round] *all the air of the room.*—If we were to swing this box round in a room without any air, would it make some air ?—*No."*

It may be of interest to examine the relations existing between the prediction of the phenomenon and its explanation, between, that is, the fact that the child does or does not foresee that the penny will remain in the box in spite of its rotation, and the nature of the explanation which the child gives of the phenomenon after the experiment, whether or not he has foreseen what would be its result. Now the result of our enquiry is very definite in this respect. In this particular case, there is no connection between the accuracy of the prediction and the nature of the explanation.

On the one hand, indeed, the explanation of centrifugal force goes through very definite stages in relation to the children's ages. Thus there is hardly a child under 8 who will attempt to introduce air as an explanation of the phenomenon. On the other hand, prediction of phenomena has appeared to us, at any rate among the children we examined, to be almost entirely independent of age. We found that one half of the children could predict the phenomenon, and that the other half could not. Now, these two groups occur in the same numerical proportion from the ages of 4 to 14, and the average age of each group is $8\frac{1}{2}$. There is therefore no relation between prediction and age ; at every age a certain number of children have made the experiment of swinging round vertically a full basket, a pail of water, etc. Cases of right and wrong prediction are to be found, moreover, at every one of our different stages. Prediction and explanation are, in this particular case, entirely independent of each other.

This is rather exceptional, and as a rule we shall find a very close relation between the degree of accurate prediction and the validity of the explanation. If in this particular case the relation does not exist, it is because the physical phenomenon which forms the subject of our experiment cannot have been observed spontaneously by the child. It is only at the instigation of their playmates that children try to swing round baskets and pails of water by themselves. But the correct prediction of the laws of inertia and movement, etc., arises from spontaneous observations that are in direct relation with the child's age, that is, with his own level of intellectual development. The particular case under discussion must therefore in no way be taken as representative.

It is none the less interesting to draw from it the conclusion which it implies. For it shows us—and this is extremely important as a justification of the method we have chosen to use—that an explanation improvised by the child during the interrogatory is, in the main, identical with an explanation based on the child's own previous observations. Whether he has thought about the matter or not, a child of a given level will, in the course of the interrogatory, arrive at the same result. There is therefore something spontaneous in " liberated conviction ", taking these two words in the special sense defined elsewhere (C.W., Introduction, § 2).[1]

Let us now turn our attention to another effect of centrifugal force. The empty box is made to swing round horizontally by the string, and the child is asked

[1] C.W. = The Child's Conception of the World. Kegan Paul.

why it goes higher (as the speed of the rotation increases). The answers obtained fall into three stages which correspond point for point with the last three stages noticed in connection with the rotation of the penny. During a first stage (average 6 years), the child answers that the box rises because it is going fast, which is a statement of the law rather than a discovery of the cause. During a second stage (average 8 years), the child answers that the box rises because of the air it creates by going round. During a third stage (average 9½ years), the child answers that the box rises because of the current of air which it produces by displacing the air of the room.

Here is an example of the first stage:

LEO (7 ; 3): "Why does the box go up?—*Because you make it go round harder and harder.* . . . *You make it go harder and then it goes up.*—Why does it go higher?—*The harder you go the higher it goes*", etc.

An example of the second stage:

BOR (9) Spontaneously: "*The air makes it go up.*—How?—*Because the box makes air when it goes round.*—Is there air in this room?—*Yes.*—In a room without any air would the box do anything by going round?—*It would make air.*"

Here, finally, are some examples of the third stage:

STOE (11): "Why does it go up?—*Because you make it go round with your hand.*—But why does it go up when I go fast and go down when I go slow?—*Because there is air in the box. It makes it fly when you swing it round with the string.*—Is there any air in the room?—*Yes*", etc.

JEL (10): "Why does it go up?—*It goes fast, then the air makes it go up. When it goes up the air comes and pushes it along still more.*"

DELESD (8½): "*The air makes it go up.*—How?—*It's the start* (Fr. *l'élan*). *The air helps the start to go up.*"

Thus the same schema reappears very clearly—explanation of movement by reflux of the air that has been displaced.

CHAPTER II

THE ORIGIN OF WIND AND
OF BREATH

THE experiments we have been describing throw a certain amount of light on the development of the notion of air. To the child, air is simply impetus or movement substantified, or, as Sully puts it, "reified." Only the substantification is of a peculiar kind, for it completely eludes any principle of conservation : the air exists only while it is blowing, and goes into nothingness immediately afterwards. Air, Bor (9) tells us, " is the current of the box when it goes round," and such definitions abound. It is true that the younger children seem to postulate a very rigid principle of conservation, more rigid even than ours, since they regard all the "currents" of air as participating with one another, the current of the box coming from the wind outside, etc. But this participation is purely dynamic, and does not involve any rational notion of conservation ; it identifies only actions or intentions and establishes only occult relations between substances separated by time and space. Participation may therefore be described in terms of conservation, but only on the condition of noting very clearly the following threefold rhythm. First, all the currents are conceived in solidarity with each other. Secondly, each one acts on its own account, emerging out of nothingness and returning to it immediately afterwards. Thirdly, the currents of air are thought of as independent vibrations of a single all-pervading substance. The initial identification and the final identification are therefore not on the same plane. The one is not derived from the other. The elaboration of the second presupposes the annihilation of the first.

The reason for this is, as we shall try to show later, that these two kinds of identification—participation and the principle of conservation of matter—are the outcome of two different kinds of logic. Participation is the result of simple transduction, of the syncretistic fusion of particular observations. The principle of conservation, on the contrary, arises from inductive comparisons and genuine deduction.

This problem of the origin of air leads us quite naturally to two of the most spontaneous of children's beliefs about air : ideas about the formation of wind, and explanations about the mechanism of breathing.

§ 1. THE FORMATION OF WIND. — The technique to be followed in order to obtain as completely as possible the child's ideas on the formation of wind is, quite shortly, as follows : first ask, " Where does the wind come from ? " then add, " There is (or there is not) a lot of wind to-day. There was (or there was not) a lot of wind yesterday. Why is that ? " In conclusion ask : " How did the wind begin ? ", " The first time there was any wind, where did it come from ? " The child begins by answering " The clouds make the wind ? " or " The trees," so it is best to ask as counter-evidence : " Do the clouds, etc., make the wind move, or does the wind make the clouds move ? " But all this is not sufficient, for the possibilities of ambiguity are without number. The most convincing counter-evidence is that which we give later on in our examination of the cause of movement, and which consists in asking the child why the clouds move along, etc., and when the child has answered : " The wind pushes them ", in asking where this wind comes from. This indirect method is indispensable as a complement to the direct method whose results we are now going to examine. But for the sake of clarity in the exposition, we shall have to deal with questions one by one, and to confine ourselves for the moment to the direct method.

The answers relating to the origin of wind can be grouped into three stages. The first is artificialist : wind is produced by man or by God, or by means of breath, or by means of machines. The average age of this stage is 5, and few children are included in it after 7. During a second stage, the child regards wind as the result of the movement of the very bodies which we regard as being moved by the wind (clouds, trees, waves, dust), etc. The average age here is 8 years and two months. During a third stage, the children refuse to explain how wind is made. They look upon it as making itself from the air, but this process appears to them inexplicable. The average age is 10½.

Here are some examples of the first stage, or stage of artificialism. Two contemporaneous types can be distinguished among these children. A child of the first type attributes the wind to the breath of men or of gods.

ZEL (4) : " How did the wind begin ?—'*Dunno.*—How do you think it did ?—*It's made by blowing.*—Where does the blowing come from ?—*From God.*—How does God make it come ?—*With nis mouth.*"

NAI (4) : It is God who " *blows.*"

RAE (6) : " *God makes the wind blow.*—How ?—*He blows with his mouth.*"

ROY (6½) : " Where does the wind come from ?—*From the sky.*—How did it begin ?—*Somebody blew.*—Who did ? —*Men.*—What men ?—*Men who it was their work.*"

TAO (7) : " How did the North wind begin ?—*It's when you whistle. It makes air come out.*"

One might be tempted to attribute such artificialist myths to pure romancing. But there are certain documents in existence which enable us to prove their authenticity ; we mean the childhood memories of the deaf and dumb. William James gives in this connection the following account of the deaf-mute d'Estrella, who became drawing-master at a school in California.[1]

---

[1] *Philos. Review*, Vol. I (1892), pp. 613-624.

D'Estrella, in order to account for the origin of the sun, had imagined that "a great and strong man" hidden behind the hills of San Francisco threw a fiery ball into the sky. It is to this great and strong man that d'Estrella refers in his memoirs as "the god." "*When there was wind he* [*i.e.* d'Estrella, who speaks of himself in the third person] *supposed that it was the indication of his* [*i.e.* the god's] *passion. A cold gale bespoke his anger, and a cool breeze his happy temper. Why? Because he had sometimes felt the breath bursting out from the mouth of angry people in the act of quarrelling or scolding. . . . He was often awed by the fantastic shapes of the floating clouds. What strong lungs the god had! When there was fog, the boy supposed that it was his breath in the cold morning.*"

But the commonest type of explanation which characterises this first stage is the artificialist type in the strict sense of the word. This type is, moreover, contemporaneous with the one preceding it. Here are some examples :

SCHNEI (4) : " Where does the wind come from ?—*From the sky when it rains.*—And where does it come from in the sky ?—*From the North wind.*—And where does the North wind come from ?—*From God.*—How is it done ? —*With a stick.*—How ?—*Like this.* (He makes the movement of fanning the air quickly), *and it blows away.* Are you making that up ?—*Yes.*—Do you really believe it ?— *No.*—Then how is the wind made ?—*God makes a hole* [in vault of the sky] *and then it flies away.*—Where does this wind come from ?—*From the sky, and inside* [the sky] *there is wind.*"

OST (4) : " Where does the wind come from ?—*From outside.*—How is it made outside ?—*By the motor cars.*— If there were no motor cars would there still be any wind ? —*No, Sir.*—Yes, there would be.—*Yes, Sir.*—What else can make wind ?—*Bicycles, trams, carts, dust.*—And what else ?—*Charabancs.* What else ?—*Clouds.*—And what else ?—*Trees.*—And what else ?—*When you blow, when you sweep.*" In these cases, along with artificial causes are others like clouds, trees and dust which, when they alone are appealed to, are characteristic of the second stage.

GAL (5) : God makes it " *with fans.*"

GEH (6) : " Where does the wind come from ?—*They blow up in the sky.*—How ?—*The things are full and then they lay down, and then they blow. It comes out at the end.*—What thing is it ?—*It's for blowing* " [a bicycle pump, as Geh subsequently showed us].

PEC (6) : " Why does the wind blow ?—*When it is going to rain so as to break off the branches for a fire.*—Do you really believe that.—*My daddy told me so.*—Why does it go on blowing ?—*Sometimes so as to make lots of little waves, and then it pushes the little boats and you don't need to row.*—What makes it blow ?—*God does.*"

GAUD (6½) : " How is the wind made ?—*By God.*—How ?—*He bends.*—What does he bend ?—*He bends the trees.*—And then ?—*That makes them move and then when there's lot of wind it makes them fall down.*—Does the wind make the trees move or do the trees make the wind ?—*The trees make the wind.*" Here we have an explanation that almost belongs to the second stage, but the actual formation of the wind is still in Gaud's mind dependent upon human or divine activity.

These first stage cases recall very closely what was said in connection with artificialism in general (*C.W.*, Section III). The root of those beliefs, namely the spontaneous element and that which alone is independent of adult influence and of the question which has been asked, is anthropocentric finalism : the wind is " made for " the rain, the trees, the boats, etc. Under the influence of the question on the origin of wind the relation expressed by the words " made for " gives rise in the child's mind to the idea that the wind is " made by " people or by God, etc. As to the ways and means of making wind which the children attribute to God, they are drawn from daily technical experience (sticks, fans, air-pumps, etc.) or they are drawn from observations which already point to the second stage, as when the wind is connected with the movement of trees, of clouds, of dust.

The second stage introduces us to a set of phenomena which are of signal importance for the understanding of the child's idea of causality. This stage is very varied in character, but it possesses one general trait in that objects in movement are believed to cause the wind. In other words, these objects are conceived as being endowed with a movement of their own, and their movement is supposed to be sufficient to engender the wind. This, however, does not prevent the wind from accelerating this movement, owing to the schema of the reflux of air or of the " reaction of the surrounding medium," a schema of which we saw the universal nature in Chapter I.

The bodies which produce wind in this way are the clouds, the trees, the dust, the waves, and even the heavenly bodies. Let us begin with the rarer cases, and then pass on to the case of clouds which will thus lead us imperceptibly on to the explanations of the third stage, according to which wind is the product of the ambient air.

In this way we shall be led to distinguish six different types of answers in the second stage. But it must be emphasised from the first that these types are not mutually exclusive. The same child may assign several different causes to the wind. There are two reasons for this. In the first place, the way very young children have of seeing participations in everything tends to make them regard movements that are quite distinct as not only related to one another but as resulting immediately one from the other. Thus the motion of the moon involves that of the clouds and of the sun, because the moon attracts the clouds and drives away the sun, and so on. Hence, the wind can be the result of the moon, of the clouds, and of the sun, etc., each of these winds having an autonomous origin, while at the same time participating with all the others. This manner of reasoning comes out very clearly in the explanations analysed in the first chapter. On the other hand, when the habits of participation are on the wane, each body in movement is supposed to produce wind on its own account, and there is no reason why each wind should be the outcome of one body in movement rather than have a number of different origins.

Only, the children rarely think of more than one origin

at a time. When at the time of being questioned they
hit upon a possible origin, they stick to it and forget all
the others. We have here one of many cases of the child's
inability to perform logical addition (see *J.R.*, Chap. IV,
§ 2)[1]. Instead of saying " The wind comes from the trees,
the clouds, the waves, etc. . . ., from everything that
moves," the child chances to fix on one element and
forgets all the others. But in his spontaneous thought,
compounded as it is of visual and motor experiences, the
different elements really co-exist, if not in a state of
synthesis, at least in one of juxtaposition or agglomeration.
This is what we discover when we come to question the
child, no longer directly, but indirectly, by trying to
make him define more closely the cause of the movements
in nature.

Here, to begin with, is a complex case, showing how
closely interwoven are the various causes that exist in
the child's mind. After that, we shall pass on to the
analysis of each different type of answer.

RE (8) : " Where does the wind come from ?—*From the
sky.*—What is it made of ?—*Dust.*—Where does the dust
come from ?—*Because sometimes the motor cars make it.*—
Is there any when the motors don't make it ?—*Yes, sometimes in the streets.*—Does the wind move ?—*Yes.*—How ?
—*By itself.*—Why does it move ?—*It blows.*—Why does
it blow ?—*When the weather is bad.*—Does it know when
the weather is bad ?—*Yes.*—Does it feel the rain falling ?
—*Yes.*—Is it alive ?—*Yes.*—Why ?—*Because it blows.*—
Where does the wind in the sky come from ?—*Because
sometimes earth gets on to it, 'cos it makes dust.*—Gets on
to what ?—*On to the wind.*—But how does the dust make
the wind ?—*It goes over the wind.*—Where does this wind
come from ?—*From the sky.*—Where is it ?—*In the sky.*—
What is the wind made of when it is in the sky ?—*Of
dust.*" " Go and open the door so that you feel the
draught.—[He does this].—What is it made of ?—*Dust.*—
But there is no dust in here, is there ?—*No.*—Then do
you think that the wind is made of dust ?—*No.*—What

[1] We shall designate by the initials *L.T.* and *J.R.* our two volumes
The Language and Thought of the Child and *Judgment and Reasoning in
the Child*, which have already appeared (Kegan Paul).

is it made of ?—*Water*.—Did the wind make you wet ?—
No.—Then what is the wind made of ?—*Sky*.—What is
the sky made of ?—*Blue clouds*.—And the blue clouds ?—
They're made of sky.—And the sky ?—*Of clouds*.—And
the sky ?—*Of the Jura*.—And the Jura ?—*Of earth*." It
should be stated that Re regards some clouds as coming
from the Jura and as having actually issued from that
mountain.

This case of Re brings us in contact with childish ideas
concerning the wind in all their complexity. It shows
how the child will stick to one explanation while at the
same time clearly showing that others are implicit in his
mind. For it is obvious that throughout the interrogatory
Re has deliberately clung to the one idea that dust is
what produces wind. Even when Re grants that the wind
comes from the sky, he maintains that the wind of the
sky is made of dust and that the sky itself is a great
big cloud made of the earth of the Jura mountain.
But it is also obvious that Re has other ideas in his head.
"The dust," he says at one point, "passes over the
wind," which undoubtedly implies that the wind is,
to a certain extent, prior to the dust. The wind is made
"of water," *i.e.* of clouds, and these clouds are closely
connected with rain and bad weather. A few months
earlier Re had told us that the wind came from bad
weather and from the cold. Behind the apparent unity
there is therefore at least duality of explanation. No
doubt all the answers we publish would, if they were
fundamentally analysed, give the same impression of
complexity. Not only this, but the reader would probably
see that for the child these various causes of the wind
participate with one another. In Re's mind certainly
it would seem that clouds, dust, air, and water participate
with one another, which means that they mutually
engender each other, but do not as yet transform themselves into one another in accordance with the process of
rational identification.

Be that as it may, it is time we turned to the enumera-

tion of the different types of possible answers, beginning
with the explanation of wind by dust, which we shall
designate by the name of " First type."

WENE (9) : " Why does the sun move along ?—*Because
the wind pushes it.*—Where does the wind come from ?—
From the dust.
CERE (9) : " What is the wind made of ?—*Dust.*—
Does it stand still ?—*It blows.*—Does it move ?—*Yes.*—
Where does the dust of the wind come from ?—*From old
rags.*—Do you really think so ?—*Yes.*—On the Mont-
Blanc there is nothing but snow, no dust. What is the
wind made of up there ?—*Dust.*—Where does it come
from ?—*From here."   " Does the wind move ?—*Yes.*—
How ?—*By itself.*—Why does it move ?—*Because it blows.*
—Where does it come from ?—*From the ground."*
GRAT (8) : " Where does the wind come from ?—*From
the dust.*—How is the wind made in the dust ?—*It blows.*
—But where does it come out from ?—*From the dust."*

Dust is therefore supposed to set itself in movement by
itself in order to produce wind. When the child is asked
how the dust moves, he naturally answers that the wind
makes it move. But this is not a vicious circle, it is a
physical circle. The dust moves of itself by means of the
wind which it has made. It is the schema of the reflux
of air with which we are already familiar. We need not
dwell upon it further here, for we shall meet with the
same problem in connection with the explanation of
movement (Chapters III *et seq.*).
We shall now deal with the children of the second type
who explain wind by the waving of trees.

GRAT (8) : " Where does the wind come from ?—*From
the trees.*—How did the wind begin ?—*Because the branches
move.*—Do the branches make the wind ?—*Yes.*—But how
do the branches move ?—*Because of the wind."*
DELESD (8) : " Is there any air outside ?—*Yes.*—
There's a lot to-day. Why is that ?—*Because there's a
wind.*—What is it ?—*It's the trees moving. It blows."*
" Where does the wind come from ?—*Because it blows."*
" But how is it that it blows ?—*Because if you go by*
[past] *a tree that is moving, it makes air.*—Why ?—*Because
it is moving.*—If there were no trees what would happen ?

—There would be some [wind] *just the same.*—Where would it come from ?—*From the air, it would be made.*—Where does the air out of doors come from ?—*From the sky.*—How is that ?—*Because it is cold. There are clouds. Sometimes they knock together and then it rains."*

TAQ (7) : "Where does all the air out of doors come from ?—*It was under the trees and then it came.*—Where does the wind come from ?—*Under the trees."* "How is it made to begin with ?—*On the trees.*—Do the trees make the wind ?—*Yes.*—If there were no trees would there be any wind ?—*No.*

These cases are all perfectly clear. They seem, nevertheless, to fall naturally into two groups. Taq, for example, thinks that the wind comes entirely from under the trees. This, incidentally, does not prevent him from saying on other occasions that the wind first began by coming from a man who whistled ; the thought underlying participation is not troubled by the lack of logical unity. Trees are therefore thought of as setting themselves in motion in order to produce the wind. This interpretation seems to us beyond question, since a number of the children have told us that trees are alive " *because they can swing themselves by themselves"*. Sully, it will be remembered, placed the same belief on record : " A pupil of mine distinctly recalls that when he was a child he accounted for the wind at night by the swaying of two large elms in front of the house and not far from the windows of his bedroom." [1]

Delesd and Grat, on the other hand, seem to admit that it is the wind that sets the trees in motion. There would seem, then, to be a circular process : the trees make wind by moving, and the wind makes the trees move. We believe, however, that it is only in course of time and after reflection that the child begins to feel this difficulty. Thus Delesd is quite unconscious of it, but nine months later he is acutely aware of it :

DELESD (9) : " Where does the wind come from ?—*I told you last year. The trees make it.*—Do you still believe

[1] Sully, *Studies of Childhood*, p. 98.

that ?—*Not so much.*—You believe it a little but not very much, eh ? Why do you believe it a little ?—*Because trees blow and make a breeze.*—Why do you not believe it very much ?—*Because even when the trees don't move, there is still a little breeze.*—How do the trees move ?—*They move with the air.*—What makes them move ?—*It's the wind.*"

The child is aware of the vicious circle. But at the time of the first interrogatory this constituted no more of a difficulty for Delesd than it did for Grat. This must have been because, in their eyes, trees seemed to move gently of themselves, and then to be more and more violently stirred by the air they had thus produced. Much as in swinging the impetus one gives oneself gradually multiplies the strength of the movement. Thus here again we have the schema of the reflux of air, which is at the root of all these beliefs. Moreover, so deeply ingrained is this schema, that even a body set in motion by a current of air infinitely more extensive than the sphere of action of this body seems to the child to be endowed with a movement that is partly spontaneous. Thus Del at 6 years old asks whether some dead leaves scattered on the road are alive, and when he is answered in the negative, retorts : " But they are moving with the wind ! " (*L.T.*, p. 206.)

To conclude : whether trees are conceived as the sole cause of wind, or whether they are considered as being partly stirred by a wind of external origin, they are capable, in the child's eyes, of producing wind themselves.

Children of the third type attribute to the waves the origin of the wind.

PAT (10) : " Is there air in this room ?—*Yes.*—Where does it come from ?—*From the wind.*—And the wind ?—*From the water.*—How ?—*The water makes the waves and the waves make a little air and then the trees do too.*—How does the water make the waves ?—*From the wind. The wind blows and then that makes the waves come.*"

FERT (10 ; 2) tells us that the air sets the sun and moon in motion : " What makes the clouds go ?—*That's*

the air too.—And what makes the wind go ?—*The sea.*—
How ?—*With the waves.*—Do the waves make wind ?—
Yes.—How ?—*When they go up high.*—Do the waves of
the lake make wind ?—*They make the North wind.*" This
is quite true as in Geneva the North wind comes across
the lake, whereas the " wind ", *i.e.* the wind from the
South or the West comes, as Fert may have learned at
school, from the direction of the sea. " And what makes
the waves ?—*The air.*—And what makes the wind ?—
The waves.—What makes the waves ?—*The air.*—Where
does the wind come from ?—*When the sea is calm, it doesn't
blow.*"

CESS (14, backward) : " Do you know what the wind
is ?—*It's air.*—Where does it come from ?—*From the sea.*
—How does it come ?—*The big waves.*—And the North
wind (*la bise*) ?—*The same thing, only harder.*—How did
it begin ?—*The waves make the North wind (la bise).*"
The waves arise from the fact that " *the water moves.*—
Why ?—*Because there's a current.*—What is the current ?
—*It goes fast, then it moves.*" " Does the wind know it is
blowing ?—*Yes.*—How ?—*I don't know. Because it is
what makes the fine weather come.*"

FALQ (8) : The sun moves because " *the wind pushes it.*"
What made the wind that pushes the sun ?—*Water.*—
How did it do that ?—*Water is cold and has a current.*"
The current of air is thus co-substantial with the air and
the current of wind.

MART (9 ; 5) also tells us that it is water that makes the
sun move. " How does it happen ?—*Because water has a
current and then it pushes.*—What is the current ?—*When
the water goes fast.*" " What water is it that makes the
sun go ?—*The water of the Lake.*—How ?—*Because it goes
fast.*—How does it make the sun go ?—*The air goes
up. . . .* " " *The current is strong. The current pushes the
air and the air pushes the sun.*" " Is the current of the Lake
making air to-day [a windless day] ?—*No, not every day.*"
In other words, the water, when moving thanks to its
own spontaneous " current ", produces air and wind. The
various possible " currents "—water, air, etc.—are not
only compared with one another, but tend to be materially
identified.

This shows very clearly that the same schema is at
work as with the children of the preceding type. The
waves make the wind, and the wind makes the waves.

The waves are partly spontaneous. They " go up high " by themselves (Fert), they are the result of a current (Cess, Falq, Mart). This movement produces wind, which in its turn accelerates the formation of the waves.

In certain cases, something more happens : the water itself produces air, because it is cold, cold being a substance issuing from the water and producing wind. Thus the dynamic schema of which we spoke develops into an attempt at identification, or at any rate at generation of the substances in question. This is what Falq and Mart led us to believe. Here are some more definite cases :

FERT (10 ; 2), whose answers we have just been examining adds : " How do the waves of the lake make themselves ?—*It's the cold.*—How ? Has the cold any force ?—*Oh, yes ! It makes the wind and the North wind* (Fr. la bise)."

FRAN (9) : " How did the wind begin ?—*When it's too cold, because of the water.*—Does the water make wind ?— *Yes.*—How ?—*Yes, when it's cold there are waves, and that makes the wind come.*—Where does the wind come from ? —*Because of the waves.*"

SUT (6 ; 7) : " Where does the air of this room come from ?—*From outside.*—And the air outside ?—*From the lake.*—What makes the air out of doors ?—*It's the water.* —How does that happen ?—*The water forms it* [the air].—How ? — *Because the water is a little bit cold.*— How is that ?—*Because it* [the water] *is made of air.*" Sut, as we ascertained in questioning him, does not know what steam is, and is unacquainted with the fact that clouds are made of evaporated water. He has simply noticed that water produces a sensation of cold and he concludes from this that the cold makes air, since air is also cold.

These explanations anticipate those of the sixth type (wind being the outcome of cold in general) which is, moreover, mainly the outcome of the fourth. Children belonging to this fourth type, which is by far the most frequent, find the origin of wind in the clouds. Here again we have a double mode of formation : on the one hand, the cloud makes wind as it moves along, on the other, the cloud becomes changed into air (smoke and steam being considered akin to air, *C.W.*, pp. 302–303, and 314). Here are some examples in which these two processes—one of dynamic formation, the other of material generation, are combined in different ways :

PEC (6) says that the wind comes " *when it is going to rain* ", which is the beginning of a link between the wind and the clouds.

ROY (6½) attributes the first origin of the wind to a man : it is " *someone who blew.*" Now the sky and the clouds are formed by the wind. Of the clouds, Roy says " *the sky made them.—*How ?*—Because it's a good thing to make some.*—How is it done ?*—Because it cuts itself in half.*" As for the sky, " *it is wind.*" But " where does the wind come from ?*—From the sky.*" " How is it made ? *—It is a cloud that has made some wind.*—How does it do that ?*—Because, when there are clouds, it is bad weather.—* How do the clouds make wind ?*—Because it is a good thing to make wind.*—Where do the clouds come from ?*—From the sky.*" Thus the process will be seen : the wind changes into clouds and the sky and the clouds become wind.

Further, Roy, as we have already seen (*C.W.*, Chap. VIII, § 1), believes that the heavenly bodies, after their birth, have grown because of the clouds, which are made of wind, and that they have grown " *because we grow.*" In the next paragraph we shall see that, according to Roy, we are full of air, because the air makes us grow bigger : " What is it that made the sun and the moon grow bigger ? *—Wind.—*Why ?*—Because it is a good thing to make us grow bigger. . . .*"

It can be seen what Roy would find to be the system of the world, if he should feel the need to systematise : the world is a society of organisms produced or fed by the air which was " blown " by a man at the beginning of things.

GAVA (6) also oscillates between artificialism and the idea that the wind is produced by the clouds ; the clouds " *are things that move about, then that makes wind.*"

PAR (8 ; 7) : " What is the wind ?*—It is air.*—Where does it come from ?*—From the clouds.*—Do they make it ? *—No. It is air which they make* [=which the clouds make], *and then it* [the air] *chases the clouds.*—Where does the wind come from ?*—From far away.*—Where from ?— From Tessin* (Par comes from Tessin).*—*How is it made over there ?*—The air makes it, or else it's the smoke from* *the chimneys* [Par thinks that the clouds are made of smoke].—Where does the air come from ?—*From the chimneys."* This case is very clear : the wind pushes the clouds, but it is the clouds, that is to say, the smoke from the chimneys, which make the wind. The air issues from the smoke.

FER (8) : The air " *comes from the sky.*—How is it made in the sky ?—*When there are clouds.*—What does that do ? —*It makes air."* " How does it make air ?—*When they move.*—That makes air ?—*Yes.*—What makes the clouds move ?—*When it is going to rain."* " Why do they move along when it is going to rain ?—*When they go to meet each other.*—Do they move along alone, or does something make them move ?—*They move alone."*

ANT (8) : " Is the air outside alive ?—*Yes.*—Why ?— *Because it blows.*—Does it know that it is blowing ?— *Yes.*—How does it know ?—*It is in the sky. When it's cold, it blows.*—Where does the wind come from ?—*From the sky.*—How is it made ?—*From the clouds.*—What do they do ?—*They open out, then they all get together, then afterwards they let the air come out.*—Where does the air come out from ?—*From the clouds."* " Where does the North wind come from ?—*It comes from the big clouds.*— How ?—*The big clouds come when it's raining. The big clouds open and the North wind comes out.*—Is there air in the clouds ?—*Yes.*—Where does it come from ?—*From the clouds.*—How do the clouds make air ?—*Because it rains. The rain makes clouds and the clouds have air."* " *The rain makes clouds and there is air inside."*

BRAS (8) : The wind comes from the clouds. " How ? —*There is air in the clouds.*—What makes it ?—*The water."*

FRAN (9), after having told us that the wind comes from the waves, because of the cold of the water, continues in this way : " How is the wind made in countries where there are no lakes ?—*Because of the sky.*—How ?— *It is when the sky is very cold, there are little bits of sky that go away, and then you can't see that they are sky any longer : so they are the wind."* Now the sky is " *a sort of cloud."*

BARD (9) : " Is the air alive ?—*Yes.*—Why ?—*Because it moves about.*—Where does the air come from ?—*From the sky.*—How ?—*It is the clouds.*—How ?—*The water that evaporates."* The sky itself is a cloud.

COMO (10) : " How is the wind made ?—*It's the clouds, when there is bad weather.*—How do the clouds make wind ? —*Because they melt."* And later : " Where does the wind come from ?—*With the clouds.*—How ?—*The clouds melt.*—Tell me, is the wind alive ?—*Yes.*—Why ?—*Because if it were not alive, it wouldn't move.*—Does it know that it blows ?—*Yes, because it is itself that blows.*"

Duss (10 ; 7) suggests, but with hesitation, that the clouds make the wind. " But is it the clouds that make the wind, or the wind that makes the clouds move along ?—*The wind makes the clouds move along.*—And do the clouds make wind or not ? — *They make wind.*—How ? — *By moving.*"

The above shows us the explanation of the formation of wind appearing under four different modalities. In the most primitive cases, which are still deeply tinged with artificialism (see first stage, cases of Schnei, Pec, etc.), there is simple participation between the wind and the bad weather : when the weather is bad, clouds and wind appear simultaneously on the scene and there is reciprocity of action between the two. The second modality is that of " generation " of the wind by the clouds : the cloud smoke, or the steam, or the water, etc., transforms themselves into wind. Or again, the cloud opens like the Cave of Æolus, and the wind escapes from it with the rain. A third modality, closely resembling the last, recalls what we observed in connection with waves : winds and bad weather together produce cold, which transforms itself into wind. Finally, the fourth modality, nearly always connected with the other three but sometimes appearing alone, is that of the genesis of air by movement : the cloud makes wind as it moves along.

From the genetic point of view it would certainly seem that the second mode arose out of the first. In other words, the schema of material generation is the outcome of animistic participation. The wind is at first thought of as " going with " bad weather on account of some intention or common purpose, and then, later, the wind is regarded as coming out of the clouds. This is a very usual order of succession in the development of childish beliefs (see *C.W.*, Chap. IX, § 5 and § 6). The analysis can even be carried a step further and a distinction drawn between " generation " and " identification ". The wind, to begin with, is simply born of the cloud. It is alive, and its exit from the cloud is comparable to the change in the state of an organism. The later cases are, on the contrary, less animistic, and the formation of wind simply becomes a material transformation of steam, smoke, or water into air.

Before dealing with the formation of wind by means of the cold, we should distinguish a fifth type of answer, according to which the wind is produced by the sun and moon. All the fourth type children attributed to the clouds the formation of wind, whatever might be the mode of this formation. Now, children from 8 to 10 generally regard the sun as a small cloud, " tight " (Fr. *serré*) and fiery. It is therefore quite natural that some of them should regard the heavenly bodies as makers of wind.

IMB (6) : The sun " *blows also* " (like the clouds).
BERG (7) in connection with an enquiry on the idea of force : " Has the sun got force ?—*No, because when it rises, there is only a tiny little bit of wind.*—Has the moon got force ?—*Yes, a little, because it makes a little wind.*"

We shall meet with other cases in connection with the problem of the sun's movements (Chap. III, § 2). But this fifth type of answer is naturally far less frequent than the former types, because the sun is warm, and the wind is nearly always cold. We shall even meet with children who maintain that the sun destroys the wind. Some, however, say that fire can produce air, as we shall see in connection with engines (Chap. X, § 1 and § 2).

Finally, there is a sixth type of answer, which, though often amalgamated to the first four we have just enumerated, occasionally even with the fifth, is to be found in a pure form at every age : wind is supposed to be produced by the cold. In order to understand this conception the reader should remember what we tried to show elsewhere (*C.W.*, Chap. IX, § 6), namely, that for the child, cold is, or tends to become, a substance.

FONT (6 ; 9) : " Where does the wind come from ?—*It comes from the mountain.*—How is it made ?—*It's the snow.* —How is that ?—*When it's all melted, that makes a wind.*" A moment after : " The wind comes out of the snow ?— *Yes.*"

EBI (7) : " *It's the snow that makes the wind.*" " How does it blow ?—*It's the snow, because it's too cold, then it makes it blow.*"

GIAMB (7) : The wind, " *it's breath*. . . .—Where does it come from ?—*From the sky.*—Why are there days when it blows ?—*It's when it's cold.*—Why does it blow when it's cold ?—*Because it makes things cold.*" Thus we find a vicious circle. The cold attracts the wind and produces it.

WENY (8) : " Why does the wind move ?—*Because it's cold.*"

FRAN (9), it will be remembered, attributes the formation of wind to the waves and the clouds. But, in both cases, he considers cold to be indispensable to the production of wind. On the one hand, there is wind " *when it's too cold because of the water.*" On the other hand, " *when the sky is very cold, there are little bits of sky that go away. . . . So it's the wind.*"

NOT (10) : " How is the wind made ?—*When it's cold, it blows.*"

It will be seen from the above that some children regard cold as a substance, and consider that snow produces wind by the mere fact of being cold. Others, on the contrary, are content to establish a somewhat loose dynamic tie between the oncome of cold weather and that of wind. As in the case of the generation of wind out of the clouds, it is obviously the vague relation uniting wind and cold (the wind " comes from " the cold) that has given rise to the idea of a material generation of air out of the clouds or out of cold weather in general.

This brings us to the close of our analysis of the answers of the second stage. These answers are of great interest for the understanding of the child's conception of movement. Superficially it looks as though the child contented himself with a very rudimentary observation of nature, and simply took effects for causes : trees, dust, waves, clouds, etc., are all supposed to make wind, whereas for us they are merely displaced by the wind. But why does the child reverse the order of things in this way ? The paucity of his means of observation is not sufficient to explain this, for, after all, these children know perfectly well that the self-same trees, dust, waves, and clouds, are themselves pushed by the wind. The impression made on the child's mind by the facts which he has observed does not therefore suffice to account for the explanations we have given. The facts requiring explanation are in reality full of what we have called pre-relations. They are seen through a schema which has been constructed on the basis of the child's own body. For it is the child's idea of material force and more particularly his animism that underlie the beliefs of this stage. Every movement is supposed by the child to contain an element of spontaneity. An internal motor is necessary if the object is to be moved by an external motor. If dead leaves " move with the wind ", it is because they are " alive ", even if driven by the wind. There is only a step from this animistic conception of things to the idea that the air that has been displaced rebounds in the direction of the movement : since things which " move with the wind " move partly by themselves, it must be that the wind comes out of them to a certain extent, and thus flows back behind them in order to push them along. Added to this is the fact that all the causes of wind are bound together by participation, both dynamic and material. The wind of the clouds attracts the wind of the trees and the wind of the waves, etc. It is enough for one source of air to function for air to come rushing in from all sides, as was made sufficiently clear in the course of Chap. I. Animistic spontaneity and dynamic or material participation are therefore sufficient to explain the answers of this second stage. But apart from these factors, which are foreign to immediate experience, the facts which the child may have collected in his observations do not account for the complex nature of these answers.

Let us now pass on to the third stage. Children at this stage say that the wind makes itself from the air that is spread out everywhere. The average age of the first stage children was 6; of the second stage, 8 years and 3 months; of the third stage, the average age is 9 years and 6 months. The answers will therefore be superior to those preceding it. The assertion that " the wind makes itself by itself " is no idle statement; it is the sign of an enforced positivism mingling with the remains of animism. Here are some examples:

BOR (9): " Where does the wind come from?—*From the sky.*—How is it made?—. . .—What makes it come? —*It's the air.*—How is that?—. . .—Can the clouds make wind?—*No.*—And the sun?—*No.*—The waves?— *No.*—The sky?—*Yes.*" " What is the sky made of?— *Of air.*" " Does the wind know that it's blowing, or does it not know?—*It knows it.*"

CUOS (10; 2): " Where does the wind come from?— *It's wind.*—Why does it move along?—*Because it goes quickly.*—Why does it go quickly?—. . .—Does it know that it moves along?—*Of course.*—Could we make a wind in this room?—*Yes, when we take a cloth* (and wave it).— Then from where does it come?—*From the air.*—Where does the air come from?—*From outside.*—And how does the air outside begin?—. . .—Where does it come from?—. . .—What do you think?—*If there weren't any we would choke. . . .,*" etc.

BAR (12): Same case. " What is the wind?—*It's air.* —Where does it come from?—*It has always existed.*" Afterwards Bar refutes all the explanations based on the replies of the second stage, that we suggest to him.

The answers of this third stage appear to be exactly like those of an educated adult, but in reality they are far from being anything of the kind. The third stage child is still animistic. At any rate, the wind is still possessed of material force in his eyes. It pushes itself along in the same way as, during the second stage, clouds are supposed to do, with the help of the wind that they themselves produce. We need only ask the children how the wind moves, to find that they will all answer in the same way as Roy (Chap. I, § 2) : " . . . *there is air, and behind there is a lot more air that pushes. . . .*"

OL (8½) : " How does the wind move along ?—*There is always more and more that wants to come, and then the one that wants to come pushes what is in front.*—And how does the part at the back move along ?— . . .—Isn't there always some at the back that pushes ?—*No, not always.*—Then how does it move along ?— . . ." " And has the air got force ?—*Air can have force because there's such a lot of it that it always wants to move.*" " And has the air got force ?—*What is behind pushes what is in front.*—Which of the two has force ?—*Both.*"

ZIM (11) : " Does the wind move ?—*Yes.*—What makes it move ?—*The air.*—How ?—*Because it pushes it.*"

In a word, the air sets itself in motion in virtue of its own force, the air behind pushing that which is in front.

We have not found any better examples than the above, apart from one very remarkable and perhaps spontaneous case which shows a great advance on the previous explanations. Here it is :

BERT (13) refuses to say where the wind comes from : it is air that is everywhere. " Why does the wind move along ?—*Because the heavier layers of air press on it. Then it escapes on all sides and makes currents of air.*—Why are these layers heavier ?—*Because they are damper.*

We have here an attempt at a mechanical explanation which is undoubtedly an anticipation of the fourth stage. But at this age, adult influences play too important a part for us to pursue the present enquiry with any profit.

§ 2. BREATHING.—Let us now try to solve a question which, in spite of appearances, is closely allied to that which we have been discussing : what ideas do children have about the mechanism of breathing ?

The various stages we obtained in investigating this question bear a strong analogy to those outlined in Chap. I. During the first stage, wind is regarded as having a double origin—internal, because we make air, and external, because we attract the air from outside or the wind which comes and settles itself in us. There is a second stage, during which the child discovers that the air is spread all around us, so that what we breathe is the air of the room, but if there were no air in the room, we should make some by breathing. Finally, there is a third stage, when the explanation is in all essentials correct.

It goes without saying that in questioning the child the word " breathing " should be used with discretion. The child should be asked to blow on his fingers and can then be questioned *ad libitum* about the air produced in this way.

Here are examples of the first stage :

Bat (4) : " Blow on your finger. Where does that air come from ?—*From my mouth.*—And where does the air in your mouth come from ?—*From the window.*"

Öst (4) : " Where does that air come from ?—*From my mouth.*—And where does the air in your mouth come from ? —*From outside.*—How did it get there ?—*By my mouth.*" A moment later : " Where does it come from ?—*From my neck.*—And the air in your neck ?—*From my body.*"

Roy (6) : " Where does that air come from ?—*From inside us.*—And where does the air inside us come from ? —*From inside our bodies.*—And the air in our bodies.— *Because you get fat, there's air that comes* (the air comes because we grow fat, it comes to make us fat, and we make it come by growing fatter).—Where does it come from.—*From outside.*"

Gava (6½) tells us, *à propos* of the air produced by the pressure of hands (Chap. I, § 1), that the air leaves the hands, because there is air " *inside the skin*", " *inside the meat*", " *everywhere in your body*". A moment later, Gava blows on his fingers : " Where does this air come from ?— " *From the body* ", etc. But on the other hand, says Gava, the air enters the body by the skin.

Geh (6) : " Where does the air in the mouth come from? —*From the head.*—And that in the head ?—*From the hands*", etc., from the stomach, and so on. " You know how to breathe ?—*When you run too much, then you breathe.*—Where does the breath come from, then ?—*You open your mouth too wide, so the wind comes there.*—Why ? —*It goes through to the stomach.*—Why ?—*Because your stomach's cold : you open your mouth to make the wind come out."*

MON (7) : " Blow. What happens when you blow ?— *Air.*—Where does it come from ?—*From outside.* [Naturally, Mon, like all the children, assumes that there's no air in the room. Besides which, the window is shut].—Is there air in the room ?—*No.*—Inside you ?—*No.*—In your mouth ?—*Yes.*—Where does it come from ?—*From outside.*—How did it come ?— . . . —How did it get inside you ?—*Through the mouth."* " Is there air in your mouth just now ?—*No.*—Blow ! Where does that air come from ?—*From outside."*

TAQ (7) : When one blows, the air comes " *from outside."*—But you can blow now ? You are not outside ?. *It comes from outside, the trees move, there's a wind.*—If you don't go outside, can you still blow ?—*Yes.*—Then where does it come from ?—*From outside.*—You have air in your mouth ?—*Yes.*—What is it for ?—*To eat with. I've eaten a egg."* " But where does the air in your mouth come from ?—*From outside.*—But where does it come from ?—*Through the window. It was on the trees, and then it came."* It will be remembered that Taq attributed the origin of the wind to someone who whistled. That does not prevent the trees from producing it also.

SUT (6 ; 7) : " Where does this air come from ?—*From outside.*—How ?—*When you open your mouth."* " But now [the windows are shut], where does the air in your mouth come from ?—*It's the air from outside."* " You know what it is to breathe ?—*Yes, when you do that* [correct].—When do you breathe ?—*When you sleep.*—Why? —*So as to sleep better.*—Why ?—*It helps us to shut our eyes."*

FERT (8) : " Where does this air come from ?—*From the body."* " But where from ?—*From the stomach.*— What is this air ?—*It's when you eat.*—Breathe ! [correct].— What is breathing ?—*When you blow.*—Where does it come from ?—*From outside.*—Why does one breathe ?— *Because one eats.*—Why ?—*To be able to swallow."*

PUR (8 ; 8) : " When you blow, where does the air come from ?—*From the mouth.*—Where does it come from ?— *We've always got some.*—Why ?—*When you drink hot milk, it makes smoke, no, air in the stomach, then it makes wind."* " If there were no air at all outside, could you blow ?— *Yes, from my mouth."*

We have given a large number of examples, because they are interesting from every point of view. Let us first of all define more closely the word "outside". It would seem at first that all the children wanted was to say that we collect out of doors the air which we subsequently breathe indoors. But some children like Taq, Mon, etc., roundly affirm that the air comes through closed windows and settles inside us, while those quoted in Chapter I proved sufficiently that this way of thinking is very general. We must therefore not read more coherence into the talk of these children than it actually contains. Just as by pressing our hands together or by waving a fan, etc., we attract the air from outside, so, by blowing, do we attract the air from outside in the street.

But it should be emphasised once more that this drawing in of wind by breathing is more in the nature of participation than of attraction. In other words, the child does not imagine that we are mere receptacles for the outside air. We make air ourselves. Not only do Roy, Taq, and the rest attribute a human origin to the air out of doors, but all our children stress the point that we can make air ourselves whenever we want to (see Par). Roy's words are interesting in this connection. Roy does not say, "The wind makes us fat," but "Because you get fat, there's air that comes." We have here participation between two autonomous wills, and not mechanical action of one on the other. If we take the children's ideas as a whole, it will be easy enough to find the right mental context for their statements.

For the reader will perceive at once the analogy existing between these answers and the material we collected in our enquiry on thought and dreams (*C.W.*, Chaps. I-III). According to several children we have met, thought is made of air, as are also dreams. This is because very young children identify thought with dreams: we think with our mouths. It is therefore only natural that thought should frequently be assimilated to breath. As to dreams, the case of Sat, in which breathing is regarded as an adjuvant to sleep, would seem to show that the child's identification of dreams with air is not an entirely verbal matter. Be that as it may, the fact remains that the children who told us that thought was made of " air ", also stated that thought was both inside us and outside us. Thought participates with the wind that blows in the trees and so on. (See *C.W.*, Chap. I, § 1, case of Ron, Brunn, etc.) Our children's answers about breathing are enough to show where the roots of these beliefs lie : breath is simply a wind, partly produced by us, partly coming from outside, and such, that between these two sources the material participation is complete.

Finally, it should be noted how wrongly the air that we breathe is localised in the organism, it is confused with intestinal gases, or again with the air which we swallow in eating.

The continuity of these answers with those of the second stage is a warrant for the soundness of our interpretation. For during this new stage, the child knows that there is air in the room and admits an unceasing interchange between the internal air and the air of the room. Only—and this is the decisive point—he continues to think that if there were no air in the room, he could make some by blowing and breathing.

Here are some examples :

ANT (8) : " *When you breathe, the air comes into the mouth ; when you blow, it comes out of the mouth again.*"— " Where is this breath ?—*In the stomach.*—Why ?— *Because we must have air.*" " *When you breathe, the breathing attracts the air.*"

RE (8½) has just discovered that there is air in the room.—" Where does this breath come from ?—*From the stomach.*—Where does it come from ?—*It goes in by the nose, then it goes out.*" " Can *we* make air, in a room without air ?—*No. . . . Yes.*—How ?—*By blowing.*"

CESS (14) : " *We have breath in our bodies, and it blows.* —Where does it come from ?—*It's the air that's in the room. When you breathe, you have air in the lungs.*—If there were no air in the room, could we make some all the same ?—*Yes*."

In the third stage, finally, the child's ideas conform entirely to our's.

The observations we have been summarising carry with them certain conclusions, in connection with which it may be useful to recall the views of psycho-analysts concerning the origin of the idea of the soul. According to Jones, whose thesis has been very ably summarised and discussed by Larguier des Bancels,[1] the comparison made by the Ancients between soul and breath arises solely from childish ideas about intestinal flatulence. Children, says Jones, cannot in any way be interested in breathing, which is automatic. On the other hand, they have every reason to be interested in intestinal gases, and this, indeed, is what current observation is always showing. Now if it be admitted, as the psycho-analysts claim, that the central ideas of primitive peoples have their origin in the mentality of the child, and if the universal character of " breath " as the substratum and transmitter of life be recognised, then it is impossible not to make the conjecture that this " breath " is simply a symbol for intestinal gases. Jones goes a step further and suggests that if fecundation is often represented in myths as due to a " breath," this must be because children have the same idea. Here, again, the breath in question can *a fortiori* be nothing but a symbol for flatulence.

Let us confine the discussion to the question of the child. In support of Jones' contention we may bring forward the fact that nearly all our children of the first stage confused ordinary breath with the gases contained in the digestive tube. But does this mean that the one is the " symbol " of the other ? There is simply identity between them. The wind out of doors and the human breath are not two distinct symbols of flatulence ; the

[1] Larguier des Bancels, " Sur les origines de la notion de l'âme à propos d'une interdiction de Pythagore," *Arch. de Psychol.*, Vol. XVII (1918).

child conceives all the air in the body as resulting from the irruption of the wind into the body, and vice versa, the wind in general as having issued from the human body. As to the hypothesis regarding fecundation, M. Larguier points out with unanswerable good sense that children can hardly be expected to have views about fecundation when primitive peoples are devoid of any definite ideas on the subject. It is quite probable that flatulence enters into children's ideas about birth, since babies are often thought to have come out of the anus or out of the fæces. Only, as always happens when we try to reconstruct a belief logically, the relations between the established facts are quite other than we could have anticipated. It is not because breath eventually plays a part in the child's conception of birth that it has become the principle underlying "spirit", "thought", or "soul" in the history of ideas. It is far rather because air plays a preponderant part in all the child's ideas about the world, and about movement in particular. And above all, it is because thought, being conceived as identical with speech, and breath, being conceived as participating with the wind in the trees, wind in general is regarded as closely connected with thought. Arguing from this, it is of course quite conceivable that participations should have been established between the soul and flatulence, as Pythagoras' proscription of beans, which is the theme of M. Larguier's discussion, seems to show. But these participations are secondary, and due to the fact that for the child there is no difference between the breath of the body and the intestinal gases.

Finally, it should be pointed out that when the child finds out how he breathes, this discovery probably has a very real influence on the explanations of movement we have already dealt with. For the ideas held about breathing show us that the child believes himself to be both making air and to be attracting the wind when he breathes. And this is so, because his breath appears to participate with the wind, since wind is breath that has come out of man's body, and breath is wind that has come in from outside. It is therefore quite obvious that such ideas closely recall the most primitive explanations of movement, in which the moving body is supposed to create air, while at the same time it attracts the wind as it moves through space.

CHAPTER III

MOVEMENT OF THE CLOUDS AND THE HEAVENLY BODIES

THE explanation of movement is the central point to which all the child's ideas about the world converge. Childish animism, in the first place, shows that the child endows nearly all bodies with a certain spontaneity of movement. It shows, above all, that the distinction between a body's own movement and that which is determined from outside is only reached after much groping and many difficulties whose causes it will be interesting to examine. Further, the affinity between artificialism and animism shows that physical objects, which are conceived both as made and as alive, are obedient to a sort of perpetual moral constraint, as well as to their own spontaneity. This means that their movement is thought of neither as fundamentally free nor as physically determined. Finally, the ideas relating to the problem of air throw a fuller light upon these difficulties. Bodies make air, but are themselves moved along by air. How are we to understand this relation? We must analyse all ideas relating to movement as fundamentally as possible, and we must also do so as objectively as possible, that is to say, without being influenced by our own adult logic and what it might be inclined to deduce from previously acquired results.

But this analysis raises technical points of considerable difficulty. The particular questions that one puts to the child in this realm are extremely suggestive. The best way is to begin with very vague questions, and then to take advantage of every answer by adding: " Why do

you say that ? " or " How does that happen ? ", and
so on. It is through this indirect method that we discovered that some children explain the movement of
clouds by the reflux of air which these bring about themselves. But it should be added that it took us three
years to discover this fact. Formerly, when a child told
us that " the cloud moved along with wind," we left
it at that. It is therefore highly probable that our present
results are still only approximately correct. The art of
questioning children requires patience above everything
else.

§ 1. THE MOVEMENT OF CLOUDS.—Five stages may be
distinguished in the explanations which the child gives
of the movement of clouds. The first stage is magical :
we make the clouds move by walking. The clouds obey
us at a distance. The average age of this stage is 5. The
second stage is both artificialist and animistic. Clouds
move because God or men make them move. The average
age of this stage is 6. During a third stage, of which the
average age is 7, clouds are supposed to move by themselves, though the child says nothing definite as to how
this movement is effected. But in addition to this, the
movement is conditioned by moral and physical causes,
which shows that the artificialism has simply been transferred to the objects. It is the sun, the moon, etc., that
make the clouds move along ; only, the heavenly bodies
determine these movements, not as a physical cause
determines its effect, but rather as one man compels
another by commanding him, with or without the addition
of physical force. During this third stage, the child says
nothing definite about the " how " of the cloud's spontaneous movement, but it is obvious that he has at the
back of his mind a motor schema which prepares the way
for the explanation which comes during the fourth stage.
For according to the children of the fourth stage, the wind
pushes the clouds, but the wind has itself come out of the
clouds. The average age of this stage is 8. When, finally,

the fifth stage is reached (average age 9), a correct explanation is found.

Here are examples of the first stage, of which traces will be found even among much older children.

SALA (8) : " You have already seen the clouds moving along ? What makes them move ?—*When we move along, they move along too.*—Can *you* make them move ?—*Everybody can, when they walk.*—When I walk and you are still, do they move ?—*Yes.*—And at night, when everyone is asleep, do they move ?—*Yes.*—But you tell me that they move when somebody walks.—*They always move. The cats, when they walk, and then the dogs, they make the clouds move along.*"

PORT (9) : " What makes the clouds move along ?—*It's God.*—What does he do ?—*When he walks, the clouds walk too. Why, Miss, even when the people in the street are walking too, it makes the clouds move.*—So *you* can make them move ?—*Yes, Miss, sometimes when I walk, I look at the sky, I see the clouds that are moving along, and the moon too, when it's there.*—Have you seen yet whether the clouds move when you are still ? Do they move ?—*No, Miss.*"

JULI (10) : " What makes the clouds move along ?—*It's when you walk.*"

These three children told us that clouds are alive and conscious. The magic in this case would therefore seem to consist in a sort of obligation which man imposes upon living beings capable of obedience. In the most primitive cases the child simply notes a relation between his own movement and the apparent movement of the cloud, and owing to the egocentric orientation of his mind (*C.W.*, Chap. IV) concludes immediately a dynamic participation between his own activity and that of the cloud.

There is only a step from this stage to the semi-artificialist and semi-animistic explanation of the second stage. The following half-way case shows the possibility of this transition :

CLI (3 ; 9), who sees, during a walk, some white clouds which are moving very quickly, exclaims spontaneously : " *It's the mechanic who makes them go.*" A few days before, he had seen a steam-roller and had been very much impressed by the mechanic and by the white smoke coming out of the chimney. Besides, Cli also calls engine-drivers " mechanics." For him, therefore, the movement of the clouds is explained by the action of the mechanic, who causes the appearance of the smoke, the cloud being conceived as a kind of smoke (see, in connection with this, *C.W.*, Chap. IX, § 3).

Such a case as this is still magical in a certain sense, since the mechanic is supposed to make all clouds move along, even those which are in the sky. But it already shows signs of artificialism, since behind the participation which Cli establishes between the mechanic and the clouds, we can already feel the presence of the idea that the mechanic *makes* the clouds (*i.e.* the smoke), and is thus the cause of their movement as well as of their appearance. It goes without saying that with many children, as with Cli himself, artificialism is almost as primitive as the magical relation. On the whole, however, it constitutes a later stage.

The second stage presents us with a paradox which is already implicitly contained in the answers of the first stage, and which we shall meet with again in the two subsequent stages. It is the idea of a double motor, both internal and external. The clouds move both of them-selves and under external influence. During the first four stages, the motor is internal and animistic: clouds move along because they are sufficiently alive and conscious to carry out their peculiar function, or office. As to the external factor, it is magical during the first stage and becomes artificialist during the second:

STEI (5) : " What makes the clouds move along ?—*God does.*—How ?—*He pushes them.*" But Stei does not think that this physical act of God's is indispensable to the cloud's movement: the clouds " *stay* [in the air] *because God wants them to stay.*" Besides, the clouds move of themselves, but by divine command : " *Some clouds are black. They go round and round. When the sun shines, they don't go round.*—Then what makes them move along ?

—*God does.*" This action of the sun on the clouds shows the inception of the second stage.

Roe (6) : " What makes the clouds move ?—*God does.* —How does he do it. Do they move by themselves or is there something there.—*They move by themselves.*"

Pen (8 ; 2) : What makes the clouds move along ?— *God does.*" But on the other hand, " *they are alive.*—Why ? —*Because they move.*"

Rey (7) : " *It is God* " who makes them move along, but they are alive, nevertheless, " *because they can see the people who are there who are not moving.*"

This shows what the second stage amounts to : God or men make the clouds move along, but the clouds are alive and conscious. There is no contradiction here. There is simply the exercise of moral constraint on the cloud which then responds with voluntary obedience. Added to this, of course, is the fact that God occasionally makes use of his hands to " push " the cloud ; but this is a personal and not merely a physical relationship.

During the third stage, this purely mental explanation remains the same, but God and men no longer play any part. It is the heavenly bodies now, that make the clouds move along. The artificialism is simply transferred to things, and things act on one another like living persons. Thus there are always two causes at work, one internal— the cloud moving along of itself, like an animal, one external—sun, moon, night, rain, and cold conditioning this movement. But this external cause acts in two ways. There is the moral way, the sun pursuing the cloud which yields before it, and there is the finalistic way, which is still moral. For rain or night making the clouds move along comes to the same thing as the clouds moving along in order to bring about rain or night. If then sun, night, etc., cause the advance of clouds, they do so much as a policeman puts a thief to flight, or as a school-bell assembles the scholars.

We can distinguish five types in the answers of the third stage. Answers of the first type attribute the advance of clouds to the heavenly bodies, answers of the second type attribute it to night, those of the third to rain, those of the fourth to the cold, to wind or bad weather, it being understood of course that these causes are supposed to act partly morally and not in an exclusively physical manner. Finally, according to answers of the fifth type, clouds move by themselves. But at the back of this explanation by pure spontaneity of movement, one feels that moral and finalistic factors are still vaguely at work.

Here are examples of the first type :

GRIM (5) : The clouds are smoke from the chimneys. " Why do they move along ?—*It's the moon that makes them move,*" but Grim cannot explain precisely how it is done. " Do they know that they are moving ?—*Yes.*— Do they know that the moon makes them move ?—*Yes.*— And does the moon know it ?—*Yes.*" Grim merely observes that the clouds accompany the moon, from which he concludes an influence which is, at the same time, both physical and moral.

BOV (6 ; 5) : We speak of the sun. " What makes the sun move ?—*The clouds.*—How ?—*Because they move and that pulls it along.*" A moment later, Bov speaks of " some " suns : " Have you seen the suns ?—*Yes, the more there are of them, the more I walk, the more I see.*— What are they like ?—*They make the clouds go, because they're stronger. They pull the clouds, because the clouds are always underneath.*" We point out to Bov his vicious circle, but this does not in the least worry him : " *It's the clouds* [which make the sun move], *because they go quicker, so the sun is stronger to make holes in the clouds.*" It will be seen that the relationship between the clouds and the sun is conceived as being a fight, during which the victory belongs alternately to either party. The following remarks confirm this interpretation : " When do the clouds stay still ?—*When there's no sun . . . I see the clouds moving,*" and even more : " *When it's going to rain, it* [the sun] *goes home quickly.*"

EB (7) : " What makes the clouds move along ?— *It's the sun.*—How ?—*With its rays. It pushes the clouds.*"

NIC (7 ; 11) : " *It's the sun that pushes.*—How ?—*With its rays.*"

In short, the sun acts on the clouds as a policeman does on a thief : he puts them to flight, not by touching them, but simply by appearing on the scene ; or else, he uses his fists. But whether the action be moral, or semi-moral and semi-physical, it always takes place between one living being and another. Let us recall in this connection the remark of Vern (*C.W.*, Chap. VII, § 3) that the clouds "try to fight the sun." Here, again, the cause of movement is both internal and external, and the motor acts through moral as well as through physical means.

The same thing happens when the child attributes the advance of the clouds to night (second type), with an added touch of finalism : night causes the cloud to approach, because it is the cloud's business to bring about night. Here is an example :

DUC (6½) has not yet been questioned by us on the nature of night. " Where do these [clouds seen from the window] come from ?—*From the sky.*—Why do they move along ?—*Because it will soon be dark.*" Later on Duc explains that night comes " *when black clouds come along.*"

CAP (7) : "What makes the clouds move along ?—*The dark.*" Same explanations.

In short, night, being made of clouds, is the motor cause, because it is the final cause or purpose, of the movement of clouds.

Exactly the same thing happens when the child attributes the movement of clouds to rain (third type).

BONJ (6½) : Clouds move " *sometimes.*—What makes them move ?—*Rain.*—How does it make them move ?—*It falls down.*—But why do the clouds move ?—*Because the rain falls down.*" A little later : " Is it the wind that makes the clouds move ?—*No.*—What is it then ?—*The rain.*" Similarly, Bonj tells us in connection with the heavenly bodies that the sun advances " *because he wants to give us light.*"

Thus the rain is both the motor cause and the final cause of the cloud's advance, showing once again that the cloud is supposed to move, like an animal, for psychical or moral reasons.

When children say that it is the cold or the wind that makes the clouds move, the problem becomes a little more complicated. "Cold" is practically the same thing as wind (see Chap. II, § 1, stage ii, type 6). It looks, therefore, as though we were dealing with a more advanced type of explanation, *i.e.* a purely physical explanation. But this is not so. Even if children of this type introduce the wind, this in nowise excludes the influence of moral reasons from their explanations: the cloud flies away from, or after the wind, because it fears fine or bad weather, etc. Further, it is not passively pushed by the wind, but makes use of it like a sailing-ship. In short, when the child says that the wind pushes the clouds, one should not accept the statement at its face value. So long as moral reasons still play a part, and so long as the child has not yet invented the schema of the reflux of air, all these cases should be classed in the present stage and present type. Here are some examples:

CAM (6½) begins by saying, about the movement of the moon, that "*the clouds walk, and the moon goes with them too.*" "Do the clouds move or not?—*They walk. It's the wind that pushes them.*—Why?—*Because the wind is hard* [=rough].—Why?—*They feel cold, so they walk.*" He adds that they walk "*because they're following us.*" This complexus of beliefs, according to which the moon and the clouds accompany us, shows that the wind acts only as an adjuvant: the cloud is still gifted with the power of movement, it follows us, it goes away when it feels cold, etc.

KRUG (6½): "What makes them move?—*It's when there's wind and snow, well then, they go. They go away, then they come back after.*"

MOS (8): "Why do they move along?—*Because they feel cold.*—Do cold things move along?—*No.*—Why does that make the clouds move?— . . .*"

DUC (8): "What makes the clouds move along?—*It's the air.*—What air?—*The air from the trees* [here we find again one of the habitual theories of the origin of wind], *and then* [when] *it's very cold. . . .*" "Are they alive or not?—*Yes . . . because they fly in the air as if they were birds.*"

Thus, although the introduction of air brings a new element as compared to the earlier types, it does nothing to destroy the idea that clouds move by themselves. They move, because "they are cold", "because they are following us" (survival of first stage), because they want to avoid wind and snow, and, above all, because they fly by themselves like birds, making use of the wind when it is there, but doing without when it is not. It will therefore be an easy task to distinguish children of this type from those who have reached the fourth and fifth stages, for then, wind has become an indispensable physical condition of the movement of clouds, whether it is produced by the cloud itself (fourth stage) or whether it is considered as having originated from anywhere outside (fifth stage).

A fifth type of this third stage is characterised by the fact that the idea of an external motor is absent, and the internal animistic motor alone comes into action. In other words, the cloud is supposed to move along " by itself." But, as a matter of fact, the idea of an external motor working for moral reasons alone is still taken for granted : the cloud has received an order whose function or office it is in the spiritual interaction of things to compel the cloud to advance. Here are some examples :

BAR (9) : The clouds move along " *by themselves,*" " *because if they didn't move along, there would never be any rain.*" " But what do they do ? Why do they not fall on our heads ?—*Because if they fell, why, we'd be dead.*—But how is that ? They wouldn't care !—*Oh, yes, they don't see. They would* [only] *feel, because it's like water* [note this spontaneous animism, in spite of a counter-suggestion].—They are not alive !—*Why, yes ! They pass by* [=they travel]. *When it hails on the mountain, it passes.*" " When it is hot, can they feel it ?—*They can feel, because they are hot too.*—Can they go where they like ? —*No.*—Why ?—*Because if they went, they'd end by staying there.* [Cf. the moral law : they must come back].—Then the clouds can't go where they like ?—*Why, yes !* "

PER (7½) : " The clouds move along. Why ?—*To go to another place.*—How ?—*All alone.* Can they go where they like ?—*Yes.*"

Clouds, therefore, move by themselves, but for the benefit of man. It is this office of theirs which determines them : they must come in order to give us rain, they must not go away but must come back again, etc. Considering that in all the preceding cases the moving cause was always closely or remotely confused with the purpose, we may say that this fifth type is the limiting case of the third stage, and *a fortiori* of all the preceding stages.

Thus during the first three stages the child confuses physical and moral laws. Such physical causes as are occasionally taken into account are the constraint exercised by one body upon another, like that of a kind of police force (as when God or the sun make the clouds move along) or non-essential adjuvants (as when the cloud makes use of the wind) which is then simply added to the force of the cloud itself as it " flies " along.

But from the fourth stage onwards, that is to say, from the age of 7-8, a new element appears in the explanation of movement : it is the idea of physical determinism. Henceforward, the movement of clouds, whatever be their private force or will, is explained solely by the action of a body external to them, namely, the wind. The wind has thus become an indispensable physical cause. Final or moral causes no longer work without a motor cause that is independent of them.

Two new phenomena, however, add to the complexity of this particular conception, and thus help to differentiate the fourth stage from the fifth. The one is the schema of the reflux of air, or of ἀντιπερίστασις, where the child thinks that the clouds themselves make the wind that drives them along. The spontaneously moving cloud creates a current of air which rushes in behind it and pushes it along. The other peculiarity of this stage is that the children, although they accept the idea of physical force, go on believing that in moving, the cloud is directed towards certain ends which make use of the wind as their instrument. These ends are naturally anthropocentric.

If we seek to trace the parentage of these two characteristics, we shall find that this remnant of finalism is inherited from the transcendent artificialism of the second stage and the immanent artificialism of the third stage. As to the ἀντιπερίστασις, it is clearly the outcome of the animism of the early stages : the cloud pushes itself along as birds fly or fishes swim. It is thus this duality of animism and artificialism which explains the complex nature of these fourth stage ideas. In this connection, the fourth stage, though it is the first to attain to the idea of physical or mechanical necessity, inherits many of the biologico-moral conceptions of the earlier stages. If a somewhat impudent comparison be allowed, this stage may be said to play the same part as the physics of Aristotle, which, laden as they are with artificialism and finalism, yet show signs of an effort at scientific explanation.

Here are some examples of the fourth stage, beginning with one which shows, it would seem, certain traces of the preceding stage :

AUD (9 ; 9) tells us, about the wind : " *It comes from the sky.*—How is it made in the sky ?—*Don't know.*—What do you think ?—*It might come from the clouds.*—How is that ?—*Because, when the clouds move along, it makes air. When they are not moving, there's not much of it.*—Why do the clouds move along ?—*Because it's the air which they make (!) that makes them move along.*—How is that ?—*Because it pushes them.*—Why ?—*Don't know. Because it pushes them.*—Are they moving to-day ?—*Yes.*—Quickly or slowly ?—*Slowly.*—Why ?—*Because it is sunny.*—What does that do ?—*When there is no sun, it makes them go quicker.*—Why ?—*Because the sun holds the air back a little.*" " Why do the clouds go slowly when it is sunny ? —*Because it's hot.*—And then ?—*It makes them slow up.*— Why ?—*Because the sun takes some air for itself.*—Why ? —*To breathe it.*—Do you believe that ?—*Yes.*—Is the sun alive ?—*Don't know. Yes.*—Why ?—*Because it can give us light. Otherwise, it couldn't.*"

The opening is clearly of the fourth stage. The introduction of the sun, on the other hand, undoubtedly shows traces of the third, but it will be seen that the sun is supposed to act physically and not only morally on the clouds.

GAL (10 ; 2) : " What makes the clouds move along ?— *The air.*" But, on the other hand, the air comes from the clouds : " How do they make the air ?—*By moving.*" In addition, the clouds follow us. " How is that ?— *Because we walk.*" But this survival from the first stage here takes on a purely physical aspect, so that the air which makes the clouds move comes partly " *from here.*— What makes this air ?—*We do.*—How ?—*By walking.*" A moment later, we ask Gal what is able to produce the air. Gal then enumerates to us all moving things : the clouds, the sun, the moon, the stars, and ourselves. Thus, to the idea of the ἀντιπερίστασις is added the idea of an interaction between various currents of air.

DUSS (10 ; 7) : " *The wind makes the clouds move along,*" but the clouds " *make a wind.*—How ?—*By moving.*" (See the case of Duss, Chap. II, § 1.)

PUR (8 ; 7) : " *It's the air which they* [the clouds] *make, and then it* [the air] *chases the clouds.*" (See also Chap. II, § 1.)

DEB (9) tells us, in relation to the moon, that it is the clouds which make it move along. " How ?—*By making a wind.*" As for the clouds, " *it's the wind that pushes them.*" The " clouds can make a wind ?—*Yes.*—How ?—*By pushing the other clouds.*"

Here is another very spontaneous case, which is probably primitive :

LEO (7) believes that the clouds are made of smoke. Now, in the explanation of a steam-engine (see Chap. X), Leo accounts in this way for the smoke rising : " *When it comes out, it makes air. The smoke makes air.*"

According to all these children, clouds advance owing to the air which they themselves produce, and the clouds make this air *by their movement.* This is the typical schema of the reflux of air. According to other children, who should be placed in the same group, things are slightly different. The cloud still moves owing to the air that it produces, but this air is inside the cloud and escapes from it. This escaping air is what drives the cloud along. Here are some examples :

ANT (8) in connection with the sun : " *It's the wind that pushes it.*—Where does this wind come from ?—*It's the clouds that let it escape.*—And how do the clouds move along ?—*It's the wind that makes them move along.*—What wind ?—*The wind of the clouds.*" This is the same idea as was held by Ant in relation to our enquiry into the origin of the wind (Chap. II, § 1).

CUR (8 ; 4) : " What makes the clouds move along ?—*The air.*—What air ?—*The air in the sky.*—Where does it come from ?—*It's the air of the clouds.*"

BOR (9) : The clouds move along " *because they have a current.*—What is this current ?—*It's in the clouds.*—But why do the clouds not fall ?—*Because it keeps them up.*—What does ?—*The current.*—Where does it come from, the current that holds·them there ?—*From inside the clouds.*—How is this current made ?—*Of air.*—And how does it hold them up ?—*It pushes them upwards.*"

This last schema is closely akin to that of the reflux of air. Which is prior to the other ? It would be hard to say. Both types are contemporaneous, and undoubtedly there is interaction between them. The idea that clouds contain air leads naturally to the idea that the air flows back in order to push them, and vice versa.

When, finally, the fifth stage is reached, the child's ideas have become identical to ours. The wind pushes the cloud, and this wind is not in any way produced by the cloud itself. Here is an example :

GUT (9½) : " Why do the clouds move more or less quickly ?—*Because of the wind. They move along by the wind.*—Where does this wind come from ?—*From the sky.*—And how is the wind made ?—*Don't know.*—And can the clouds make a wind ?—*No.*—Can they make a wind by moving ?—*No.*—And when there is no wind, can they move along alone ?—*No.*"

These last questions were necessary to make sure that the child had really reached the fifth stage. The answer " The wind pushes the cloud " may belong to the third, fourth, or fifth stage. But the criteria we have given should suffice to ensure an objective classification. All one need remember is that very young children often complicate things by bringing in the possible participations between the various sources of air, but this does not constitute an insuperable obstacle to the task of questioning and classifying these children.

In conclusion, we should point out that the results obtained by Mlle Rodrigo on some hundred Spanish children from both town and country, entirely confirm what we have been saying. Particularly frequent is the first stage answer : " What makes the clouds move along ? —We do when we walk." We also find a whole group of answers which attribute this movement to the sun, to thunder, to the stars, to rain, etc. (third stage). It is not until about the age of 9½ that a decisive part is attributed to the wind.

§ 2. THE MOVEMENT OF THE HEAVENLY BODIES.—The question of the movement of the heavenly bodies is naturally more obscure for the child than that of the movement of the clouds, but for the younger children it is of exactly the same order, since the heavenly bodies are situated on the same plane as are the clouds. The answers obtained may be roughly classified, and the interesting thing is that we shall find the same schema of evolution as we have just been analysing in connection with clouds.

Thus the five stages appear again. During the first, the cause of movement is magical and animistic—we make the heavenly bodies move when we walk, and they obey us consciously. During a second stage, this movement is due to God or to men, but magic is replaced by artificialism. Of course, the heavenly bodies are still regarded as alive and conscious, and they still follow us when we walk. But it is no longer so much because we make them do so by magic as because they " want " to come with us. During a third stage, these two features are retained as such, but the artificialism is transferred to the things: clouds, night, rain, etc., are supposed to set the heavenly bodies in motion for reasons that are moral as well as physical. During a fourth stage, the heavenly bodies move in virtue of the reflux of air, of fire, or of heat which they make themselves. The cause of movement has thus become physical. Nevertheless, the heavenly bodies are still regarded as alive and conscious, and as a rule they are still believed to follow us about on our walks. When, finally, a fifth stage is reached, the movements of the heavenly bodies find a purely mechanical explanation, such as the wind, etc.

The average age of the first stage is 5, of the second, 6, of the third, 7, of the fourth, 8, and of the fifth, 9½.

Here are examples of the first stage:

NAI (4½): " When you go for a walk in the evening, does the moon stay still ?—*It comes with me, it follows us.* —Can the moon go where it likes, or is there something that makes it move along ?—*It's me, when I walk.*"

The daughter of Rasmussen, R., at 4 years old, exclaims, on seeing the moon: " *It's the moon, it's round . . . it walks when we walk.*" It was explained to R. that this was not true, but three months later she made the same remark in connection with the stars: " *What are those little bright things up there ? When we walk, they walk too, but they don't really do it.*" [This final restriction has been merely learned.] [1]

The heavenly bodies are therefore both alive and compelled by us to move along. This twofold cause explains their advance. The passage from this stage to the second, *i.e.* to that of artificialism takes place imperceptibly. For there is every shade of transition in passing from the idea that we make the sun and moon move by walking to the idea that we give them orders to obey, and again between this and the idea that the makers of the sun and moon compel them to move. Here are some examples of the second stage.

[1] Rasmussen, *Psychologie de l'enfant. L'enfant entre quatre et sept ans*. French transl., Cornet, Alcan, 1924, pp. 25-26.

GAND (6): " Why does the sun move along ?—*To keep us warm.*" " Is the sun alive ?—*Yes, because it moves along.*" " And the moon, how does it move along ?—*It's God. . . . It's God that does it.*"

CAUD (9): " Does the sun move or not ?—*It moves by itself.*—Can it go as fast as it likes ?—*No.*—Why ?—*It's God.*—Can the sun see the daylight ?—*Yes, of course it can, as it gives us light ! It hides to make the night.*" The same explanation is given for the moon : it doesn't come out, during the day " *because during the day the sun comes.*" " Could the sun not move along by itself, without God ?—*Yes, if it wanted to.*"

In a word, sun and moon move of their own free will, but their advance is controlled for moral reasons by God or by man.

This bipolarity reappears in the second stage. On the one hand, the sun and moon still move along owing to a living and conscious force within them. On the other hand, there is an external motor, no longer God or man, but clouds, or rain, or wind, etc. The interesting thing is, that the external motor does not yet act in a wholly physical manner, for moral influences are still at work between one body and another. The artificialism is simply transferred to the objects. The average age of children at this stage is 7.

As was the case in connection with clouds, this third stage is of a very complex character. In order to interpret it aright the three following circumstances should be borne in mind. The first is that up to the age of 8, children go on believing that the sun, moon, and stars, follow us about on our walks (see *C.W.*, Chap. VII, § 2). This fact alone is sufficient to show that the heavenly bodies retain their spontaneity, even when the explanation appears to be purely mechanical. For, if they follow us, it is in order " to look at us ", " because they are curious ", " because they want to know what we are doing ". Secondly, the following should be remembered : owing to his difficulty in performing logical addition and multiplication (see *J.R.*, Chap. IV, § 2), the child will always

point to a single cause of movement when in his spontaneous thought there is an agglomeration of causes.
Thirdly, it must be realised that from the age of 7-8, the
child thinks of the heavenly bodies as in the nature of
compact clouds, something like the smoke of chimneys.

This will enable us to understand the complexity of the
answers of this stage. We shall distinguish five chief
types of answer, according as the movement of the
heavenly bodies is due to clouds, to night, to rain, to wind,
or to an entirely spontaneous cause. Answers introducing
the wind will be classed in this stage only in so far as
to this explanation is added another of a definitely moral
order.

Here are examples of the first type :

Roy (6½) : " How does the sun move along ?—*It's the
clouds.*—How ?—*Because the clouds move along.*—Do they
touch the sun ?—*No.*—How do they make the sun move
along ?— . . . ." " What does it do at night ?—*It hides.*
—How does it move so as to go and hide ?—*It's the
clouds.*—How ?—*It makes the sun move along.*—How is
that ?—*The cloud makes the sun move along because the
cloud walks.*—And then ?—*It brings bad weather.*" " Does
the sun know when it's fine weather ?—*Yes.*—Why does
it know ?—*Because there are no clouds.*—Does the moon
move along or not ?—*It moves. It's the clouds that make
it move along too.*—How ?—*Because the clouds move along.*
—What does the moon do when you go for a walk ?—
It walks too.—Do the stars move ?—*Yes.*—Why ?—
Because we move sometimes.—What makes them move ?
—*It's the . clouds.*—Can they move when there are no
clouds ?—*No.*—Not at all ?—*Sometimes they can move
because we move.*—What makes them move when there
are no clouds ?—*It's because we move.*"

Bov (6 ; 5), as we have seen (§ 1, 3rd stage), says sometimes, that the clouds make the sun move " *because they
walk and that pulls it along,*" and sometimes, that the sun
" *makes the clouds walk because it's stronger, it pulls the
clouds, because the clouds are always underneath.*—Which
do you think is right ?—*It's the clouds* [which pull the
sun along] *because they go quicker, so the sun is stronger to
make holes in the clouds.*" Thus the sun is capable of
spontaneous movement : " *When it's going to rain, it goes*

home quickly." It can be seen that the sun follows the clouds as one animal follows after another but not as a mechanical cause is necessarily followed by its effect.

BUL (7 ; 6) : " Where is the sun to-day ?—*Behind the mountain.*—Why ?—*Because it's bad weather.*—Does it not appear when it's bad weather ?—*No, because it rains.*— Why does it not come ?—*Because it gets* [=it would get] *wet.*—How does the sun move along ?—*It's the clouds that make it move.*—How ?—*It's the wind . . . because they push it.*" Thus the cloud acts mechanically, but the sun remains free to come or not to come, to allow the cloud to push it, or to go away.

FRAN (9, backward) : " Does the sun move ?—*Yes.*— Why ?—*Because it wants to make strong sunshine.*—Why ? —*Because sometimes there are ladies and gentlemen who are going for a walk and they are pleased when it's fine.*—Does the sun see them ?—*Yes.*—How does it move along ?— *Because of the clouds. Sometimes they push the sun, because sometimes the clouds move along. That makes the sun move too.*—When there are no clouds, what does the sun do ?— *It moves along too.*—And when we walk, what does the sun do ?—*Sometimes it looks at us ; then sometimes it follows us.*"

BRUL (8) : " *The clouds push it,*" but without wind or clouds " *it goes all the same.*" . . . " *It goes by itself.*"

DEB (9) : " *It's the clouds that push it.*—How ?—*By making a wind.*—And when there are no clouds, does the moon move along or not ?—*It moves by itself.*—How ?— *It's the stars.*—What are the stars ?—*A little lightning.*— What makes the lightning ?—*When the clouds meet each other.*"

LUG (12, very backward) : " *The clouds push the sun,*" but it can also go by itself, " *because it's made of fire.*"

There are two possible interpretations. The first is mechanical : the clouds push the sun and moon, and in this way cause them to move along. The second is moral : the sun imitates the advance of the clouds or flees before them, etc. Which of these two are we to choose ? Clearly, the originality of these children resides in their unwillingness to exclude anything. The clouds incite the sun and moon to movement as one animal does another, sometimes by force, sometimes by example, sometimes by fear. The proof of this is that several of these children say that when there are no clouds, we suffice to set the heavenly bodies in motion (see Roy). On the other hand, the heavenly bodies move by themselves when there are no clouds (Bov, Fran, Brul, etc.). These answers are therefore the exact counterpart of the beliefs held during the third stage in relation to the movement of clouds. In a word, the sun makes use of the clouds to move along, but it can leave them or flee from them, and retains in their absence a considerable capacity for self-movement.

According to other children it is " the sky " that makes the heavenly bodies move. But there is nothing to be gained by classing this type of answer apart, for it is closely related to the preceding type, of which, indeed, it constitutes only a special case. The sky consists of " tightly packed (*serré*) clouds."

RE (8) begins by stating that the sun moves along " *all by itself.*" He then defines his meaning more closely : " *It's the sky.*—How ?—*It moves too.*" The sky is made of clouds : " *There are lots of little clouds close together.*"

Thus the sky is a large cloud which drags the sun along with it, but the sun makes use of this motor without being entirely subject to it.

Answers of a second type appeal to night and are chiefly concerned with the moon, although night is also regarded as chasing the sun away.

Here is an example :

LUG (12 ; 13, very backward) : One half of the moon has gone " *to a country where it is night.*—How is it that she has gone ?—*She had to go into the other country.*— What makes her go away ?—*The dark.*—How does this happen ?—*She goes away when it is light here.*" According to Lug, the moon " follows us " on our walks.

This shows that night acts chiefly morally, " *she has to* . . ." In other cases it acts physically, being conceived as a great dark cloud that envelops the moon.

A third type of explanation consists in accounting for the movements of the heavenly bodies by the action of the weather, and more especially of the rain.

KRUG (6½) : " Does the sun move ?—*Yes.*—Why ?—
Because sometimes it goes to France and everywhere.—How
does it move ?—*The rain drives it along.*—And why does
it move when there's no rain ?—*Because it is going to drive
the sun away.*—And when it isn't raining ?—*It can always
move.*—How ?—*It goes away.*—Does it move alone or does
something make it move ?—*It moves by itself.*—Do you
really think so ?—*It's the air that makes it go away.*—How
does the air do this ?—*It* [the air] *is strong, then it blows
very hard and makes the sun go away.*"

The movement in question is clearly that of living beings
who chase and pursue one another. Krug's later utter-
ances introduce us to a fourth type of answer : the air is
what makes the sun and moon move along. This is a
type of which, like the preceding type, the average age
is 7. But when the child brings in the wind as cause of
the movement of sun and moon, there are, as with clouds,
three different cases. Sometimes the wind is simply an
adjuvant of the movement, the real cause being of a moral
order ; sometimes the wind is an indispensable condition
of the movement, but is produced by the heavenly bodies
themselves ; sometimes the wind is an indispensable
condition and has an origin that is outside the heavenly
bodies. The first case alone comes under the third stage.
The second case, on the contrary, characterises the fourth
stage, and the third case characterises the fifth stage.

Here are some examples of this fourth type in the
answers of the third stage :

HUB (6½) : " How does the sun move ?—*It goes with
me.*—Why ?—*To give light. So you can see clearly.*—
When you go to C., where does the sun go ?—*Towards
me.*—How does it go with you ?—*Because I look at it.*—
What makes it move along when it goes with you ?—*The
wind.*" Thus the wind is only an adjuvant, for the sun
remains free to follow us wherever we go.

TAC (6½) : " What does the moon do when we go for a
walk ?—*It rolls along with us.*—Why ?—*Because the wind
makes it go.*—Does the wind know where we go ?— . . .
Yes.—And does the moon know ?—*Yes.*—Does the moon
go with us on purpose or is it forced to go ?—*It comes to
light us.*"

GAV (8½) : " *Sometimes, but not always, you see it* [the sun] *go up early in the morning, and then it sets in another place.*—Why does it set in another place ?—*When the winds blow.*—Why ?—*Because they push it.*—Can it set where it likes ?—*No.*—Why ?—*Because there are places which aren't good* [cf. the argument which appeals to moral reasons and not to a physical determinism]." On the other hand the sun follows us : " *It follows me.*—Why ?—*Because it watches over us. It watches what we do* [confusion with God !]." We then ask Gav how the sun is able to follow us if it is the wind that pushes it. " *It goes where the wind pushes it.*—But you told me that it follows us ?—*Perhaps it has wings.*—Do you think it is the wind, or wings ?—*I think it has wings, because if it wants to go on one side, and then the wind pushes it on the other. . . .*" It is clear that for Gav there is no contradiction between the spontaneous movement of the sun and the idea that the wind pushes the heavenly bodies. When we confront Gav with an unsuspected difficulty, he invents a trick explanation so as to retain the two aspects of the sun's movement : an internal motor, which is the will of the heavenly body, and an unnecessary external motor, which is the wind acting as a physical cause.

ACK (8 ; 7) : " Does the sun move ?—*Yes.*—How ?— *It's the wind that pushes it.*—And when there is no wind ? —*It goes by itself.*—How does the wind make it move ?— It pushes it, it chases it.—And when there is no wind ?— *It goes by itself.*—How ?—*All by itself.*"

These cases are all perfectly clear. The wind is an adjuvant of the movement, but the heavenly bodies retain all their spontaneity : they follow us or go where they will. A boy of 8, for example, maintains : " *As the sun is not moving* [at this moment] *the air is not making it move.*" In other words, " As the sun does not want to move, it does not call upon the wind, and the wind blowing at this moment is not strong enough to force it to move." In short, the heavenly bodies make use of the wind as do sailing-ships or aeroplanes ; they do not make wind, but they use it, sometimes at the risk of being blown away, but more often with the certainty of guiding themselves so as to keep the same direction as before. They do more than this, they have the faculty of moving by themselves when there is no wind at all, though the child says nothing definite as to how this is to be done. But one feels that ἀντιπερίστασις is close at hand. Once allow that the sun moves by itself and can make use of the wind, and you are only a step removed from admitting that the sun's movement makes or attracts wind that is capable of adding to the strength of the movement. This will appear more clearly presently, when we examine the answers given during this fourth stage.

But first, let us deal with yet a fifth type of answer, belonging to the third stage, and one according to which the sun and moon move " by themselves." This type, like the one immediately before it, is by far the most numerous and its average age is also 7. It cannot therefore constitute a stage of its own. This type, moreover, stands in the closest relation to those preceding it. For, after all, the distinction we have drawn between the five different types of explanation in the answers of the third stage is highly artificial. In reality, these types enter into every possible combination. Each child tends to emphasise one or other type of answer, but not to the exclusion of others. On the contrary, these explanations all have a common schema, which is the combination of spontaneity in the movement of the heavenly bodies with the moral obligation to move to which they are subjected. On the one hand, the sun and moon move by themselves, making use of the clouds, the wind, etc., but not determined by them. On the other hand, the sun and moon have to move in order to give us light, to follow us, etc. The fifth type of answer gives us the quintessence of these ideas, the children in question simply saying that the sun and moon move along by themselves, and do so for our benefit. Here are some examples :

CAM (6) : " Why does the sun move ?—*Because it shines.*" It follows us, says Cam, to give light. " Why does the moon move ?—*Because it's night.*—Yes, but why does it move ?—*Because there are people outside.*—And then ?—*Because there are people who want to work.*— And then ?—*It's time to go to work. So the moon comes.*" This again is almost the second, or even the first, stage.

ZAC (6) : The sun moves "*to light us.*" " But how does it move along ?—*Because it rolls.*—Why ?—*Because it's round.*—Does it roll by itself, or does something make it roll ?—*By itself.*—Is the sun alive ?—*Yes, because it rolls.*" It is made of air, wind, or cloud. Same explanations for the moon. " Could it go away if it liked ?—*Yes.*—Why does it stay ?—*Because we couldn't see.*"

EILL (9) : " Does the sun move along ?—*Yes, because it has to light us.*"

MOC (10) : The sun moves along "*by itself.*" " Does it know it is moving ?—*Of course. It turns itself round. Of course it knows it !*"

The dual origin comes out clearly in all these explanations. Animism impels the child to consider the sun and moon as advancing by themselves. On the other hand, artificialism, which has become immanent, impels the child to explain this movement by a finalism to which all things are subject and before which the sun and the moon must bow their wills. Thus all the answers of the third stage are homogeneous.

The idea expressed by Zac and Moc, etc., and according to which the heavenly body " rolls " and " turns itself round," leads us on to the fourth stage. Children of this stage believe that the sun and moon, by advancing or by turning themselves round, produce a current of air which flows in after them and drives them before it.

The ἀντιπερίστασις schema is thus the characteristic of this fourth stage. The wind has become an indispensable physical cause, but in virtue of animism and the spontaneity attributed to the heavenly bodies, this wind is believed to be produced by the sun and moon themselves. We have before us a fourth stage which is exactly parallel to the fourth stage of explanations relative to the movement of clouds. Only, in the case of the sun and moon, this type of explanation is less frequent than in the case of the clouds, for the very simple reason that according to a great many children, the sun and moon, being hot,

cannot produce wind, which is cold.   The habitual schema
is merely transposed so as to be adapted to the conditions
of the heavenly bodies : the " heat " is supposed to push
the sun and moon.   Heat is thought of by some children
as a warm substance emanating from the sun and moon
and pushing them along by reflux.   The answers of this
fourth stage belong, therefore, to two types, one bringing
wind, the other heat, into its explanation.   Here are some
examples of the first type, of which the average age
is 8 :

GIAMB (8½) said, at 7 years old, that " *it's us* " who
make the heavenly bodies move along " *by walking.*"
But a little later he added that " *it's the wind that does it.*"
The wind is the instrument and we are the cause.   A year
and a half later, he refers back to the schema of the reflux
of air.   " How does the sun move along ?—*It's the air that
makes it move.*—Why ?—*Because when people feel cold it*
[= the sun] *warms them, and for the people who are hot, it
makes shade.*—How ?—*It turns and goes further.*—How is
it that it turns ?—*Because it* [= the sun] *makes air, and
that makes it turn.*"   As for knowing how the sun makes
air, Giamb has a curious notion on this point : air " *it's
wind, it's shadow.*"   Thus the sun makes both shadow and
air at the same time.

GALL (10 ; 2) : " How does the moon move along ?—
By the air.—How does it do that ?—*Because in the evening
the air is fresh.*—What makes the air which makes the
moon move along ?—*It's the freshness.*—And what makes
this freshness ?—*It's the movement of the moon.*"   Nothing
could be clearer.   In the same way, says Gall, the sun
makes air because " *it blows,*" and clouds make it " *by
their movement,*" and the stars move along by " *the air of
the stars.*"

BRAS (8 ; 8) says that the sun moves along because
" *the wind pushes it,*" but the sun makes this wind " *because
it moves.*"   Bras adds " *it walks with us.*—How does it
manage to follow us ?—*It runs.*—How ?—*The wind pushes
it.*—But when you turn right round ?—*Because the wind
pushes it.*—But what makes the wind turn round when
we do.—*Because it* [= the sun] *walks.*"

MART (9 ; 5) : " *The wind pushes the sun.*—And when
there's no wind, does the sun move along ?—*Yes.*—What
makes it move along ?—*The air.*"   We then ask Mart

where this air comes from. Mart replies that the sun is " *blown out with the air.*" The sun, says Mart, has " *a current.*" This is analogous to what we saw in connection with the clouds, which push themselves along by means of the air of which they are full.

BERG (7 ; 2) says of the moon : " *The wind blows to make it move,*" but he adds, that the moon has a little force " *because it makes a little bit of wind.*"

The analogy with the corresponding cases in connection with clouds is striking. For between the years of 6 and 7, there are children to be found who believe that the sun and moon make air. It will be remembered, moreover, that according to children between 8 and 10, the heavenly bodies are made of clouds, or even of compressed air (*C.W.*, Chap. VIII, § 3). Thus Roy, whose answers have frequently appeared in these pages, is of opinion that the clouds have made the sun grow bigger thanks to the air they contain, etc. Several children, however, deny that the sun can make air although it does contain a current.

DUC (7 ; 5) thinks that there is " *a current* " in the sun, but no air, because " *when you light a fire it doesn't make any wind.*"

FALQ (8) : " Can the sun make wind ?—*No, because it is hot.*"

This leads us on to the second type of answer of this stage : the sun is pushed along by the heat or vapour which it throws off. We have here a new form of the reflux schema. It should be noted, moreover, that for some children there is complete continuity between this form and the last, since vapour, smoke, and air are all more or less confused. Here is a clear example :

ANT (8) : " What does the sun do when you are out for a walk ?—*It follows us. It goes the same way.*—Does it move along ?—*Yes, it does.*—How ?—*The heat makes it move along.*—What is the heat ?—*It's a flame that comes out of the sun.*—How does this flame make the sun move along ?—*Because it pushes it.*—How does the flame move ? —The sun makes it move.*—How ?—*When the sun moves*

along the flame moves.'' But Ant does not confuse heat
and wind : " Can a flame give wind ?—*No, it gives heat.
—But wind too ?—No, it would be too hot.''*

BRAS (8 ; 8), whose first type answers were given above,
also says in explanation of the sun's movement : " *It
gives heat and that makes steam.''*

The close analogy to the preceding type is apparent.
Apparent too (as in the case of the clouds) is the essential
part played by moral causes, right up to and during this
fourth stage, in spite of the fact that physical causes are
beginning to be thought of as necessary conditions of
movement.

When, finally, a fifth stage is reached, moral factors
are eliminated, and physical factors begin to be conceived as the only true causes of movement.

These physical causes are, of course, wind and air,
since the sun is a fiery cloud at the same height as other
clouds. But the wind has come to be thought of as
produced by the sun, and the sun has ceased to be considered as alive, conscious, or under any moral compulsion.
Here is an example :

TAU (9) : " *The North wind drives the clouds and the
sun along at the same time.*—And when the North wind is
not blowing ?—*Then the clouds don't move.*—And the sun ?
—*It doesn't move.*—Can the sun make air ?—*No.*—When
you are out for a walk do the sun and moon follow you ?
—*No.*—Do they know that you are moving ?—*No.*—Do
they feel that they are going to rise or set ?—*No.''*

Of course, after the age of 8 to 9, children begin to
repeat things they have heard said, so that it is very
seldom that one can catch a fifth stage answer pure. The
extraordinary custom followed by some pedagogues of
teaching the system of Copernicus to children of this
age has given rise to the quaintest distortions. The child
concludes from what he hears in class that it is the earth
that makes the sun go round. Or else, he concludes from
the fact that the sun is stationary, that the clouds are so
too (since they are on the same plane and also seem to
move). A feeble-minded subject of 25 once told us that

he had never believed that the earth went round the sun, and was of opinion that they had been " pulling his leg." It would be useless to reproduce these answers, which have none of the spontaneity of those we have quoted in this chapter.

CHAPTER IV
WATER CURRENTS AND MOVEMENTS DUE TO WEIGHT

IN studying the explanations which children give of the movements of the heavenly bodies and the clouds, we are led to a very definite result. It is that the cause of movement is not simple, but rests on a kind of bipolarity. Every movement presupposes an internal motor force which is the moving object's own life or will power. We are thus faced with a conclusion which has been established elsewhere by different methods (*R.J.*, Chaps. V and VI). But every movement also presupposes an external motor force which can be magical, artificialist, moral, or physical, and is generally both moral and physical. It is only in the later stages that the explanations attain to the mechanical simplicity of adult schemas.

It may be of interest to see whether similar phenomena are to be found in other spheres. We shall therefore study, from this point of view, the movements of water, beginning by a very simple case, that of the waves. The study of the current of rivers will lead us to the analysis of the causes of the fall of bodies, and finally to an examination of the explanations which children give of why the clouds and the heavenly bodies remain suspended.

It is not from any desire for mere symmetry that we are going so thoroughly into these matters. It is because children's explanations exhibit a very general tendency, which takes on a new form in each particular case, to introduce living and personal forces where we should make use only of weight and inertia.

§ 1. THE WAVES OF THE LAKE.—All our children know

the Lake of Geneva. They have bathed in it and sailed on it, they have observed its waves and probably asked questions about them. They are therefore in possession of the necessary data of observation for their explanations, and it will be interesting to see whether in this case too we find the same types of causality as before.

An examination of the questions asked about the waves shows that the child is interested in the problem.

DEL (6½) : " *The waves are only at the edge of the lake. Why ?* " " *Are the waves on the lake naughty ?* "

These children therefore regard the waves as alive and conscious. Is this impression confirmed when we come to question them ? It would seem so. During a first stage, of which the average age is 4–5 years, the movement of the waves is attributed to combined animistic and artificialist causes. During a second stage, which extends from 5 to 8, the waves are due, on the one hand, to an internal motor force, on the other, to an external motor force, such as stones or wind. Some explanations of this stage involve a vicious circle : the wind drives along the waves, but is made by the waves. This is the familiar schema of the reflux of air, but here it characterises only one type of the second stage, and not a whole stage. The children do not all go through this particular phase of explanation, seeing that its average age, about 8 years, is that of other second stage types. When, finally, a third stage is reached, the cause of the waves is thought of as entirely mechanical : the wind pushes the waves, which have no movement of their own. The average age of this stage is 9 years.

Here are some examples of the first stage. The cause of the movement is conceived, on the one hand, as being the life of the water itself, on the other, as being some human or artificial action, such as the movement of oars or of ships, etc.

DON (5) : " What are waves ?—*They go up, then they go down.*—Where do the waves come from ?—*It's the water.*—Why does the water make waves ?—*To make the boats go.*—How does the water make waves ?—*It's the oars."*

GRIM (5) : " What are waves ?—*Water.*—What makes the waves ?—*It's because they row.*—That's right. But some days there are no boats but all the same there are waves. Where do they come from then ?—*It's the wheels* [which make the waves], *and that* [the waves] *makes the boat go."*

REVAT (6) : " Why are there waves on the lake ?— *Because they've been put there.*—What is a wave ?—*It's like that, lying down* [gesture to show how water rises and falls].—Where do the waves come from ?—*From under the water.*—Why are there waves ?—*So you don't fall* [= so that boats and swimmers shall not sink], *so the lake isn't all down below* [= so that the lake shall not be flat].—Why ?—*So you don't fall, because the water is at the bottom* [= so that the boats and the swimmers shall not touch the bottom, as they would if the level of the water sank].—What makes the waves ?—*A man.*—Is it always men ?—*My Daddy makes waves* [movement of swimming].—When there are no men, how are they made ?—*It's the water.*—Why ?—*Because it doesn't like it because it's like that* [= because it doesn't like to be horizontal : Revat makes a horizontal gesture].—Why does the wave move along ?—*Because the water moves along.*—Does it feel that the water moves along ?—*Yes, it feels it. It comes down in a slope, the water does."*

These explanations will be sufficient to show what is the starting-point in all ideas about waves. The waves are " made for " boats and swimmers. They are among the many adjuvants which nature supplies for man. Integral and anthropocentric finalism is the spontaneous root of these explanations. Hence, two ideas which emerge under the pressure of the interrogatory : on the one hand, the waves are due to the will belonging to the water itself, on the other, they are due to man, since they are made for man.

During the second stage, this bipolarity of explanation persists entire, but the artificialism of the external motor force is transferred to the objects. This gives rise to four types of explanation.

The first type is interesting, and shows very definitely the nature of the child's spontaneous ideas : stones and rocks are supposed to produce the waves. This is not a casual explanation. We have met with this particular type too often not to give it close attention. To the question asked by Del (*L.T.*, Chap. V), " What makes the lake flow ? " a child of 7 answered, " *The rocks do* " (*L.T.*, p. 295).

CHAL (9) : " What are waves ?—*It's the stones that make it go up* [the water] *and make it go down again.*—But what makes the waves on the lake ?—*Stones also.*" It is in this way that Chal explains the current of a river : " *Because the stones that are in the Rhone, make it go up and down ; and that makes the current.*"

NOT (10) : The pebbles " *are high. The water goes on top and that makes waves.*—There must always be pebbles to make waves ?—*No.*—How are they made ?—*Yes, there must be pebbles.*"

This shows very clearly what the child means by cause of movement : it is the occasion for which the internal motor force is set going. The obstacle to be overcome is the source of energy, and calls for a special effort, just as the sun is the cause of the motion of the clouds which work against him, and night is cause of the movement of the clouds it draws after it.

According to the answers of a second type, waves are produced simply by the current of water. Added to this is the idea of quantity of water : when there is a lot of water, a current is produced which increases the strength of the waves :

PERET (7) thinks that the water in the lake is " *alive* " : " *It moves. It makes waves.*—Does it feel the heat, when it's a hot day ?—*Yes.*—Why ?—*Because it makes little balls* [like most children Peret thinks that air bubbles are made of water].—How does the water go along ?—*It's the waves that make it go along,*" etc.

LU (5½) : " Why are there waves on some days, and on other days none ?—*It's the water that pushes.*"

BAB (8½). The waves on the lake " *are a current.*"

" *When there are a lot of them, it makes a current.*—But why are there waves on some days and none on others ? —*Because sometimes there's not much water, and sometimes there's a lot.*"

Waves, therefore, are a manifestation of the spontaneous force of water. The advent of the notion of the depth or quantity of water is not, as it seems to be, an unequivocal criterion of purely mechanical explanation. We shall see later, in connection with floating bodies, that depth of water is thought to be the cause of a force or disturbance, more precisely of a current going upwards, and capable of producing waves (see, also, Chap. VII). To this same stage belongs a type of explanation by reflux of air analogous to that examined in connection with the heavenly bodies and the clouds : the waves are produced by the wind, but this same wind is produced by the waves. Such explanations occur between the years of 5 and 10, but the average age is 7–8.

FRAN (9) : ". . . *When it's cold, there are waves, then that makes the wind come.*—Where does the wind come from ?—*Because of the waves.*" (See context, Chap. II, § 1.)

FERT (10) : "And what makes the waves ?—*It's the air.*—And what makes the wind ?—*The waves.*—What makes the waves ?—*It's the air.*" Previously Fert told us that the waves made wind " *when they lift up.*" (See Chap. II, § 1.)

PAT (10) whose replies have already been seen in § 1 of Chap. II, tells us, several months later : "What are waves ?—*It's when the water goes too hard, it meets itself and that makes waves. It's the cold wind that lifts the water up a little.*—Where does the cold wind come from ? —*From over there.*—How ?—*It's the big waves and that makes a lot of cold wind.* Where does the wind come from ?—*Also from the water.*—From what water ?—*Over there.*—What water ?—*Also the lake.*"

The explanation contains a vicious circle : the waves make the wind, and the wind makes the waves. Does the child simply mean that air comes out of the water in making the waves ? If so, according as one asked for the cause of the waves or for the cause of the wind, the child would in each case answer by the other term, and would run the risk of arguing in a circle. But the circle is probably more physical than logical : as they rise, the waves produce a current of air which animates them on its rebound. This, at least, seems to be what is indicated by Fran's expression : " That makes the wind come ".

It may be that further research will establish this type as a genuine stage of its own, but our examples are too few to make more of it than a special type of the second stage.

Besides the examples we have quoted, some more primitive cases are to be found, in which the waves are supposed to result simply from the air which is in the water, the child not appearing to have thought of a reflux of the air so produced :

BLAN (6) : The waves are due to the " *current*." " What is the current ?—*It's the wind. . . . The cold wind.*—There's a current in the water ?—*Yes.*—There's wind in the water ?—*Yes.*"

BOUV (9) : The waves rise because of the " *current* ". " What is the current ?—*It's the wind.*" This wind is also in the water.

CESS (8 ; 6) : " Where do the waves come from ?—*It's the air that's in the water.*—You think there's air in the water ?—*Air travels about. There's always some in the water. The air pushes the water. When there's a lot it makes it rather high.*" The proof : " *When you make soup, when it boils it makes bubbles.*"

The waves of the lake rise and fall, therefore, like water that has been brought to the boil. This type of answer is intermediate between the former and the fourth.

According to children of the fourth type, wind produces the waves. But the wind is not enough, a moral factor is added to it. The waves are alive and move spontaneously, and they are in general endowed with intentions or duties which are useful to man. Here are examples :

HAUSM (5) : " *It's the wind that does it.*" But : " Why do the waves move along ?—*To go further.*—Why ?—

Because there's lots of them." As for " how ", Hausm
specifies that the water " *wants to go further.*"

GAV (7): " *It's the wind that pushes,*" but, says Gav,
when there is no wind, there are some waves all the same,
because waves " *are for the boats.*"

Thus the wind is a mere adjuvant. It is the means
to be put at the service of the real cause, which is the
moral necessity that there should be waves for the boats.

In conclusion, it will be seen that all the types of the
second stage, even those which introduce definitely
physical causes, have this in common that they all endow
the waves with a certain spontaneity, of which the aim
is moral. After the third stage, on the contrary, the
explanation is entirely physical: the waves are produced by the wind, and have nothing spontaneous about
them. Here is an example :

SCHAN (10): " Where do the waves come from ?—
From the wind.—Do they know they are moving ?—*No.*—
Can they make wind when there isn't any ?—*No.*"

§ 2. THE CURRENT IN RIVERS.—It was necessary to
make a study of children's ideas about waves in order to
understand the explanations they give of the current in
rivers, for, as will presently be seen, the two questions
are closely connected in their minds. And it is also
necessary, so as to avoid any suggestion by perseveration,
to allow an interval of time to elapse between the two
interrogatories, or to carry them out on two different
sets of children.

The questions spontaneously asked by the children
show from the first not only interest in the matter we
are about to deal with, but also a definitely dynamic and
artificialist mental orientation. Thus a 4-year-old child
asks : " *Auntie B., how do rivers ever start going ?* " Del
(*L.T.*, Chap. V) asks at the age of 6 : " *Who makes the
Rhone go so fast ?* " He also asks whether there is always
water in the rivers, and when he is told that there is,
he adds : " *It* [the water] *can go away, then why* [is there

always some left] ? " It would seem that in the child's mind water is something both alive and subjected to man by ties of moral obligation.

Now it is possible, in classifying the explanations given in answer to our interrogatory, to establish four distinct stages, of which the first two confirm what we have just anticipated. During a first stage, of which the average age is 5, the child explains the current by the collaboration of an external, artificialist motor force (people or men) with an internal, animist force (the water's obedience). During the second stage, reached at about 7 and 3 months, the external force is thought to be the wind on the stones, etc., and the internal force is still the water's own spontaneous current. During a third stage, the water is supposed to run because of the slope, but the child is not yet able to understand that the weight of the water is what makes it move along. When, finally, at 10 or 11 a fourth stage is reached, the child understands everything. The analogy will at once be seen between this schema of evolution and that embodying the explanations of the movement of clouds and heavenly bodies.

Here are examples of the first stage :

GRIM (5) : " Why does the water in the Arve [1] move along ?—*Because people make oars. They push.*—Where are the oars ?—*In the boats there are men who hold them. They make it go.*—Do men make the water in the Arve go ?—*With boats, great big boats* [there are a few skiffs down-stream].—Does the water run without boats ?—*No, because that holds it back.*—Is the Arve running to-day ?—*No. . . . It is moving along a little.*—Why ?—*Because there are a few boats.*" The water, says Grim, is alive, and knows that it is flowing.

ROY (6) : " Why does the water in the Arve move along ?—*Because there are boats going by.*—And when there are no boats, does it move along ?—*Yes.*—Why ?—*Because there are big fish which swim.*—How does the Arve flow ?—*From over there* [right direction].—Why ?

---

[1] These children were questioned at a school situated on the banks of the Arve. The current is fairly strong at this point and the slope obvious to the eye.

— . . . —You know ?—*No.*—Does it always go like that, or not always ?—*It always goes like that.*" We invent for Roy an imaginary river on an inclined piece of cardboard : Roy says that the water will flow "*because it leans down*". We return to the Arve, Roy tells us that it moves along because of the "*current*". "What is the current ?—*Water.*—What makes the current ?—*Men when they swim in the water.*—And without men ?—*The fishes.*—And without fish ?—*The boats,*" etc. All the same, Roy insists that the water is alive.

CAM (6). Same explanations. In addition, the water flows "*to make the fountains flow*", "*to make a big lake*", etc.

Some children at this stage have noticed that the Arve always flows in the same direction. Others have noticed nothing. They can all say that the water goes down an inclined plane, but some believe that, if necessary, it can go up. With all these divergences, they agree in maintaining that water flows for the good of man and because man compels it to do so.

The second stage shows us the same dualism of external and internal motor force, but on a more immanent plane. The explanations of this stage may be divided into four separate but contemporaneous types.

Children of the first type attribute the current to stones, stones being the stimulus of the water's activity.

ING (5 ; 8) : The water in the Arve flows "*because there is the water in the mountain which pushes it. Then, when the waves come, that pushes it.*—Where do the waves come from ?—*From the water, from the stones.*—What makes the water move along ?—*The rain, then the stones.*—How do the stones make the water move along ?—*Because they make waves.*—How do the stones make waves ?—*Because the water . . . because the stones make waves because they're hard. Sometimes you don't see the stones because the Arve is too deep.*—What do the stones do, when you can't see them ?—*They go to the bottom. . . . They are covered with water.*—How do they make waves ? —They hold the water back, then the water goes over and that makes waves.* [Here Ing is describing what can be seen round the stones of which the summit projects slightly].—But how do the stones make waves ?—*They're heavy, it goes, the water swims.*—What does it matter that the stones are heavy ?—*The stones are too* [= very] *big, to prevent* [= in order to prevent, or, so that they should prevent], *it* [the water] *to go by.*—Why ?—*Because it* [the stone] *is not light. Because the stones which are heavy, make everything go along.*—How ?—*It makes the water go.*" Ing had told us, not long before this interrogation, that the stones make waves " *because the stones can't make the water go without waves.*"

VEL (7 ; 8) says that " *it is the current which . . . makes it* [the water of the Arve] *move along,*" and that the current is due to the stones " *because they're standing up,*" and that " *the water goes on top and that makes the current.*" " What makes the Arve flow, to-day ?—*Stones.* How ?—*It's when the water goes up* [on the stones] *and comes down.*—Where does the current come from ?— *From the water.*—How has the water got a current ?— *Because it goes up on the stones and comes down.*" Vel indicates correctly the direction of the current of the Arve, but adds : " *Sometimes it goes the other way.*— Why ?—*Because sometimes it turns right round.*"

CHAL (9) : " Does the Rhone flow ?—*Yes.*—Why ?— *Because the stones that are in the Rhone, make it go up and down, and that makes a current.*"

These explanations are interesting from many points of view. In the first place, they show us the exact relation between the external and the internal motor force in all cases where the external force merely occasions or acts as a stimulus to the internal (as when the sun and night make the clouds move along). The stone incites the water to spontaneous action, making it clamber over the stone, thus gaining further impetus from its fall. Such data are of the utmost value in tracing the origins of explanations that argue in a circle or of explanations by " reaction of the surrounding medium " (ἀντιπερίστασις). For, while it does not constitute an actual reflux, the action we have been describing points very clearly to the self-starting capacity of which, in the child's eyes, the water is possessed when faced with an obstacle. This automotricity, which can be liberated by an external body is obviously the starting-point of the schema of explanations by reflux.

The case of Ing, on the other hand, introduces us to a notion which we shall analyse at great length later on (Chap. VII), and whose central idea is that a stone under water produces a current by the mere fact that it is heavy and weighs on the water. The stones, says Ing, " make everything move along ", " make the water start ", which means that they create the current. We shall see that, in the child's eyes, a pebble immersed in a glass of water raises the level of the water, not because of its volume, but because of its weight, in virtue of which it produces a current running from below upwards. We have here an integral dynamism, of which the first traces appear in the case of Ing.

A second type of answer, closely allied to the former, consists in saying quite simply that rivers move because of the waves they make. This shows an improvement on the explanation which may now be described as " circular ", and which takes us straight on to the schema of the reflowing current (reaction of the surrounding medium). Here are some examples :

PERET (7) : " Why does the water move along ?— *Because it makes waves.*—The water is alive ?—*Yes.*— But how does it move along ? Does it go by itself or does something make it move along ?—*It's the waves that make it move along.*—But why does the water flow ? —*Because it moves.*—Why ?—*Because the waves make it move.*" As for the waves, they are due, on the rivers as on the lake (see § 1), to the water itself : " *it makes waves.*"

BAB (8 ; 11) : " Why does the water in the rivers move along ?—*Because there's a current.*—Because there's a current ?—*It's the water that has made it.*—Why has it made it ?—*To make the water move along.*"

BOURG (6½) : " *It's the current, as it goes away, it makes the water go.*"

Naturally, we always try to make the child discover the part played by the slope. But children at this stage take no interest in it. It will be seen how strongly this second type anticipates the explanation by reflux. Just as the clouds are supposed to advance because of the air which they make, and the sun because of the flames which escape from it, so the river advances because of the waves which it produces itself. Here are some examples :

STEI (5½) : The water in the Arve moves along " *because it goes hard. There's a current.*" The current is " *a current of air.*—Where is the current of air ?—*In the Arve.*—Where does this current of air come from ?— *From everywhere. . . . It's the water that makes the current.*" And again : " How does it make a current of air ?—*Because it goes hard.*—But why does it go hard ?— *Because sometimes there's the wind that pushes it.*"

BLAN (6) : The Arve moves along because " *the wind carries it*", " *because the wind went back into the water.*" But, on the other hand, when there is no wind, the water " *flows by itself*", because " *it has made a current.*" " What is the current ?—*It's the cold wind.*"

FALQ (8) : " *It's the wind that pushes it.*" But the wind comes from the water, because "*the water is cold and it has a current.*" [See Chap. II, par. 1.] See also Chap. II, § 1, the case of Mart (9 ; 5) : The water in the rivers makes a wind " *because the water has a current, then it pushes.*" So it is by reason of its " current " that the water moves along.

The resemblance to the explanations of the same type quoted *à propos* of the clouds or the heavenly bodies will strike the reader at once.

Finally, a fourth type of answer consists in attributing the current of rivers to the wind, whatever may be the origin of the wind. This type is, of course, more or less amalgamated to the last one ; both, moreover, are contemporaneous. Nor does this explanation by the wind exclude moral factors. On the contrary, the wind is a mere adjuvant in the service of the force belonging to the rivers themselves. Here are some examples, beginning with a very curious case of participation between the wind, the rivers, and the fishes. This case is intermediate between the first and second stages :

GEH (6) : " Does the wind know it is blowing ?—*Yes, because the water runs quickly all the time, like that. When the wind stops, the water stops, because it runs with the fishes.*—Why ?—*If the fishes stop, the water stops too.*— The fish can stop the water ?—*Yes, they go like that.*— The wind makes the water go along ?—*Yes.*—What makes the wind go along ?—*It stops, and the water stops too.*— Does the wind know where it's going ?—*Yes. It goes in the Arve. The fish goes in the Arve too. . . . If the fish goes anywhere, the wind goes anywhere too.*"

DON (5½) : " Can the water in the Arve go where it likes ?—*No. It can't go over there, it can go towards the quay* [right direction].—Why ?—*Because it's the wind that pushes it towards the quay.*—Why ?—*Because they want to go towards the quay.*—Why ?—*So as to go further* [into the Rhône]," etc.

GUT (9) : " *It's the wind that pushes it.*" Gut indicates correctly the direction of the current of the Arve. The water flows thus " *because it can't go backwards.*—Why ? —*Because the Rhône is over there* " [=Because the Arve must flow into the Rhône].

What strikes one in these answers is the absence of any concern as to " how " the phenomenon in question occurs. The child may know perfectly well that the wind blows in every direction, and that the Arve always flows in one direction (two-thirds of the children know this), he will maintain, none the less, that the wind is sufficient explanation of the current in rivers. Much the same was said in connection with the heavenly bodies. The sun goes where it wants to and not where the wind blows it, but it is the wind that drives it along. In other words, the wind is only an adjuvant, and the moving body is still spontaneous. This comes out very clearly in the earlier cases like that of Geh, according to whom there is simply an agreement or participation of intentions between the wind and the river.

In short, up to the age of 7–8 the explanation of the movement of rivers is the same as that of the movement of clouds or of the heavenly bodies. It is a pre-causal explanation, which means that it is as much moral as physical, and as much finalist as causal. For during the first two stages, movement is explained by the collaboration of an external and of an internal or spontaneous motor force, and the mutual adjustment of these two forces can only be accounted for by teleological reasons. After 7–8 years, on the contrary, a third stage sets in, of which the average is 9, and during which the movement of rivers begins to be thought of as determined by purely physical causes : the slope explains the current. But naturally, this stage is only approached gradually and through a succession of intermediate stages. Moreover, the part played by weight has not yet emerged : the river goes down the slope, simply because it has not the strength to go up. Here are some examples :

DUC (6 ; 11) : The river moves along " *by the current.—* Why is there a current ?—*Because the river is sloping.—* Why does it flow when it's sloping ?—*It slides.*"

HEND (9 ; 8) : The river flows because " *it's sloping, so it goes down.—*Why does it flow when it goes down ?— *Because there's a slope.—*But why does it not go up the slope ?—*It can't. It isn't strong enough, because there's another* [water] *which will come down and another* [water] *which comes. That would push.*" " *It can never go up. When there's a hill, it makes zigzags.—*Why can't it go up ?—*Because it isn't strong enough to go up again.*" " *Why not ?—Because when it's strong, it can't turn sharply.*" " *Why ?—Because it's not strong enough. When it's strong it comes down quite straight.*" Notice the reversal of values : it is strength which explains the descent of the water, and not the slope which explains the strength of the water !

BAR (9 ; 5) : " How does the water in the Arve flow ? —*Because if it didn't move along, you wouldn't have any water !* " Bar, in spite of this finalistic approach to the subject, indicates correctly the direction of the current. " *It always flows like that.—*Why ?—*Because if it flowed* [in the opposite direction], *it could not climb the mountains. —*Why does the water go down ?—*Because if it went up, there would be no hollow to keep it up above !* " We ask

Bar whether water or mercury would go the faster down a slope : " *It's the water,*" says Bar, " *because it's lighter* " !

BURD (9) : " Why does the water in the Arve go along ? —*Because it goes down.*—And then ?—*It has a current, it is strong.*—Why does it flow when it goes down ?— *Because there is pressure.*—What does that mean ?—*It's when it goes down.*—Why does the Arve always go down ? —*Because. there's no other way.*—Why does it not go up again ?—*Because it must* [!] *go and flow into the Rhône.*— Why ?—*So that the Rhône can flow into the lake.*—Why cannot the water go up again ?—*Because it has no current when it goes up.*" It can be seen, that as used by Burd, the word " pressure " is purely verbal. Burd has not understood the role played by weight ; for him, the slope produces an impetus, and that is sufficient explanation for everything.

AUD (9) : The Arve moves along " *because the other* [water] *which comes after, pushes it, then it makes it move along. The other pushes itself inside hard, and that makes it go along.*—Why does that other water flow ?—*Because it goes quickly : it comes down from the mountain.*"

NOT (10) : " *It always comes from the water, so it always pushes.*" There is a current " *because the water is strong.* —What does that mean ?—*It's energetic.*—Well ?—*It goes quickly.*—Why ?—*It comes from the mountain, then it goes down.*—Can the water go up again ?—*Not always.*—When ? —*When it comes down, it goes up again to go on the other side.*"

BU (12) : " *It's pushed by the other that comes from the mountains.*—Can the water go up ?—*Oh no ! . . . because if it went up it would overflow.*" " *It goes along where it ought to go.*—Where ?—*With the other rivers, to go into the sea.*—But why cannot it go up ?—*Because it has no strength.*"

The reader will see how deeply tinged with dynamism these early physical explanations still are. It is the cumulative drive and thrust that explain the current, not the weight of the water. There is, moreover, in the background a very definitely finalistic and moral tone : the water " must " go down, it must not overflow, etc.

During a fourth stage, finally, *i.e.* only at the age of 10–11, the child becomes capable of giving the correct explanation of the movement of rivers.

HEI (11 ; 1) : " Why does the water in rivers run ?—
Because of the slope.—Why does it not go up ?—*It can't.*
—Why not ?—*Because it hasn't enough strength to go up.
It's too heavy.*—Why does the water go down ?—*Because
the water is heavy. When it goes downwards then it goes
fast.*"

The proof that children of the third stage have not
even implicitly reached this explanation is that when it
is suggested to them they are highly astonished. Here is
an example :

HEND (9 ; 8), whose answers are given above, cannot
explain why the water " *has not the strength* " to go
upwards. We then show him a pebble and ask him why
it falls to the ground when we let go of it : " *It's going to
fall down. It can't stay in the air.*—Why ?—*Because it is
heavy. . . .*" Then, thinking about the rivers, Hend
exclaims spontaneously : " *Ah, now I see !* " and adds :
" *It is because water is heavier than air, and so it has to go
downwards.*"

Thus it is not until the age of 10–11 that the idea of
weight enters definitely into the explanation of the movement of rivers. Between the thought of the child and
our own there is therefore an actual reversal of values :
what seems to us simple is complicated for the child,
and vice versa.

Nothing teaches us so much in this connection as the
ideas of children about the rise of water in the pipes of
a room. We have questioned fifty-odd children on the
subject, and it is not until about the age of 11 that the
child realises that there is any physical difficulty about
the matter. According to the youngest, the water rises
" *to go into the taps* ", " *so that we can wash our hands*",
as though the water's utility explained its movement.
Others answer : " *The wind drives it up* " (age 5), " *There
is air* " (age 8), " *It is the force of the water* ", " *It is the
current* " (age 8), as though the water went where it
wanted to or the wind blew where it had to. This is
decisive as counter-evidence of the interpretations we
have given of the answers quoted in this chapter.

§ 3. THE SUSPENSION OF THE SUN AND MOON, AND THE FALL OF HEAVY BODIES TO THE GROUND.—The preceding results have shown what difficulty children experience in making any precise use of the notion of weight. It may therefore be interesting to ascertain what explanation is given of the suspension of the clouds and heavenly bodies, and, more generally, of the fall of heavy bodies and the movements of light bodies. We shall see that here again, the dynamic explanation definitely precedes the mechanistic.

With regard to clouds, four stages can be distinguished in very clear gradation. During the first (average age 5), the suspension of the clouds is explained by both artificialist and animistic reasons. During a second stage (average age 7), clouds are regarded as either stuck on the sky or as inserted into a mass sufficiently solid to hold them. During a third stage (average age 9), clouds are supposed to remain in the air for dynamic reasons : the wind drives them along or sustains them, the clouds glide like birds, and so on. When, finally, from about 10 onwards, a fourth stage is entered upon, the child calls in the notion of weight : clouds stay in the air because they are light, light, that is, in the absolute sense, not lighter than air.

Here are examples of the first stage :

GRIM (5) : The clouds do not fall down, " *because they hold, they stick* ", " *because God is there and takes hold of it* " [the smoke of the clouds].

STEI (5) : " Why do they not fall down ?—*Because they stay . . . because God wants them to stay.*"

The second stage is merely a prolongation of the first, the artificialism being transferred to the objects.

KRU (6) : " How do the clouds stay in the air ?— *They are inside the sky.*—Why don't they fall down ?— *Because they stay* (se tiennent) *high up in the air. They almost touch the sky.*"

PAI (7) : " *The sky holds them up.*"

PERET (7) : " *Because they are held with the sky.*—How ? —*They are stuck.*"

BAR (9) : "*Because they are held fast.*—But why don't they fall on our heads ?—*Because if they fell, we'd be dead, so there.*" "*Something stops them from falling.*— What ?—*Big blocks of stone.*" (Bar regards the sky as formed by a vault of stone.)

This stage is clearly still very close to the earlier one : the clouds are stuck on to the sky or tightly wedged into it because, obviously, everything is organised to be of the greatest benefit to man. The curious thing is that nearly all the children belonging to these first two stages regard the clouds as " heavy ", and this, " because they are big ". Nine-tenths of the children examined told us this. There is nothing surprising, therefore, in their regarding the clouds as being stuck. According to some, it is even the weight of the clouds that is supposed to explain their suspension in mid-air. Here is an interesting case intermediate between the second and third stages :

BORS (5½) : The cloud "*keeps up there by itself.*— How ? Why does it [a book we have allowed to drop] not stay in the air ?—*Because it lets itself go.*—Why do the clouds not let go ?—*It keeps up.*—Why ?—*Because it keeps up by itself. They are too big* [to fall].—What does that mean ?—*They are too heavy. They are too long.*"

This type of answer is no isolated case. It represents a transitional case analogous to what we shall find in connection with floating boats. To Bors, weight is the symbol of force and solidity : a large and heavy object keeps its place by itself, because it has sufficient resistance and strength. This is only absurd if we compare the weight of the cloud to that of the air that surrounds it, but if one thinks of weight without any relation to the surrounding medium there is no reason why this idea of absolute weight should not carry with it the idea of a force sufficient to resist the air and remain suspended in it. We shall have occasion presently, in connection with the fall of bodies to the ground, to show that originally the idea of weight in no way implies the idea of a downward tendency. The connection between these two ideas is due to the fact that the idea of absolute weight gradually gives way to the idea of the relativity of weight to the density of the surrounding medium. Now, this is a much later discovery. It is therefore far more natural, in Bors' view, that the cloud should stay in the air because it is heavy.

During the third stage, the child begins to bring air and wind into his explanation of the suspension of clouds. But the interesting thing is that, as the case of Bors has just led us to foresee, the relation between cloud and air is in nowise a static relation, involving respective specific weights, but a dynamic relation : the cloud's own weight is what enables it to float, because the cloud moves fast enough to stay on the air, the suspension of clouds being thus made comparable to a sort of gliding flight. Or again, the wind drives the cloud along with sufficient vigour to allow it to remain suspended. In both cases, suspension is related to the forward movement of the cloud. Here are some examples :

GUT (8 ; 9) : " Why do the clouds not fall ?—*Because the wind pushes them.*—And when there is no wind ?— *It rains* [so they fall].—Does it always rain when there is no wind ?—*No.*—Then how do they stay up when there's no wind ?—*Because there's a current inside.*"

BOR (9) : " Why do the clouds not fall ?—*Because the air holds them.*—How ?—*It* [= the air] *pushes them so they don't fall.*" See Chap. II, § 1 : Bor believes that this air is " a current " which comes from the clouds themselves : " But why do the clouds not fall ?—*Because it holds them.*—What ?—*The current.*—Where does it come from, this current that holds them ?—*From inside the clouds.*—How is the current made ?—*From air.*—And how does it hold them ?—*It pushes them up above.*"

BARD (9) : " Why do the clouds not fall ?—*Because the wind's there and lifts them up.*" Bard also tells us, with regard to the rain, that when the clouds are too heavy they burst. Thus, the clouds are heavy, but the wind lifts them up.

BAL (11 ; 8) : They stay up " *because the wind makes them go up* ", " *because the wind holds them up a little* ".

This explanation of suspension by a gliding flight through the air is all the more interesting because we find an analogous version of it in a completely different sphere, *viz.*, the problem of how boats float on the water. In the case of the clouds, this belief is connected with the fact that very young children believe smoke (of which clouds are made, *C.W.*, Chap. IX, § 3) to rise, not because of its lightness, but owing to the air, to the wind, or to a current produced by the accumulation of smoke that comes out of chimneys.

HANS (5) : " Why does the smoke go up instead of falling to the ground ?—*It's the wind.*"

BORD (5½) : " *Because it smokes and it goes up.*—Why does it not go down ?—*Because there's still some at the bottom that smokes* [that presses against the first lot and makes it go up]."

BLAN (6) : " Why does it go up ?—*It's the wind.*"

NOT (10) : " Why do the clouds not fall ?—*Because it's made of smoke.*—And then ?—*It doesn't fall, it goes up.*—Why ?—*It's the air that makes it go up from the chimneys.*—How ?—*By blowing.*"

Finally, during a fourth stage, the children discover that the clouds remain suspended, not because of their movement, but because of their lightness.

GEI (9 ; 3) : " Why do they not fall ?—*Because they can't fall.*—Why ?—*Because they are light.*"

BUSS (10 ; 3) : " *Because it's light.*"

ROSS (10 ; 7) : The clouds do not fall because they are made of vapour. " And the vapour ?—*Because it's light. It's lighter than water* " [Ross does not say : lighter than air].

CAR (11 ; 7) : " *The air pushes them because it's light.*"

BAR (12 ; 7) : " Why do the clouds stay in the air ?—*Because they are like air.*—Why does the air not fall ?—*Because it goes everywhere.*—Why does it go everywhere instead of falling ?—*Because they* [the clouds] *are light.*"

These ideas follow an evolution that proceeds from artificialism to dynamism, and thence to a mechanistic way of thinking. This is exactly the same sequence as we shall meet with later in connection with floating boats, and which will occupy us now in the question of the suspension of the heavenly bodies.

On this last subject we questioned some sixty children, none of whom had been examined on the suspension of clouds. Not only did we discover the same stages, but the average age of each stage was noticeably the same as in the case of the clouds. During a first stage (average 6 years), sun and moon remain suspended for reasons both artificialist and animistic. During a second (average 7 years), they remain suspended either by the sky or by the clouds in which they are swathed (much in the same way as the clouds themselves are regarded as stuck on to the sky). During a third stage (average $8\frac{1}{2}$ years), the wind is supposed to keep the sun and moon in place through causes of a dynamic order (gliding flight). Finally, during a fourth (average 10 years), sun and moon are regarded as light, and as remaining suspended because of their lightness.

Here are examples of the first stage :

BONJ (6) : " How does the sun stay up there ?— *Because it wants to give us light.*—How is it that it does not fall ?—*Because it wants to give us light.*" Bonj does not worry as to how. It is true that he declares that the sun stays up " *with a stick* ", but he admits that he does not believe it. It is the moral reason which is the true cause of the suspension of the heavenly bodies.

RO (6) : " Why does the moon stay in the sky ?— *Because it is alive.*—Why ?—*To make light for us.*"

FONT (6 ; 9) : " *It's God that makes it stay up* [the sun].—How ?—*It keeps up.*"

GRAT (8 ; 2) : " Why does the sun not fall ?—*Because it doesn't want to come down.*" And if it does not want to come down, it is " *to make light for us.*"

PIE (9) : The sun does not fall " *because it is used to staying in the sky.*"

Note the habitual coupling of animistic with finalist and artificialist factors.

Answers of the second stage, while still very dependent upon these primitive factors, introduce the idea that the heavenly bodies do not fall, because they are clothed, as it were, in the clouds or in the sky. Here are some examples, beginning with one that is transitional between the first and the second stage :

KRU (6 ; 5) : " *It's above the clouds* [the sun] *and it peeps* [= it watches stealthily].—And if there are no clouds ?—*It doesn't fall, because it's between the sky.*— What holds it ?—*It holds on to the sky a little.*—What ? —*Some of the rays of the sun.*—Why ?—*Because it* [the rays] *is big and strong."*

WYD (6 ; 6) : " Why does the moon stay in the air and not fall ?—*It holds itself back.*—How ?—*It goes into the sky.*—What is the sky made of ?—*Sort of smoke.*— And the sun ?—*It's in the clouds.*—And when there are no clouds ?—[It is held back] *by the sky. When it touches a little, it's held back."*

ZAQ (6) : " *It holds by the clouds, and the moon too.*— And when there are no clouds ?—*It is held above the sky.* —How does the sky hold the sun ?—*It holds on towards the mountain* [= the sky leans on the mountain].

CAM (6) : " How does the moon stay up ?—*Because at night there are clouds and they hold the moon."* " *Because the sky holds it nicely."*

ACK (8) : " Why does the sun not fall ?—*It is held.*— How ?—*By the clouds."*

RE (8½) : " How does the sun manage, so as not to fall ?—*It always keeps still.*—How ?—*Because there's the sky to hold it.*—How ?—*It* [the sun] *is all surrounded.*— How ?—*The sky goes above.*—What is the sky made of ? —*It's blue.*—What is it made of ?—*Of clouds."*

GAVA (8½) : " How does the sun stay up in the sky ?— *Because up there, it's as though you were on the ground. So it goes as though it were walking on the ground. It doesn't fall."* Gava then explains to us that the sky is a " *blue flower-bed* " made by the smoke from the boats. " Is the sky hard ?—*It's like a sort of earth.*—Is the sun above or below the sky ?—*It runs all along the sky as though it were stuck on to the sky, then it travels.*—How is it that it doesn't fall ?—*The sky moves, so the sun moves with it."*

This last remark leads us on to the third stage. According to Gava, the sun is still enfolded in the sky and dragged along by it. For children of the third stage,

however, this insertion of the sun into the sky is not
sufficient to explain the fact that the sun does not drop
down. But the actual movement of the sun, partly
spontaneous and partly derived from without, becomes
sufficient cause of its suspension : the wind, driving the
heavenly bodies before it, is what keeps them in the air,
or else the heavenly bodies themselves move along by
means of a sort of gliding flight.

BOURG (7 ; 8) : " Why does the moon not fall ?—*The
wind pushes it into the air.*"

WEUX (8) : " Why does the moon not fall ?—*Because
the wind carries it.*"

BRUN (11 ; 11). The sun and moon do not fall " *because
they go quickly.*"

LUG (12 ; 3) : " Why does the sun not fall ?—*It's the
air that holds it.*—Why ?—*The air prevents things falling.*—
The note-case falls, if I drop it ?—*Yes, there is less below
than there is above. The air flows on top.*—On top of
what ?—*The sun.*—What does that do ?—*It stops* " [= it
makes it stop].

Thus the notion of weight plays as yet no part. On
the contrary, during the fourth stage, the heavenly bodies
are believed to be suspended on account of their lightness.

MART (9 ; 5) : " Why does the sun not fall ?—*Because
it's made of fire.*—Why does fire not fall ?—*It stays in the
air because it's light.*"

CHAL (9 ; 5) : " Why does the sun not fall ? If you
were up there you would fall . . .—*Because the sun is
lighter than I am.*"

The succession of these stages is interesting, and shows
that mechanical reasons, that is to say, those which bring
in the weight of the heavenly bodies in relation to the
weight of the air in which they hang, are the last to
appear. It may even happen in the third stage that the
celestial bodies are regarded as " heavy " and as staying
in the air because they are heavy. In the eyes of the
child, their weight actually points to the existence of
a force, of a capacity for movement, and this force is
precisely what enables the sun and moon to advance,

and in this way to remain suspended. It is even in this way, strange as it may seem, that the child explains the suspension of those little balloons of skin which are known to all children. We thought it desirable as a means of controlling our results to ask the children why these balloons rise. We were able to classify the answers into three stages corresponding to the stages I, II and IV that we have just been studying. And there is a transitional stage during which the child maintains that the balloon rises because it is " heavy ". Here are examples of these three stages :

First stage. NAI (4) : Balloons go up " *because they want to fly away.*" LE (6) : They go up because " *they like the air. So when you let go they go up in the sky.*"

Second stage. Bov (6 ; 5) : The balloons go up because " *there's gas inside.*—How is it done ?— . . . *When there's a lot of gas, it's heavy, it's very strong and then it flies.*"

Third stage. NE (8½) : The balloons go up " *because they're light.*"

It is sufficiently obvious in the case of Bov to what extent weight is assimilated to force. Again dynamic reasons prevail over mechanical considerations. If this schema is correct, it must admit of additional proof by means of questions put to the children about the fall of bodies to the ground. As it happened, the facts here proved decisive. According to the youngest of our set of children (on the average under 7), bodies fall to the ground, not because they are heavy, but because they want to, or because nothing holds them back. Only the older children bring in the idea of weight as cause of the fall.

Here are examples of the first of these two stages :

HANS (5). We let a book fall from a certain height. " Why does it fall ?—*Because you don't hold it.*—But why does it fall ?—*Because it doesn't stay up in the air.*—Why ?—*Because there's nothing* [to hold it].—Why does it fall ?—*Because it's not clouds.*" Same experiment with a box : it falls " *because it wants to go there* [on the ground].—Why ?—*Because it's a good thing.*" (Cf. the peripatetic doctrine of the " right place.")

Lu (5½) : " If I let go, will that [a book] fall, or not ? —*It will fall.*—Why has it fallen ?—*Don't know. Because you made it fall.*—But why did it fall ?—*Don't know.*—If I put some smoke on the table, will it fall ?—*Yes.*— It will fall, or it will go up ?—*It will go up.*—Why ?— *Because the smoke goes away.*—Why does the book fall and the smoke go up ?—*Don't know.*—Why did the book fall ?—*Because you made it fall.*"

Gut (8 ; 9) : " If I let go of that, why does it fall ?— *Because you let go of it.*—Yes, but why does it fall ?—*It can't keep up.*—Why not ?— . . . *It can't stay.*—Why ? —*Because you let go of it.*—Yes, but why does it fall when I let go of it ?— . . ."

We shall now give two cases of the second stage, but it will be noticed how the rôle played by weight is still connected with that of the other factors.

Hen (9 ; 8) : A pebble, " why does it fall ?—*Because it couldn't go up,*" etc. " But why does a flame go up and this goes down ?—*Because that* [the flame] *burns on the wood and not underneath* [=because the flame is forced by the wood to go up]." " But this, if I let go of this [metal object], what will happen ?—*It will fall down, because it can't go up in the air.*—Why ?—*Because it's heavy. . . . Ah ! I've got it !* "

Schan (10 ; 8). We show him an object which we allow to fall on the table. " Why has it gone down ?— *Because it's the wind. Because it's heavy.*—What wind ? Did you think there was a wind in the room ?—*No.*— And that [sheet of paper], why does it fall ?—*It's the air.*" In the end, Schan appeals to weight alone.

This shows how hard it is for children to isolate the part played by weight. Schan, in particular, tends to bring in factors of a dynamic order, such as the air produced by the actual fall of the body. According to our materials, it is at about the age of 7 that explanation by weight tends to become general. But children of this age still cannot say that smoke or flame rise because they are light. They still appeal to the air. " *The air is what makes them go up.*" Or again they rise " *because they are moving all the time.*" It is only at about the age of 10 that light bodies are supposed to rise because of their lightness.

Here is another conclusive experiment in connection with the fall of heavy bodies. The child is shown two objects, one heavy (*e.g.* a hammer's head), one light (*e.g.* a roll of ribbon). Each object is then attached to a ring and preparations are made before the child to make them descend along a string two metres long and set at a sufficiently steep angle. The child is asked to weigh the objects and to say which will descend quickest. All the children over 7 answer that the heavy object will descend quickest, "*because it is heavy*" (only one-twentieth of the children gave a contrary answer). Of the children under 7 or under 6, on the other hand, two-thirds were of opinion that the ribbon would go down quickest "*because it is light*".

This rapid survey of the explanation of the fall of heavy bodies, together with what we saw of the difficulty experienced by children in discovering that rivers run downwards because water is heavy, would seem to justify us in drawing the following conclusions. According to the child, movements of rise and fall are originally explained in virtue of dynamic reasons which are innocent of any concern with weight : bodies sustain one another by means of their own movements, they raise themselves by means of an inner force, they fall through lack of this force, and so on. As to weight, the child does not misjudge its importance, but weight is regarded as a symbol of absolute force or resistance, independently of the direction of movement. A heavy object possesses, by the mere fact of being heavy, as much the power of remaining in the air as of taking a downward course. As we saw, certain bodies (clouds, balloons) remain suspended, or even rise in the air, because they are heavy. We shall meet with this explanation again in connection with the way boats float on water. It means that heavy bodies are capable of impetus, and of resistance to pressure from outside, and that in this way, they can stay where they like. We have also had occasion to note that stones weigh on the water, and by their downward thrust bring about a current, and this is a view which we shall meet with again (Chap. VII). The child, in short, is not ignorant of weight. On the contrary, he attributes to it an even more important rôle than we do. But this rôle is of a different order : weight simply implies a latent force, which is both thrust and resistance, and can be used in the service of each and every end.

CHAPTER V

THE CHILD'S IDEA OF FORCE

It now remains for us to establish a few general ideas from the foregoing pages, to ascertain how children define for themselves the notion of material force, and to discuss the problem of the sources of this notion in the mind of the child.

§ 1. How the child explains movement.—The most striking characteristic of the explanations we have been studying in the last few chapters is their complexity. One would have thought that if any notion were impressed upon the mind by its surroundings with the maximum of clearness and simplicity, it would be the idea of movement. This, at least, is how things would happen if the Empirical Theory of Knowledge which goes with, say, the psychology of Herbert Spencer, were correct: the mind should from the first reach, not the scientific idea of inertia, such as it has been accepted since Descartes, but the modern commonsense notion, according to which bodies can do nothing of themselves to alter their movement or their state of rest. Now, in the first place, the further back we go in the intellectual evolution of the child, the less occasion have we to find even the smallest trace of this commonsense idea, according to which every movement is controlled from outside. The child fills the world with spontaneous movements and living "forces"; the heavenly bodies may rest or move as they please, clouds make wind by themselves, waves "raise" themselves, trees swing their branches spontaneously to make a breeze, water flows in virtue of a force residing within it. In short, all movement is conceived of by means of pre-notions and pre-relations. It is life and will, activity and spontaneity. It is therefore much more than what can be seen of it by direct perception; or rather, the problem arises as to why primitive perception endows nature with life rather than with inertia, why the " immediate " data of the external world are of a dynamic and not of a mechanical order. In the second place, these initial data of the perception of movement are not even " simple ". One would have thought that to every movement there would be attached from the first a single cause, external or internal, and that each movement would constitute an elementary unit. But the facts show, on the contrary, that the further back we go in the mental life of the child, the more movements are perceived as complex and conceived as due to the participation of many and various accumulated influences.

The most general characteristic of these primitive explanations of movement given by children is what may be called their bipolarity : the movement of a body is regarded as due both to an external will and to an internal will, to a command and an acquiescence. The starting-point of these ideas is both artificialist and animistic. If we go back further still, we may say that this bipolarity is originally of a magico-animistic order : on the one hand, we issue commands to things (the sun and moon, the clouds and the sky follow us), on the other hand, these things acquiesce in our desires because they themselves wish to do so.

This bipolarity endures long after the early stages have been passed. Even during the stage when the child is trying to explain the movements of nature by nature herself, every movement is still explained by the co-operation of external and internal motor force. The internal motor is always the free will of the objects. The external force is the sum of bodies morally attracting or repulsing the moving object. Thus the lake attracts the rivers ; night and the rain attract clouds ; sun and clouds repel each other ; rocks help water to flow, and so on. It is simply the artificialist-animist complexus prolonged, but the artificialism is transferred to external objects.

During a later stage, movement is explained by causes that are more physical than psychical, in the sense that the external motor force is supposed more and more to act by contact, *i.e.* by push or by pull. But the explanation is still far from being mechanical. It remains dynamic and bipolar, in the sense that the internal motor force is never abolished : the moving body retains the initiative and may utilise the external force or remove itself from its influence. Thus the sun is driven along by the clouds, but at the same time it follows us and uses the wind for its own ends. And the same is true of the clouds.

A special instance of this duality of influence is the schema of the " reaction of the surrounding medium " (ἀντιπερίστασις) which assumes most interesting proportions in the child. The moving object advances of itself, thanks to its own internal force. But in doing so, it produces a current in the surrounding medium (air or water), and this current, which constitutes the external motor force, flows back behind the moving object and accelerates its progress. Thus, clouds advance, thanks to the wind they make, and so on ; often indeed, when there is ἀντιπερίστασις there will be participation of the whole medium in that the wind begins to blow in the direction of the moving object which is producing wind. In short, this is the extreme form of the bipolarity we have just been talking about.

Finally, comes the fourth and last period, during which the child simplifies his conception of movement, and gradually reaches a mechanical causality based on inertia, whose advent coincides with the disappearance of the animist and artificialist mentality.

The first conclusion we may draw from this examination is that the idea of material force has a far wider connotation and denotation for the child than it has for us. As our mind becomes accustomed to the principle of inertia, we are led to dismiss many forces as imaginary or simply as useless. For the child, on the contrary, there is no movement, however simple, that does not call for the intervention of special forces. Thus the evolution of physical ideas is marked by a progressive diminution of " forces ", and not by their multiplication. What is the nature of these " forces " in the mind of the child ? To answer quite shortly, they are alive (*i.e.* not only teleological, but efficient through the very fact of their being teleological) and they are substantial.

On the first point there can be no possible doubt. During the stages when the child is still multiplying the number of forces, most movements are held to be conscious and to emanate from living bodies. This is true of the sun and moon, of clouds, rivers, and wind, etc. It will be remembered (*R.J.*, Sect. II) how closely the child assimilates movement to life, and vice versa. Even when, in the early stages, movements are not explicitly declared to be conscious, they are always regarded as intentional. The sun moves along " to give us light," the clouds " to give us rain," or " to make it night," the rivers " so that we can have water," etc. As a general rule, movement is inconceivable apart from an aim, and force apart from a function or office. Moreover—and herein resides the close connection in the child's mind between the ideas of force and those of life—the aim is both the final and the efficient cause of the movement. Just as in a living being the satisfaction of his desires is both the end and the cause of his activity, so for the child the usefulness of physical movements implies a force capable of producing them.

Nothing is so tempting in this connection as to compare a certain number of childish habits of thought with the well-known tendencies of Greek physics, that of Aristotle in particular. Like the Stagyrite, the child feels, for example, a very definite repugnance for the ideas of physical necessity and chance. To our eyes, nature is simply the totality of necessary sequences and of their interferences, which interferences characterise what we call chance. For the child, on the contrary, the world is a realm of ends, and the necessity of laws is moral rather than physical. Physical necessity certainly does appear, and even very early. The child admits the presence in the cosmos of unharmonious movements, of struggles, and even of disorder. But the interesting thing is that the child tends to regard such violent movements as " unnatural". A boy of 6 tells us that the clouds are not " clever " because " they try to fight the sun ". The sun, on the contrary, is clever, and being clever means that " you don't do what you ought not to " (see *C.W.*, Chap. VII, § 3). Necessity, during these early stages, occurs only as an obstacle ; it characterises the sum of the various traps and snares which things must avoid if everything is to function normally.

The same applies *a fortiori* to chance, as we have shown elsewhere (*L.T.*, Chap. V). The very way in which the child frames his questions before the age of 7–8 is evidence of an implicit belief in a world from which all chance is proscribed. The study of the explanation of movements entirely confirms this view. Sun and moon, cloud and wind are always supposed, whatever they may do, to be acting with some intention or other. Their will may be capricious, but there is no element of chance in the transaction.

In a word, child dynamism is a sort of panpsychism or hylozoism. This leads us on to a second characteristic : the idea of force is substantial. The chief mark of our adult, mechanistic conception of the world is that energy is transmitted : this body loses its energy in communicating it, that other increases its energy by receiving it from outside. This substance, for example, is warmed from outside, and then loses its thermal energy by warming the surrounding medium. In child dynamics, on the contrary, every substance is endowed with a *sui generis* force, unacquired and untransmissible, constituting the very essence of its activity. Every body, since it is alive, is the seat of personal activity. One living being may very well " give force " to another living being, but there is no question here of any transmission. The one simply excites or awakens the force of the other. This is why, if we try to find out exactly what a child means when he says that a force sets an object in motion, we always discover the idea of mutual excitation : the external force simply calls forth the internal force which belongs to the moving object. Thus stones make the rivers move along by calling forth the impetus of the water. Paq $(4\frac{1}{2})$ tell us "The road makes the bicycles go ". We make the sun move across the sky, night attracts the clouds, bad weather rouses the wind, etc. The process is everywhere the same. There is no transitive movement, there is only excitation of one living being by another. Force is not transmitted, but awakened.

We must beware, of course, of systematising over-much. The child often contradicts himself, and above all, he does not see the problems raised by his statements, his thought being innocent of all conscious or intentional coherence. But what we can say is, that in the more elaborate explanations which he gives, the idea of force is more akin to that conceived by the ancient Greeks than to that which is embodied in our present-day way of thinking.

One more point. In the eyes of the child, does force act with or without contact ? The idea of contact seems foreign to childish dynamics in some of its aspects : when we compel the sun to follow us, when the sun pursues the clouds, etc., there would seem to be action at a distance. But in other aspects, childish dynamics seem to require contact : when the clouds drive the sun before them, it is because a breath issues from them and goes to the sun ; and when the movement of the hands produces a current of air in a closed room, it is because air has simultaneously entered the room through the closed window. The antinomy is analogous to that which we find in primitive peoples. Everything acts upon everything else, but everything is omnipresent. In point of fact the question does not arise for the child, or at any rate, it takes quite a different form. For in one way the action of the motor on the moving object is of a psychological order : the external force commands or arouses a desire or a fear. In this sense, it acts at a distance. On the other hand, the actions are for the most part accompanied by material transferences, and in this sense, there is contact. Thus to the extent that there is action at a distance, the explanation is psychological, and to the extent that there is contact, the explanation is physical. But originally—and this is why one is apt to be misled—the two activities are not differentiated, because of the lack of any precise boundaries between thought and things, between the ego and the external world.

In conclusion, it should be noted that this analysis of child dynamics entirely justifies the interpretation to which we were led by our study of the questions of a child of 6 (*L.T.*, Chap. V). In other words, child dynamics are based on pre-causality. Children's questions showed evidence neither of any search for the mechanical cause of phenomena nor of the search for any logical justification of their judgments, but pointed only to a search for motivation, which was conceived as the only possible explanation. In a world filled and animated with intentions, such as the child conceives it to be, the true cause of a phenomenon is the moral reason for its happening. Every end calls forth the very force which is to realise it, and in looking for the " why " of things, the child is also exploring the manner of their production. The " how " is of no interest to him and raises no problems. The features to which we have drawn attention in child dynamics seem to confirm these views, and there is no need to dwell any longer upon the subject.

§ 2. DEFINITION OF THE IDEA OF FORCE.[1]—Since the idea of force or strength plays so important a part in

[1] Throughout this section we have retained the word " force " for the French *force*, although it can hardly be said to form part of an English child's vocabulary, and has the further disadvantage of possess-

forming the child's picture of the world, it may be of interest to enquire how children define it. In order to solve this question, we have made use of a method which had already served us in our study of animism : the child is given the names of a certain number of objects, and is asked about each in turn : " Is it strong (*fort*) or not ? ", and after the answer : " Why is it strong ? ". Care must naturally be taken to avoid suggestion by perseveration.

We had hoped in this way to discover the various stages in the evolution of the idea of force as we had done in connection with the definition of the word " alive ". On this point, however, our enquiry led to an entirely negative result : we could detect no evolution as the child grew older. The different types of answer obtained always yielded the same age average and presented the same frequency at every age up to 10–11.

The real point of interest about the answers was to show that the child defines material force almost exactly as he defines life, with one or two slight deviations which we shall presently note. This explains why these definitions undergo no development : when everything is regarded by the child as alive, the ideas of force and of life completely overlap, and the notion of force gradually inherits all the features originally attributed to life. It is true, of course, that the use of the idea of force develops, since the child advances from integral dynamism to an increasingly mechanistic outlook, but the verbal definitions, *i.e.* the child's own conscious realisations develop much more slowly, and indeed do not appear to do so perceptibly much before the age of 11–12.

One of the first characteristics of a thing which enable the child to pronounce it " strong " is the capacity for

ing no corresponding adjective like the French *fort*. At the same time, it conveys a shade of meaning which is intermediate between " strength " and " power ", and not adequately rendered by either. The reader must therefore remember that this experiment was designed for French-speaking children, to whom verbally it is particularly well suited, and that the dialogue inevitably loses some of its spontaneity in translation [Translator's Note].

movement. Here we recognise a criterion frequently used in connection with the definition of life

TAÏ (7 ; 1) : " Has water got force ?—*Yes, it moves along.* — Has petrol got force ?—*No, it doesn't move.* [Taï knows the use of petrol, but for the moment he neglects the idea of activity in favour of that of movement.]—Has a bicycle got force ?—*Yes, because a gentleman makes it go.*" " Has a table force ?—*No, it doesn't go.*—And wood ?—*No, because it doesn't move along.*" " Has the water in the lake force ?—*Yes, because it moves towards the rivers.*" " Has the moon got force ?—*Yes, because the clouds drive it along hard.*"

RŌ (6) : " Is the sun strong ?—*Yes, because it moves rather fast.*—Are rivers strong ?—*Yes, because they move. And a bench ?—No, it doesn't move.*" We suggest to Rō that the bench is strong since we are sitting on it. Rō agrees, but soon after returns to his idea of movement : " Is an aeroplane strong ?—*Rather ! It goes fast.*—Is an aeroplane standing still, strong ?—*No, because it hasn't got a start yet* (il n'a pas encore ses élans).—What does that mean ?—*That it doesn't go very fast.*—What do you mean by having a start ?—*When you walk fast.*—Have you got a start [Tu as des élans] ?—*Yes, when I'm running.* —What does it do ?—*It goes fast.*—What is it like ? Have you got one now ?—*No. I make it happen myself* (C'est moi qui les fait faire).—How ?—*When I run.*—How do you do it ?—*I give myself a start. It's when I run.*" " Which is strongest, an elephant or a fly ?—*A fly, because it goes faster.*"

BERT (9 ; 1) tells us that force is " *current* ". " Has a motor-car a current ?—*Yes, because it goes fast.*" This current is " *air*—Where does it come from ?—*It's the air that the motor-car makes.*"

This shows to what extent force is assimilated to movement and how much these definitions recall those of life (*C.W.*, Chap. VI, § 2). It shows, above all, to what extent force is substantified and reduced to a current or to air which emanates from the powerful object itself. Such answers as these are not without their use in throwing light upon the explanations of movement examined in the foregoing chapters, and in particular on the origins of the schema of the " reaction of the surrounding medium ".

A second type of schema confines force to bodies that move of themselves.

HELLB (8½) gives, as an instance of strong objects, the wind : " *It moves because it is strong.*—Tell us something else that is strong ?—*Water, when there is a current.*" " Are clouds strong ?—*No, because it's the wind that makes them move.*—Is a bicycle ?—*No, because you have to work the pedals.*" We ask Hellb : " Are life and force the same thing ?—*Life is lasting a long time, force is when you can hold things up.*"

OL (8½) : " Has the moon got force ?—*No, because that's the way she moves : it's the air that makes her move.*—What does it mean to have force ?—*It's something you have in your body.*"

BRUN (11) : " Has the sun got force ?—*No, because it isn't alive.*"

These children define force exactly as they define life. According to a third type of answer, which is by far the most common, force is defined as activity in general and useful activity in particular. These answers recall very closely those of the first stage of animism (*C.W.*, Chap. VI, § 1).

TIE (10 ; 10) : " Has the sun got force ?—*Yes, because it gives light.*—And fire ?—*Yes, because it burns.*—And a stick ?—*Yes, because it can keep a house up.*—And glass ? —*Yes, because it can cut.*—And trees ?—*Yes, because they make the fruit grow.*" " Has grass got any force ?—*Yes, because it is useful.*—And a spoon ?—*Yes, because it is used for all sorts of things.*" " Have clouds got strength ? —*No, because they do nothing.*—And rain ?—*Yes, because it makes the seed go into the earth.*" Once a child has embarked upon a definition of this kind, there is no getting him off it, but the interesting thing is to see the mental orientation which led him to this view

KRUG (6) : " Are flowers strong ?—*No, they are only pretty, but they can't do anything.*—Is a seed strong ?— *Yes, because it can make things grow for us (!).*" " Is a fish ?—*No, because they do nothing, they can't do anything.*"

Note to what an extent it is only from our point of view that things are alive and have force. In all other cases things are regarded as being endowed with force only when their activity is dangerous, but this again is a form of anthropomorphism.

BOURG (6) : " What is force ?—*It is something strong* (fort) *that can kill us.*" " Is the water in the lake strong ? —*Sometimes. The lake and the stones, when you go and bathe they hurt.*" " Has a motor got force ?—*Because it can run us over, sometimes it runs us over.*" " Are clouds strong (fort) ?—*No, because they haven't got an eye.*—And if they had an eye ?—*Yes, they would see and would be just a little bit strong.*"

DA (7) : " Is a bench strong (fort) ?—*Yes, you hit each other.*"

According to a fourth type of answer, force is defined by the action of carrying something. But in point of fact this activity is taken in a purely anthropocentric sense. This type of answer is also connected with the preceding type by a number of intermediate cases.

BOUR (7 ; 8) : " Has the moon got force ?—*Yes, because she carries the old moon in her arms.*—Is the wind strong (fort) ?—*Yes, because it sends the moon up into the air.*— Is water ?—*Yes, because it can drag us into the Rhône.*— Has petrol force ?—*Yes, because it can clean.*—And the window-pane ?—*No, because it hardly carries anything.*— And birds ?—*No, because they are little. They have no arms.*—Has rain got force ?—*No, it does nothing.*—And stones ?—*No, they carry nothing.*"

TASS (8 ; 2) : A fly has no force " *because it can't carry anything*", a fish " *because it can't do anything*", etc.

PURR (7 ; 11) : " Has the sun got force ?—*No, because it can't raise itself* (ne se soulève pas).—And a plant ?—*Yes, because it carries flowers on its stem.*"

Answers of a fifth type seem to have left all traces of animism behind them : those things are strong, have force, which resist, which do not break. This is the characteristic most frequently referred to after activity and movement. But, curiously enough, this resistance is not thought of by the child as passive : it is a real activity, closely akin to life itself.

SART (11 ; 5) : " Is a house strong ?—*Yes, it can stand up by itself.*—And a cloud ?—*No, because it falls down in rain* [= it does not hold together].—Is fire strong ?—*Yes, because it is difficult to put out* ". Boats are strong " *because they can stay on the water* ", thought (la pensée), " *because when you want to keep something, you keep it and you don't say it* ". Words are not strong " *because they go away at once* ", but trees are " *because you can't tear them up easily* ". The moon has force " *because it couldn't stay up in the air if it hadn't any* ", but a fish has " *not much ; because when it is out of water it can't live* ".

BORI (7) : " Is a bicycle leaning against the wall strong ? —*Yes, because there is no one on it.*—And this bench ?— *Yes, because there's no one there.*—And if you go and sit on it ?—*Then it isn't strong any longer.*—Why not ?—*It's not.*"

This shows what is meant by resistance. It is self-preservation. the fact of remaining what one is. The moon is strong because it remains in the air. the bench because it resists pressure, and so on.

In a sixth and last type the answers characterise force by size and weight (two criteria which we may regard as interchangeable). But the interesting thing is, that in conformity with what was shown in the last chapter, weight retains a far more dynamic meaning for the child than it does for us : to be heavy means to be capable of pressure, of impetus (*élan*), of resistance, etc.

MONT (8 ; 4) : " Has the wind force ?—*No.* . . . *Yes, it has, because it's heavy.*" Mont goes on to say that the wind is heavy " *because it goes fast* ". " Has a bicycle force ?—*Yes, because it is heavy.*—A boat ?—*Yes, because it is heavy.*—And a little boat ?—*Also, because it is heavy.*" To be heavy means, therefore, to be capable of swiftness, of pressure, of resistance, etc., the wind is heavy because it blows hard, the boat because it remains on the water, and so on.

PEC (7 ; 3) : " Has a stone got force ?—*No, because it is light. You can break it with a hammer.*—And a big stone ?—*Yes, it can crush your feet and flatten them out.*" Weight, here, means something resistant or capable of pressure.

HEND (8) : " Has a stone got force ?—*No. It has when you throw it because* [then] *it is heavy.*"

Clearly, weight is still closely allied to power in general, and therefore to life. It should be noted, moreover, that the same criteria often serve to characterise life. Thus a boy of 7½ tells us that clouds are not alive " because they are not carrying anything ", and that of two bodies "*the biggest*" is the more alive.

But we must press this point no further, for the perpetual contradictions indulged in by children and the dangers of suggestion by perseveration bar the way to a more thorough-going analysis. Besides, the results we have reached, such as they are, and in spite of their defects, are sufficient to confirm the interpretations put forward in § 1 of this chapter. For the idea of force seems to be the prolongation of the idea of life. The concept of force is the residue left by animism : once consciousness has been eliminated from things, such life as the child still bestows upon them constitutes the actual content of the idea of force.

§ 3. ORIGIN OF THE IDEA OF FORCE.—The fact that the idea of force owes its existence to inner experience seems to be beyond dispute. To Maine de Biran belongs the merit of having stressed this origin. It matters at bottom very little whether the feeling of effort is, or is not, bound up with sensations of innervation, in other words, whether it is afferent or efferent : without the feeling of our own muscular effort we should not be able to explain the movements around us by the idea of force.

This being so, the thorny problem still remains as to how an inner experience could ever lead us to endow external things with forces, for it is far from proven that the child begins by noticing the existence of force in himself. It would seem rather that force, while it is the result of a transposition or transference, is first of all discovered in things, before being felt in the self. In other words, it may very well be that from the point of view of conscious experience, the order of succession in the various moments is the reverse of what it is from the point of view of the objective construction of the idea.

According to Maine de Biran, the order of succession in the conscious realisation coincides with that in the objective construction. To put it differently, force is first of all grasped in the self and then inferred in external objects. On the one hand, the notion of force comes from the intuition of self, which is prior to it. On the other, it is by means of an inference that we transfer to external objects this force felt within ourselves. The original runs as follows. On the one hand : " Before the self or without it there is no actual or possible knowledge. Everything, therefore, must come from this source or join issue with it." [1]   " For the idea of *force* can originally only be taken from the consciousness of the subject who is making an effort ; and even when it is abstracted from the fact of consciousness, carried outside and altogether removed from its natural seat, it still retains the traces of its origin." [2]   The idea of force is opposed in this sense to the idea of substance " which is more mixed in its origin and may be derived equally from one and the other of the two elements that make up the fact of consciousness ",[3] *viz.*, from the self which makes efforts and from the term that resists these efforts. On the other hand: " In virtue of a first induction, founded on our immediate sense of effort, or—what does not concern us here—in virtue of a primitive law inherent in the human spirit, we interpret this change, the actual object, of which our own effort or self is not the *cause*, as due to a force or to an efficient external cause." [4]

Now, if we confront this process thought out by Maine de Biran with the facts—not as they come to be observed in the mind of a philosopher but as they are seen to take place in the development of the child, we are led to an

[1] *Œuvres inédites de Maine de Biran*, published by Ernest Naville, with the collab. of M. Debrit, Paris, 1859, t. I, p. 248.
[2] *Ibid.*, p. 249.   [3] *Ibid.*
[4] " Rapports des Sc. Nat. avec la Psychol.", quoted by Brunschvicg, *Expérience humaine et Causalité physique*, p. 34.

exact reversal of the order of things. For everything happens as though the child began by attributing forces to all outside bodies, and as though he only ended by finding in himself the " I " that was the cause of his own force.

After all, nothing is less likely than that the feeling of the self should originate in very young children. All that we have seen of child realism, of the confusion between physical and psychical, of the origins of magic (*C.W.*, Sect. I) seems rather to indicate that our earliest experiences are not referred to a central " I ", but float about in an undifferentiated absolute. The self would thus be the result of a gradual and progressive dissociation, and not of a primitive intuition. This dissociation is due, no doubt, to the very effort which enables the mind gradually to oppose the world of external resistances to the world of inner tendencies and desires, but the effort is, in all probability, not to be thought of as personal or connected with an " I ". It must be felt as absolute, as bound up with the whole universe before being understood as subjective.

As a matter of fact—and this is the only point of any practical value, disastrous though it be of the Biranian psychology—the more the feeling of the " I " develops in the child, the more does the idea of force lose in wideness of application.

In the early stages during which the child's realism, *i.e.* his ignorance of his own ego reaches its highest point, childish dynamism is complete : the universe is peopled with living and substantial forces to a degree that adult commonsense would find it hard to imagine. During the later stages, as the child gradually becomes conscious of the inner world and of the specificity of his ego, dynamism is ousted from the child's conception of the world by a more mechanical way of thinking.

This direct ratio between the development of subjectivity and the reduction of dynamism bears a close resemblance to what was shown in connection with animism. In the measure that the child is ignorant of the existence of his own thought, he attributes life and consciousness to every object that comes his way, and in the measure that he discovers his own thought, he withdraws consciousness from the things around him. The analogy, moreover, is easy to understand, since the idea of force, as we have just had occasion to show, is closely bound up with childish animism.

If, then, we analyse the facts in the order of their appearance and genesis, and not in the fictitious order of adult introspection, we shall find that they admit of an interpretation which is the opposite of that put forward by Maine de Biran. Seen in natural perspective, the " primitive fact " is a derivative fact. Genetic analysis joins issue at this point with the critical analysis which M. Brunschvicg has used with such skill and subtlety, and in which he shows how powerless was the dogmatic psychologism of Maine de Biran to lay the foundations of the ideas of cause and force.

It cannot, therefore, be in virtue of any " induction " that we transfer to things around us the feeling of force derived from our inner experience. If force were really in the first instance experienced in the " I ", and only subsequently projected into things, then we could speak of induction. We could say that we never conceive of physical bodies without " hypothesising in them up to a point that individual force which constitutes our " I " [1]

But if it is in the things around him and before knowing his own " I " that the child discovers force, it behoves us to express the matter in different language. Now, the vocabulary of Maine de Biran seems to reduce itself to two sets of terms : those that connote immediate experience, internal intuition or introspection, and those that connote inference or induction. Thus the " I " is grasped immediately by intuition, and external force is inferred in things. But M. Brunschvicg has shown [2] very clearly

---

[1] Maine de Biran, Œuvres, édit. Naville, I, p. 249.
[2] L'expérience humaine et la Causalité physique, livre II.

how deluded was Maine de Biran in his belief that a substantial ego could be reached by intuition : the " I " is not a fact of experience that can be isolated, it is the condition of experience, and can only be reached by reflection. We have just recalled the circumstance that the " I " is slowly built up throughout childhood rather than immediately given at the outset of conscious experience. What, then, of the idea of force ? It is the result of internal experience, but not of an experience which is felt as internal from the first. Force, then, is not a fact given in direct intuition since, coming as it does from the sense of effort, it is originally localised in objects. Further, the idea of force cannot be the result of an induction, since during the early stages, that is to say, during those which mark its zenith, there is little or no boundary between the ego and the external world. For there can only be induction from one term to another in so far as the terms are distinct. What, then, is this reality due to the feeling of muscular effort and yet situated in external objects ? How are we to explain this objectification of a schema of organic origin, without falling back upon the convenient but ineffectual ideas of " projection ", of " introjection ", or of " ejection " ?

From the psychological point of view, things would seem to happen as follows. Every thought is the product of sensorial elements resulting from the pressure exercised on the organism by its immediate surrounding, and of motor schemas which organise these sensorial elements into bundles which we call perceptions, ideas, mental experiences. Thus every thought presupposes an external contribution, due to sensible reality, and an internal contribution due to the organism itself, *i.e.* to the movements it has made in order to perceive, to virtual movements which it carries out mentally in order to reconstruct passed scenes or to foresee future scenes, and so on. Now these two kinds of contribution are, of course, completely undifferentiated from the point of view of the subject's consciousness : every perception and every idea will necessarily appear to be objective, so long as the mistakes and failures of action have not led the mind to discern what is subjective and what objective in a given point of view. In other words, reality is perpetually being "assimilated" by the motor schemas of the organism, without it being possible for consciousness to take part in this assimilation. Assimilation is therefore not an induction. It is the expression of the complete continuity which binds the organism to its biological environment. It is prior to any distinction between the external world and the ego.

From this point of view the idea of force consists in one of the possible schemas of assimilation. In order to build up the idea of objects and to distinguish the different physical objects from one another, the mind proceeds by a series of the most laborious experiments, of which the essential task is to become conscious of the innumerable resistances set up by the external world.

Thus, reality is conceived by means of schemas which have been built up by the accumulated muscular experiences of the subject, *i.e.* by the residue of all those of his movements that have been accompanied by a sense of effort. The idea of object is undifferentiated from the idea of resistance. And the idea of resistance itself is undifferentiated from the ideas of activity, of will, of purpose, in short of living force.

From the point of view of behaviour, this description comes to the same thing as the theory of Maine de Biran : the idea of force is of internal origin and it is by transference that we attribute force to the things around us. But from the point of view of consciousness, the process is reversed : there is neither direct intuition of internal force, nor induction allowing us to pass from the ego to the external world. There is simply assimilation of the world by the ego " I " ; and there is consciousness of the product of this assimilation before there is any consciousness of the " I " as a seat of force. Only by means of a derivative process does the mind come to dissociate the

" I " from the world around it, and in the measure that this dissociation takes place, force becomes gradually withdrawn from external objects and confined within the ego.

If this view is correct, the difficulties raised by Ribot which we mentioned in connection with the origin of animism (*C.W.*, Chap. VII, § 5) vanish of themselves. The feeling of effort, says Ribot, is afferent : thus we are conscious of the effect produced by muscular effort but not of its cause ; how, then, could the feeling of effort lead us to imagine causes and forces in the external world ? How in general are we to interpret that tendency, " well-known though unexplained ", which leads the subject to endow everything with life and with activity ? In the psychology of personality taught by Ribot, and which is in a sense a translation into the language of cœnesthesia of Maine de Biran's spiritualist psychology, such a tendency is indeed inexplicable. But if we say that that consciousness of self is the result, as it were, of carving consciousness out of the object, and that the object present to primitive consciousness has already been moulded by unconscious effort—in other words, if we say that this object is conceived by means of motor schemas which the conscious subject precisely does not localise in the " I ", then the afferent character of the feeling of effort, far from rendering inexplicable the objectivity of the idea of force, will supply ample support to the interpretation which we have outlined above.

PREDICTION AND EXPLANATION

WHEN one leaves the field of verbal enquiry and begins to perform little experiments before the children and ask questions about them, one is astonished at the wealth and constancy of their ideas. For this reason we cannot in the present section of this book deal with the problem of child physics as a whole. There is a multitude of phenomena which children have had occasion to notice in nature or in industry which give rise, not to spoken explanations, but to visual and motor schemas which fill and satisfy the child's mind.

We shall confine ourselves here to the analysis of three groups of phenomena : the floating of boats, the displacement of the level of water by the immersion of a solid body, and the problem of shadows. These phenomena have not very much in common, but they will enable us to analyse the relations between the logic of the child and the causal explanations which he gives. In carrying out this analysis, we shall adopt a special point of view—that of the relation between the prediction and the explanation of phenomena. M. Claparède has made the following very useful suggestion in this connection. He asked himself up to what point children (in virtue of their more or less conscious bodily experiences) were able to foresee events in the domain of elementary physical law. The same problem is being investigated in several German laboratories. Messrs. Lipmann and Borgen have published a highly suggestive book [1] describing ingenious devices for inducing children to perform certain movements

[1] O. Lipmann and H. Borgen, *Naïve Physik*, Leipzig, 1921.

which presuppose the practical knowledge ("physical intelligence" as these authors call it) of mechanical relations. The problem we have set ourselves here is of an appreciably different order. We shall endeavour, first of all, to get the children to say what is going to happen in certain given physical circumstances, and then ask them to explain what has taken place. We shall then compare the prediction with the explanation, so as to be able to grasp the relations existing between what these authors call "physical intelligence" and "gnostic intelligence." The psychological problem involved in this way develops into an epistemological problem, that of legality and of causality, a subject which M. Meyerson has dealt with in well-known terms.

CHAPTER VI

THE FLOATING OF BOATS

THE interrogatory, the results of which we are going to analyse, contains a purely verbal part—that which bears upon the floating of boats on the lake. But it is possible to make this part more concrete by playing with bits of wood, with stones, with nails, etc., and by asking the child whether these objects will or will not float, and why they do or do not float. One can also help the child to build little boats in clay, so as to study the relations between form, volume, and the capacity for floating. Above all, when the child says that wood floats because it is light, one can bring forward two equal volumes of wood and of water, and then ask the child to say which will be heavier.

By combining the interrogatory on boats with these more concrete practices we were able roughly to distinguish four stages in the evolution of explanations about floating. During the first stage, which ends at about 5 years, floating is explained by animistic and moral reasons. During a second stage, extending on the average from 5 to 6, the child thinks that boats float because they are heavy. During a third stage (average age 6–8), on the contrary, the child says that they float because they are light. But this explanation is still fraught with reasons of a dynamic order. Finally, at about 9 years, the child begins to understand the true relation between the weight of the boat and that of the liquid element.

Moreover, the earlier the explanations are, the less simple we shall find them. There is an over-determination

of factors which is very interesting to observe. In
addition, it should be noted at once that, in spite of
appearances, these experiments on floating are subject to
a schema of evolution completely analogous to that
which we found in our investigation of explanations
relative to the suspension of clouds and the heavenly
bodies, and to the fall of heavy objects to the ground.

§ 1. FIRST AND SECOND STAGES : BOATS FLOAT FOR
MORAL OR DYNAMIC REASONS.—We need not trouble at
this point to lay any stress on the answers of the first
stage. In this particular case they exhibit all the usual
features. Here are two examples :

FRE (4 ; 10) : " Will this little boat [made of wood]
lie on the water or go to the bottom ?—*It will lie on the
water, because they always must lie on the water.*—Why do
big boats lie on the water ?—*Don't know.*—And this
match ?—*It lies there because it must lie.*—And a stone ?—
It will go to the bottom.—Why ?—*Don't know.*—And a bit
of glass ?—*It will go to the bottom.*—Why ?—*Because it's
not allowed to put glass on the water.*"

VERN (6) realises that a piece of wood will float, that
a stone will sink, etc. " Why does a boat not sink. It
is heavier than a stone, yet it doesn't sink.—*The boat is
cleverer than the stone.*—What does it mean to be clever ?
—*It doesn't do what it ought not to.*—Why do rowing-boats
not go to the bottom ?—*Because the movements of the
oars keep them up.*"

According to the child, boats remain afloat because of
some moral necessity, which is connected both to the
will of their makers and to the obedience of the boats
themselves. There are therefore laws which regulate the
way in which bodies float, and these laws are accompanied
by a feeling of necessity which renders them explicative.
But this necessity is still purely moral : law has not ceased
to be mixed up with social obligation.

The second stage is much more complex. Its outstanding
feature is dynamism, but this appears in several distinct
forms. The child begins to introduce weight as an
explanation of floating, but he does so in a confused and

often contradictory manner. As a general rule, boats are regarded as able to float because they are heavy. The word " heavy " means that the boats have the strength to keep themselves up, that they are capable of resistance, of impetus (*élan*), etc. An equal volume of water is, of course, considered lighter than wood, but water, when it is deep, is sufficiently " heavy " to raise the boats. These, moreover, have also sufficient force to keep themselves up, because people row, or because there is an engine. Thus in the end, and by devious paths, floating comes back to a sort of gliding flight, entirely analogous to what we described in connection with the suspension of clouds and of the sun and moon.

Here are a few examples, in which boats are quite definitely considered to be floating because they are heavy :

HEL (5) does not yet speak of weight, but in his mind size and weight are still synonymous. Hel anticipates that a plank and a pebble will both sink to the bottom of the water. We make the experiment : " Why does the wood stay on the water ?—*Oh ! I know, it's because it's big.*—And the rowing-boats on the lake ?—*Because you make them move along.*—And the big boats, why do they stay on the water ?—*It's because you make them go with a motor. If the motor stops, the boats go to the bottom.*—But in port ?—*It's because they're tied up* " [Hel is thinking of the anchor chains]. " And this wood will go to the bottom or stay on top ?—*It will stay on top because it's big.*—And this pebble ?—*It will stay on top.* [We make the experiment.]—Why did the pebble fall and the wood stay ?—*Because the pebble is thin and the wood is big.*" Later Hel predicts that glass, metal, etc., will remain on the water. Seeing that they sink, he exclaims : " *It's because there's not enough water that it always goes to the bottom.*"

COL (5 ; 9) Rowing-boats " *stay on the water because they move.*—And the big boats ?—*They stay on the water because they are heavy.*"

GEN (6½) : When the boat " *is heavy, it presses all round and it swims quicker.*"

HEI (5 ; 7) : " Why does the boat [a toy] remain on the water ?—*It stays on top because it is heavy.*—Why does it stay because it is heavy ?—*I don't know.*" " *The rowing-boats stay on top because they're big.*" Fifteen days later Hei says, on the contrary, that the boats stay " *because they're not heavy.*" But comparing a pebble with a plank, Hei again says : " *This pebble will go to the bottom because it isn't big enough, it's too thin.*" Finally, Hei says that a stone goes to the bottom because " *it's stronger* [than the wood].—And the boats, why do they stay on top ?—*Because the water is strong.*"

AN (5 ; 9) : " *The wood holds itself up.*—Why ?— *Because the water is lighter than the big bit of wood.*" " Why does the wood stay on the water and the pebble go to the bottom ?—*It's not so light as the pebble.*" Thus, weight is a sign of strength : what is heavy " *sticks together.*"

M. To (7 ; 11) : " Why does the wood stay on the water ?—*It's light and the little boats have sails.*" Of the two equal volumes of water and wood, To believes the wood to be the heavier. " And the little boats without sails, why do they stay on the water ?—*Because they are light.*—And why do the big boats stay ?—*Because they are heavy.*—Then heavy things stay on the water ?—*No.* —A big pebble ?—*It goes to the bottom.*—And the big boats ?—*They stay because they are heavy.*"

To these examples must be added the case of this little boy, who is always passing from one explanation to another, but whose hesitation in itself is highly significant :

PETA (5 ; 7) : " If I let go of this [a little wooden boat], does it stay on top or go to the bottom ?—*I don't know. I think that it goes to the bottom because it's too small.*—And a bigger one ?—*It will go to the bottom because it's big.* [We make the experiment with the little boat.] *It's small and it isn't heavy. The heavy things fall.*" Nevertheless Peta predicts that a pebble will stay on top of the water. " Why did it go to the bottom ?—*This pebble is too heavy . . . no, this pebble is too small ; that's better* [to say that it's too small].—Why does this nail go to the bottom ?—*It's too small, too thin.*—Why does this hammer [the head of a hammer] go to the bottom ? —*It's too big, too heavy.*" " Why do the rowing-boats float ?—*I don't know. Because the water is too heavy*

[=too strong !]. *Is that right ? "* " Why does this pebble go to the bottom ?—*It's too small, too thin.*"

This gives some idea of the complexity of the answers at this stage. The child seems to be contradicting himself at every point. At one moment, he appeals to the weight of the boat to explain the fact of its floating, at the next, he appeals to the weight of the water to explain how it manages to support the floating object. But, disregarding these hesitations, let us see whether behind the confused language of this particular child there is not some characteristic trait common to all children at this stage. Now, there is one statement that is constantly recurring in the talk of the youngest children : whatever is strong (*fort*), *i.e.* capable of movement can float. Floating is assimilated to swimming : rowing-boats float " because you make them move along " (Hel), " because they move " (Col), " because they have sails " (To), and so on. There is no need to draw particular attention to these statements here, as we shall come across them repeatedly during the third stage. But, this being so, children of the second stage add—and this addition is their peculiar contribution—that they float because they are heavy. What does this mean ? Clearly, that weight or size is to them a sign of strength : heavy bodies have more strength than light ones, and can therefore swim better, press better on the water, resist more strongly, and so on. Gen tells us that when a boat is heavy " it presses better ", An maintains that a heavy piece of wood sticks together. Hei says that a stone is not big enough or too thin, and Peta that it is too small to stay on the water surface. We are thus brought back to the same explanation as the youngest children gave of the suspension of clouds : clouds stay in the air because, being heavy, they have the strength to keep in place or to move along fast enough to glide. Once admit the identity of weight and strength, and this interpretation raises no difficulty.

Only, and this is what makes for the complexity of these answers, the child's explanation carries with it no correct prediction of the event. At every turn, experience gives him the lie : a stone that should have floated because it was heavy sinks to the bottom, a small light piece of wood floats on the surface, and so on. So that the child is constantly being obliged to adapt his conception to new and unforeseeable events. In order to do this, he simply applies the idea of weight in a new way. If a light body floats, this is because the water is heavier than it is and has sufficient force to sustain it. This is why Peta comes to say that the rowing-boats stay on the water because the water is " heavy " and Hei " because the water is strong (*forte*)." Thus, heavy bodies will float because, being heavy they can keep themselves up, and light bodies will float because they are light and the water will be heavy enough, *i.e.* strong enough to bear them. This double and contradictory explanation will fit every case, and the child will always contrive to justify the most widely opposed facts. Hence the tentative and hesitating statements of Hei, of Peta and, in fact, of all the children belonging to this stage. But under this incoherence there is a fixed and definite conception : the identification of weight and force, and the assimilation of floating to a sort of gliding flight.

From the point of view of the relations between prediction and explanation, this stage, as compared to the last, shows an interesting reversal in the order of things. Explanation here seems to dominate prediction. The child is in possession of an explanatory schema : bodies float because they are heavy. He therefore predicts that the stones will float, that matches will sink, and so on. The law obtained in this way is false, but it follows from the explanation, once the latter is admitted. Apart from the dynamism which this explanation imposes upon the facts (and which has in nowise been culled from pure observation) the prediction would be completely different. Now, during the first stage, things happen the other way

round : the child predicts nothing. He confines himself
to observing certain partial laws and to explaining them
without going beyond them : since boats float, it *must*
be so ; since the pebble sinks, it *cannot be allowed* for it
to float, and so on. We grant that the explanation is
moral, but it is entirely dependent upon the observed
law. Moreover, in the third stage, as we shall presently
show, prediction once again separates itself from explanation. Thus between law and explanation a reciprocal
action is continuously at work, in accordance with a
rhythm which it is easy to observe : legality precedes
causality, and then causality overflows the limits set by
legality and calls for the formation of new laws ; the
correctness of these new laws necessitates the appearance
of fresh explanations, and so on. What we have yet to
ascertain, is how far these two terms mutually imply one
another. In other words, our task is to establish whether
and up to what point the laws observed by the child
contain implicit explanations, or whether, on the contrary,
they go against the type of explanation characteristic of
the particular level of mental development in question.
The sequel will show us what to think.

§ 2. THIRD STAGE : BOATS FLOAT OWING TO THEIR OWN
OR TO ACQUIRED MOVEMENT AND BECAUSE THEY ARE
LIGHT IN RELATION TO THE TOTAL MASS OF WATER.—
The criterion of the third stage, as compared to the first
two, is that the child begins systematically to attribute
to their lightness the fact that boats float on the water :
wood, skiffs, etc., float because they are light ; nails,
stones, glass, etc., sink because they are heavy. But
what is the true meaning of these expressions ? As we
shall presently see, it is far more dynamic than static. Let
us examine the following questions in succession : the relation of weight to volume (specific weight, or density), the
relation of the weight of a submerged body to the corresponding volume of water (principle of Archimedes), and finally,
the part played by movement in floating (gliding flight).

Beginning with the question of density, we show the children two equal volumes of wood and of water (in small glass vessels). We say : " You see, there's the same amount of wood and of water. Which is heavier of the two, the wood or the water ? " All the children of this stage, like those of the preceding stage, in other words all the children under 9, answer that the wood is heavier. And yet children of the third stage say that wood floats because it is " light " !

KLEI (8½) : " Which is the heavier ?—*The wood.*—Why ? —*Because it weighs more than the water.*"

LO (6½) : " *The water is lighter because it is thinner* " [=less condensed].

RE (8) : " *The wood is heavier.*—Why ?—*Because it is bigger.*" Re knows quite well that the volumes are equal. " Big," according to him, means " condensed ", or " solid ".

CHAL (8½) : The wood is heavier " *because it is full* " [same meaning].

MUS (9 ; 8) : " *The wood is heavier because it is thicker* " (*id.*).

FALQ (7 ; 3) : The water is lighter " *because the water is liquid* " (*id.*).

LUG (11 ; 3) : The wood is heavier " *because it is bigger* " (*id.*).

CESS (12) : " *Because it's a bit bigger, and because water is water* " [=it is liquid].

The motives behind the choice of answer are constant : the child has, as yet, no notion of the specific weight of bodies. True, weight is no longer, as it was in some cases of the first stage, directly proportional to volume, but it is proportional to condensation : wood is heavier than water because it is closely packed and water is liquid. Density is a matter of compression. We met with the same phenomenon in connection with stones : a stone is " packed " and with its parts one could make a larger stone which would be less dense. (See *C.W.*, Chap. X, § 3.)

In short, at equal volumes, wood is heavier than water. What, then, is meant by the statement : " Wood is lighter than water ", which the children appeal to in order to explain why boats can float. In some cases, it simply means that wood is light in an absolute sense, and quite independently of any comparison with water. In others, curiously enough, the child is thinking of the total volume of the water. The boat floats because it is lighter than the lake or than the Rhône, etc. Only, in most of these cases, this conception has a dynamic meaning which it is all-important to notice : the lake, being heavy, produces an upward-flowing current which sustains the lighter body. Here are examples :

BAB ($7\frac{1}{2}$) : " Why does a boat not go to the bottom ?— *Because it's not heavy enough.*—Why does it stay on the water ?—*Because there is a current.*—Why does this boat [a toy] stay on top [on the water in a basin] ?—*It is big* [the basin] *and there's some water.*—And there [a glass] ? —*It will go to the bottom, because it's little* [the glass], *it's not the same as there. There is no current. There* [basin], *there is a little current.*—And if there were none ?— *It would go to the bottom.*" Later, Bab is very astonished to see that the boat floats in the glass. He exclaims : " *It's because it's not heavy.*" " Why does a little boat not go to the bottom, on the lake ?—*Because there's a current.*"
ZWA (8 ; 3) also predicts that certain pieces of wood will sink : " *This wood will go to the bottom because it's heavier than the others.*—If I put it in the lake ?—*It will not sink because the water* [of the lake] *is stronger than in a tin* " [=than in the basin]. Zwa also predicts that a little pebble will float because it is light. We make the experiment, and Zwa says that it has fallen " *because there is not much water there, but in the lake there is more.*" Zwa also tells us that the pebble will stay at the bottom of the water : " *It will not go up again because the water will hold it down.*" " *The water is strong, so it holds the boat on top.*—Why does it stay there ?—*Because the water presses from underneath and that holds it up.*—But you told me that the wood was heavier than the water ?— *Because the wood is lighter than the rest* [the rest of the lake]." And again : " Why does the boat stay on the water ?—*Because the water is strong.*—Why ?—*Because there's a lot of it.*—If I put it in a pond ?—*It goes to the bottom because there's not enough water.*" Zwa predicts

that a nail will stay on the water " *because the water is stronger* [than the nail]." Zwa is surprised that the nail sinks, and exclaims : " *It won't sink in the lake !* "

MEY (10 ; 8) predicts that a piece of wood will sink in our basin, but will float on a pond. The boats float " *because the water makes waves come up . . . because there are waves that hold it up.*" Various objects, according to Mey, will sink in the basin " *because the water is not strong enough to hold them.*" Briefly, when the water is deep, it is strong, because it makes " *waves come up* " ; if not, it is weak.

KLEI (8½) : " A little boat on the lake, why does it lie on the water ?—*Because the water is heavier.*—The water is heavier than it is ?—*Yes.*—Because it is light ?— *No, because there's a lot of water.*"

A. To (7½) : The boats float " *because the water is rather solid in the lake.*—If it were put on a pond ?—*It would not swim. There's not much water.*" A big boat would sink on the lake, but floats on the sea " *because there's more current in the sea than here.*—Why ?—*Because the lake is too small.*" Similarly " *a pond has not so much current as the lake.*" A. To concludes that " *the water* [of the lake] *is heavy* ", and that it is because of this that the boats float.

FALQ (7 ; 3) : Rowing-boats float " *because they are not very heavy* " and " *because the water is strong.*"— And why does this [a metal object] go to the bottom [we put it on the water in the basin] ?—*Because there's not enough water.*—On the lake ?—*It stays up, because there's a lot of water.*" " Why do the big boats stay on the water ?—*Because they go where there's a lot of water.*"

BIZ (10 ; 3) : " Why do the little rowing-boats stay on the water ?—*Because the wood is light. They can stay on the water.*—And the big boats ?—*Because the water is high. That holds the boat up, it's very deep.*"

WIR (10 ; 11) : The wood floats and the stone sinks, because " *the wood is lighter than the water. It isn't strong enough, whereas the pebble and the iron have more strength to go through the water and they go to the bottom.*" As for the big boats, " *that also depends on how much water there is. It's not the same in the Léman as in the sea. The boats swim better in the sea, because it's very deep.*—Why ? —*In the lake, the boat will sink more easily, because there is less water, and the boat is heavier for the lake than for the sea.*" [!]

All these cases are singularly instructive. In these children's minds there is a struggle between the weight of the body and the weight of the water. Heavy bodies try to pierce through the water, but if the water is plentiful and deep, it produces a " current " or " waves " which flow from the bottom upwards and is thus enabled to carry floating objects even when they are heavy. The existence of this current is indispensable in the eyes of the child. It is really the current that explains the fact of floating, and the weight of the water is only brought in as cause of the current.

Or again, boats may be thought to float the more easily because they are big, which is a survival of second stage beliefs. But the size or the weight of the floating body are no longer called in as signs of the strength or power belonging to the boat, they are simply regarded as liberating a greater thrust on the part of the water. This is almost the same as the principle of Archimedes, only there is no relation between the weight of the floating body and the weight of the displaced water ; there is merely a relation between the force of the floating body and the total force of the water in the containing vessel. The whole thing is therefore conceived in terms of dynamism : the body tries to slip into the water, but the water drives it back with its current, with its waves, etc. The best confirmation we can give of this interpretation rests on the fact, which we shall examine presently, that boats in movement are supposed to float merely owing to their movement.

In the meantime, let us try to check the hypothesis we have put forward, according to which there exists in the child's mind no preoccupation whatever with the weight of a floating body in relation to its volume. The control is easy enough. One has only to ask the child to model some boats in clay or in plasticine to realise that he will call light the boats that are so in the absolute sense, and not those that are light in relation to their size. The opposite of this will take place in the fourth stage. Here are some examples of the present stage :

RE (8) makes two boats, one small and the other large, and predicts that the small one will float because it is light and that the large one will sink because it is heavy. We make the experiment and it is the opposite which happens. Re is astonished, is unable to understand, and so imagines, having recourse to the explanations of the second stage, that the little boat sinks because it is light and the large one floats because it is heavy.

GRAN (8 ; 11) declares that a lump of plasticine will sink because it is heavy. To make the boat float, he tries to make smaller and smaller skiffs and is surprised that they sink in spite of their increasing lightness. In the end he thinks of making a hollow boat and observes that this boat floats. But Gran does not explain how it floats by saying that the boat floats because it is light [light in relation to its size] : he declares that the boat stays on the water " *because the water can't get in* ", as though the rims were enough to explain the floating.

NOT (9 ; 7) : " If I put this piece on the water ?— *It will go to the bottom, it's too heavy.*—What must we do to make it stay on top ?—*Make it smaller.* [Not makes a small ball, puts it on the water and finds that it sinks.] *It's still too big!* [he places a smaller ball, which sinks]. *Can't do it ! Must make it flat* [he places a little flake, which floats]. Why does that stay up, when it is flat ?— *Because it's light.*" We make a much larger boat, but hollow, with the whole piece of plasticine. " Why does that stay on top ?—*Because the water doesn't get inside.*— Why does it not sink ?—*Because you make that* [rims] *all round.*—But why does it not go to the bottom ?— *The water can't get in.*—But why not ?—*Because there's no water inside* ", etc.

The relativity of weight to volume has been completely overlooked. Most of the children we examined made smaller and smaller lumps, thinking that they would float in virtue of their absolute lightness. Others made thin and hollowed-out boats—thus showing a correct anticipation of the law—but they explained the fact of their floating simply by the existence of the sides : the sides " prevent the water from coming in ", etc. The real problem as to why the sides remain above water is thus completely left out. We shall see later what is the significance of the factor " form of the boat " which some of the children introduced in the course of these experiments. For the moment, all we need say is that we have here once again a dynamic factor, and that there is no proof that the child is in any way concerned with the relation of weight and volume.

So far, we are in possession of two elements of the problem. For the child who has reached the third stage is already beginning to take the specific weight of the floating body into account, since the stone is generally held to be heavier than wood : the stone " *is full inside* ", wood " *what's inside wood is light* ", and so on (Falq, 7 ; 3). But this specific weight is entirely a function of the condensation of bodies, stone is considered as " closer " than wood, and the true density of bodies is still unperceived. Wood is thought of as heavier than water for the same reason as stone is thought of as heavier than wood : wood is " full ", " thick ", " fat ", etc., whereas water is " liquid ", " thin ", etc.

Moreover, the water displaced by the floating body does not come into play, but only the total mass of the water in the containing receptacle. In other words, the weight of the moving body is estimated, not in relation to its volume, but in relation to the whole of the lake or of the basin, etc. This is a beginning of relativity which marks a great advance upon the second stage, but it is still a very rudimentary form of relativity, and finds expressions in such phrases as : " *heavy for the lake* " (Wirt), " *light when the water is deep* " (Re), and is peculiarly well summed up in the remarkable formula of Lev's (6 ; 7) : " *The pebble goes to the bottom because it is heavier* (than a big boat) *for the water, and less heavy for our hands.* " In other words, the pebble seems less heavy than a boat, but the water has less hold on it.

In conclusion, we may say that weight has not yet acquired any static significance : what enables wood to float is not its low density, that is to say its weight compared to that of the same volume of water, it is its capacity for pressure as compared to that of the bulk of the water in the lake. The essential point of the explanations given so far by the children consists in their saying that the boats float in the measure that the water in the containing vessel is able to produce a current that will sustain them. If the boat is too heavy, or if the supply of water is not sufficiently plentiful, the boat will sink. Otherwise, it will float. On the whole this explanation proves satisfactory. When it comes to details, there may be a certain difficulty in understanding why the small pebble sinks (though it is light absolutely, whereas the big boat floats). But when this is pointed out, the child makes use of second stage explanations and declares that the boat, being bigger, the water is better able to keep it up (the pebble, on the contrary, succeeds in slipping in through the waves, and so on).

The third stage is thus characterised by explanations which are intermediate between the outspoken dynamism of the second stage and the static explanations of the fourth stage. The best proof of the importance still retained by the dynamic orientation during this stage is that in a large number of the explanations given, floating is reduced to a sort of swimming or gliding flight, such as is supposed to take place in the boat's movement. This new aspect of third stage explanations is perhaps the most important if we take into account the frequency of these answers. It is, of course, closely related in each particular case to the statements of the preceding types. Indeed, after having said that boats float because they are light, most of the children add that they also float because they are moving.

This movement may be due to two causes—the current of the water, or the action of the oars or of the engine, etc. Here are examples of explanations which bring in the current of water. They resemble very closely those we dealt with a little way back, except that the current in question is horizontal, and does not run from the bottom upwards :

MULL (8½) : The boats float " *because the water pushes the boat . . . when there are waves.*" As for large barges, they float " *because the water is strong,*" . . . because " *the water moves. It can't keep still.*" " *There's a current.*"

VUIL (7½) says that the boats float on the Rhône " *because there's a current.*"

PERE (11) : The barges float " *because the water pushes them, pulls them.*"

But the most frequent explanation is that which appeals to the actual movement of the boat. We may say that nearly all the children make use of it at this stage, especially with regard to steamers, whose capacity for floating is always felt to be particularly mysterious.

BAB (7½) : " Why do the steam-boats stay on the water ?—*Because there's an engine.*—And when the engine doesn't work ?—*They're tied up, and anyway there's a current.*" Bab is thinking here of the current of water in the port of Geneva.

MART (9 ; 7) : " Why do the big boats stay on the water ?—*Because they've got machinery.*—And when it stops ?—*They tie it up, they put big chains.*—And the little boats ?—*It's by rowing.*—And if one stops ?—*It's the impetus that makes them stay up.*"

TAC (9 ; 10) : " Why do the big boats stay up ?—*Because they're stronger* [than the little ones].—Why ?—*Because there are machines that make them stay up.*"

ZWA (8 ; 3) : " *Because they have a big wheel* [paddle-wheel], *and that makes the water go away.*—Why ?—*Because that makes the water go away and at the same time it moves along.* . . . —And the little boats ?—*They move along because you row. It's the impetus that keeps them on the water.*"

KEN (7½) : " *It's the wheels which make them stay up.*—And if you take off the wheels ?—*It sinks.*"

CESS (12 ; 10) : " Why do the skiffs stay on the water ? —*Because there are sails, and then they have to row ; because if there's no wind, the boat would sink.*—If one stops rowing ?—*If one didn't row, it would go to the bottom.*— But *I* have done it. I have been in a boat, and stopped rowing.— . . . *It's because the water in the lake isn't strong. . . ."* Now Cess, who has such backward ideas, is actually the son of a hirer of boats.

In all these cases, floating is explained as gliding, exactly as it was in the case of the clouds and the heavenly bodies.

One last factor invoked by the child is the form of the boat. But this is considered important, not from the point of view of the relation of weight to volume, but solely as a factor in creating speed.

RE (8) says of a boat that it floats because of *" that "* [the keel]. *" What is that for ?—To make it go fast.— Why does it make it go fast ?—Because it is heavy."*

CHA (9 ; 8) : The skiffs travel *" because the sails make them move along, the water is deep, and underneath they are pointed."*

Or again, the children refer to the existence of the sides, as though they prevented the water from coming in independently of the weight of the boat.

§ 3. FOURTH STAGE : BOATS FLOAT FOR STATIC REASONS.—All the factors which the child appeals to throughout the third stage have, directly or indirectly, a dynamic significance, with the possible exception of the intuition of specific weight, of which the child gives proof in regarding a stone as heavier than wood. The fourth stage is marked by a general reversal of values. Factors such as the current of the water, the impetus (*élan*) of the boat are no longer appealed to. For now *all* boats are believed to float because they are lighter than water. In addition, the intuition of density and the relation of weight to volume stand out more and more clearly.

First, take density. It will be remembered that we show the child two glass vessels of the same volume, one of which contains a disk of wood, the other water. We say : " You see, it's the same amount of wood and of water. Which of the two is heavier ? Now, whereas the children of the first three stages invariably answer

" The wood is ", for the reasons given above (wood is more compact than water), those of the fourth stage all give the answer " The water is ". It is, on the average, after the age of 9½ that we have obtained this answer. Here are some examples :

PERN (10 ; 11) : *" The water is the heavier, because the water is heavy, and then the wood isn't."*
STUCK (10 ; 5) : The water is, *" because the water is heavier."* Of two equal volumes, one of water, the other of stone, it is the water which is lighter.
MIÉ (10) : *" The water is.*—Why ?—*Because the wood is lighter than the water, so* [the water] *is heavier, the water has more weight than the wood."*
CLE (12 ; 11) : *" The water is, because the water is heavier than the wood."*

The fourth stage, therefore, is marked by the appearance of the relation of density. So that when children of this stage say (later on) " the wood floats because it is lighter than water ", the word "·light " will have taken on a new significance : weight will have become relative to the corresponding volume of water. We shall therefore not expect that during this fourth stage very much attention will be paid to the total volume of water in the containing vessel. And our expectation proves correct. According to the material we collected, three-quarters of the children who said that a body could float on a lake but not on a pond, or else in a basin but not in a glass, were children of the second and third stages. Only the remaining quarter belonged to the fourth stage, showed, that is to say, signs of a correct intuition of the density of wood.

If, now, we pass on to an analysis of the relation of the weight of a floating body to its volume, we shall find that the great majority of children of the fourth stage succeed in regarding large boats as lighter than the corresponding volume of water :

CLE (12 ; 11) : " Which is the heavier, big steam-boats, or the same volume of water ?—*The water is heavier.   When you put a box with water in it, it goes to the bottom."*

LUG (11 ; 3) : A big boat stays on the water *" because it's light.*—Which is the lighter, a big boat or a pebble ? —*The pebble.*—The pebble goes to the bottom ?—*Yes.*— Then why does the boat stay on the water and the pebble go to the bottom ?—*Because the boat is lighter than the pebble.*—Which is the heavier if you lift them up in your hands ?—*The boat.*—Why does the boat stay on the water ?— . . . —It's because the boat is strong ? [We put this suggestive question to see if Lug will be able to avoid the trap.]—*It has an engine.*—That makes it stay on the water ?— . . . [No]. *It's because the boat is empty."* One can see, in this last affirmation, the correct intuition of a relation between weight and volume.

CHAN (10 ; 7) begins by telling us that the big boats do not sink because of their shape, which is a conception belonging to the third stage : *" They are pointed so as to cut the water."* But later, Chan delivers himself of this explanation : " If they were round, could they stay on the water ?—*They couldn't. Oh ! Yes, they could.*— They would sink ?—*I don't think so.*—Why ?—*Because they are lighter than the water.*—Which is the heavier, this pebble or a big boat ?—*The big boat.*—Why does this pebble sink ?—*Because it's heavy, because it's heavier than the water.*—Then the pebble is heavier than the water and the boat is lighter ?—*Because the pebble can fall more easily : the big boat has air in it, the pebble is thick."* Thus the boat is conceived as being light because it is empty.

These last answers should be borne in mind. We were setting Lug and Chan a formidable question in forcing them to compare the weight of a little stone to that of a big boat. It was a direct incitement to them to place themselves at point of view of absolute weight. In spite of this, Lug and Chan maintained that the big boats were lighter than water, and that they were, in consequence, relatively lighter than the stone. We have here a discovery, confused indeed, but fertile, and one that constitutes the peculiar achievement of the fourth stage.

But we must take care not to exaggerate the significance

of these expressions, and to assume that the child has attained forthwith to a definite realisation of the relation of weight to volume. If we look more closely into the answers, we shall be able to discern without straining the material three quite distinct types of judgment which very probably constitute three successive sub-stages. Only, considering the difficulty of correct diagnosis, we have not a sufficient number of results to establish these three sub-stages statistically. Probability alone seems to point to their existence.

During a first sub-stage, the statement that big boats are relatively lighter than pebbles still retains a dynamic meaning. The child does no more than say that big boats, being hollow, contain air, and that this air is what makes them float. Here are some examples :

AUD (8 ; 8) : " Why do the boats lie on the water ?— *Because they are open on top.*" " Why does that make them stay up ?—*Because the air gets in, and they are lighter than if there wasn't any.*"

PERN (10 ; 11) : The boats float " *because the inside is empty and the wood is light.*—Which is the heavier, this pebble or a big boat ?—*The boat.*—Then why does the boat lie on the water and the pebble sink ?—*Because there's just a little air in the boat. There's air in the inside.*—But it can get out ? . . . —*There's a lot more air than . . . than the stuff all round* [=there is more air than wood or metal, etc.].—What does that matter ?—*The air is stronger than the boat by itself.*—Why ?—*Because it's more difficult to make the air go into the water.*"

STUC (10 ; 5) : " Why do the boats lie on the water ? —*Because they're made of wood, because they're hollow inside.*—And the big boats ?— . . . —*They are hollowed out inside. There is air. The air prevents them from going to the bottom of the water.*"

Of course, these conceptions contain the idea of a relation of weight to volume : a big boat is light because it is hollow and full of air. But the examples show how deeply coloured is this notion with the dynamism of the preceding stages : the air keeps the boats up because it is strong, because it dislikes going into the water, and so on.

During a second sub-stage, the child rids himself of all traces of dynamism. He roundly affirms that the boat is "light," meaning thereby that it is relatively lighter than a small but full object. Only, at the risk of seeming to complicate matters, we must at this point bring in an essential distinction. Take two pellets of plasticine of the same size and weight. Out of one of these we model a large bowl. The other is left as it was. The child will say that the bowl is lighter than the lump. By growing in size and hollowing itself out, the original pellet has become "light" in changing into a bowl. Does the child mean that the bowl is lighter than the pellet relatively to its volume, or that the bowl has grown lighter in the absolute sense? In the second case, the pellet would have been regarded as having lost some of its absolute weight in becoming a bowl: the child would then appear to be ignorant of the principle of the conservation of weight.

This is not the place to solve this problem in its totality. It requires a more general enquiry into the idea of weight, an enquiry which we shall undertake some day, and of which the results will appear elsewhere. We shall simply say that among the children we examined, both types of belief were found, and that they can be said to characterise the second and third stages respectively.

During the second sub-stage, a body, while retaining the same quantity of matter, is therefore supposed to lose some of its absolute weight in increasing its size. Boats lose some of their absolute—not relative—weight in proportion as they are large and hollow. Here are two examples of these conceptions : [1]

---

[1] We may as well mention at this point the experiment which seemed to us decisive in this matter and of which we shall publish the results elsewhere. We give the children—independently, needless to say, of any interrogatory concerning boats—two pellets of plasticine both of the same size and weight. We make a long sausage out of one and a short cylinder out of the other. Most of the children under 10 say that the sausage is lighter than the cylinder. Children of 10-11, on the contrary, say that the weight is the same in both cases.

LUG (11 ; 3), it will be remembered, told us that a big boat "*is lighter than the pebble.*" We show him a lump of plasticine : "*It -goes to the bottom, because it's full.*— What must be done to make it lie on the water ?—*It must be empty.*—Try [Lug hollows it out, till it floats].— Why does it stay up when it's empty ?—*Because it's light.*" Then we make a boat with a thick hull, which sinks. "Make it stay on top. [Lug then increases the volume of the boat, but without removing the least particle of plasticine, thus not at all diminishing the absolute weight.]—Why does it stay up ?—*It's empty and it's thin. That makes it lighter.*—Does it actually make it lighter ? Is it really and truly lighter, or only for the water ?—*Really and truly.*" Thus it would seem that, for Lug, the absolute weight of the boat has diminished in proportion to the increase in volume.

BUS (10 ; 6) : We make a boat from plasticine, which floats. We decrease the volume, and it sinks : "Why does it go to the bottom ?—*Because it's tighter* (plus serré).—Why does it go to the bottom when it's tighter ? —*It's heavy.*" We ask Bus if it is really heavier than before. Bus says yes, and seems convinced that the boat has increased in absolute weight. The proof is, that after reflection, Bus succeeds in saying the opposite, and adds that up to now, he had thought that in "tightening" one increased the absolute weight.

These data may seem insufficient to justify our interpretation. But when they are compared with those mentioned in the footnote of p. 154, they seem to admit of no other reading. On the one hand, these children grasp perfectly well the fact that the boat is light for the water in the measure that its volume is big in relation to the density of its material—and this is what places them in the fourth stage. On the other hand, absolute weight is not distinguished from relative weight, and as a body expands, or increases its volume, it is considered to have become lighter in the absolute sense.

What is the origin of this curious conception ? It would seem that we have here a very general feature of child logic, and one that we have investigated elsewhere in connection with the logic of relations.[1] The child finds great difficulty in reasoning by means of relations. He reasons with absolute concepts. Such terms as right and left, dark and fair, etc., seem to him to denote absolute qualities and not relations. Now, once the child has come to understand the relativity of a notion or idea, he, as it were, hypostatises this relation and makes of it a fresh absolute entity. Here is an example. Take the test : " Edith is fairer than Suzanne and darker than Lili. Which is the darkest of the three ? " The child begins by finding the problem impossible of solution, for one cannot be both dark and fair. This is the stage of complete conceptual realism. Children at a more advanced stage, however, succeed in solving the question : this is the stage of relativism. Now, between these two stages we find answers of this type : " *Edith is fairer than Suzanne, so she has ' something more '. Edith is darker than Lili, so again she has ' something more '.*" (Car, 13 ; 5).[2] Fairer and darker have already become relative terms, but the relation itself is hypostatised, or taken as a new absolute term. This is what we have called the stage of pre-relation.

Exactly the same thing happens in the case of weight. The child begins by making of weight an absolute entity, and does not understand that big boats can be lighter relatively than small pebbles. He ends up by making of weight a relative entity, in much the same way as the children we mentioned just now. And between these two stages he says that a body grows lighter as it increases in size (which is a gain for relativism) but grows lighter in the absolute sense (which is a survival of realism).

During a third sub-stage, the children seem at last to reach a purely relative idea of weight. They seem to understand that a pellet of plasticine when it becomes a bowl, loses in relative weight (*i.e.* relative to its volume)

---

[1] See Piaget, " Une forme verbale de la comparaison chez l'enfant," *Arch. de Psychol.*, Vol. XVIII, pp. 141-172. Also *J.R.*, Chap. II.

[2] *Arch. de Psychol.*, Vol. XVIII, p. 161.

while retaining the same absolute weight as before. One child, for instance, declares that the plasticine bowl floats because it is " *lighter* " than the pellet of which it was made, and when we ask him whether it is " really and truly lighter or only lighter for the water," he says that " *it's the same thing, but it's bigger.*"

Here is a very suggestive case :

IM (10 ; 1) : " You see this big bit of wood and this penny. Why does the penny go to the bottom and not the wood ?—*Because they are not the same metals.*—But these are the same metals [a lid which floats, and a penny]. —*It's because it is small* [the penny] *that it sinks, and that* [the lid] *is a little bit light all round. That* [the penny] *is all in the same place. It's as I said just now, it's because it is round* [he said ' small '] *and it is all in the same place, and then the wood takes up a lot of room.*"

Under these clumsy expressions one can discern the intuition of the relativity of weight to volume : the material of the penny is condensed " at the same place ", that of the lid is not less heavy but " takes up more room ". But are we not putting into the children's minds more than is actually there ? It is hard to tell. All we can say for certain is that before reaching the third sub-stage—that in which the explanation is entirely correct—the children go through the devious by-ways of the first two sub-stages.

This brings us to the end of our study of the fourth stage, about which we may say in conclusion that it is marked by the progressive elimination of dynamic factors and the equally progressive establishment of the notions of weight and volume.

§ 4. CONCLUSIONS.—The foregoing results are not easy to synthesise, for their most obvious feature is their complexity. Nor must the reader be misled by the systematic appearance we have given to these explanations : they are turgid and muddled, more akin to the over-determination of autistic thought than to the sophisticated complexity of rational thought. We have dealt at sufficient

length with this subject elsewhere (*J.R.*, Chap. IV, § 2)
for any further purpose to be served by dwelling upon
it here.

At the same time, analysis points to certain broad
lines of classification. In the first place, there are certain
very interesting connections between the prediction of
physical events and their explanation. As M. Meyerson
has shown with such profound insight, in the philosophy
of science, law and explanation are two separate things.
Pure legality never satisfies the mind. There is an
irrepressible tendency that causes the mind to deduce
phenomena instead of merely predicting and observing
them. And this attitude receives entire confirmation
from the earliest of the results we have been discussing
in this chapter. As soon as the child has discovered the
first laws about floating bodies (those of the first stage)
his mind seeks to justify them, to feel them as necessary :
the necessity he invokes is moral, but this is already a
first step in justification. But a correct prediction or
prognosis of phenomena does not always entail a correct
explanation. We have here two distinct moments of
intellectual activity. For example, during the third stage,
the phenomena of floating are quite correctly predicted.
But the explanation, in order to account for the laws
observed in this way, has to take in all the curves and
vagaries in the outline of raw fact, just as it did during
the first stage, but with all the more difficulty because
the number of observed facts is greater. The child then
invents a series of juxtaposed explanations, bearing no
relation to one another, and often even contradicting one
another.

We do not wish at this point to discuss M. Meyerson's
thesis as a whole, but there remain two remarks to be
made about our own children. The first is that reciprocal
action is perpetually taking place between law and explanation. We have already drawn attention to this in
the first two stages : during the first, law dominates
explanation, whereas in the second, the reverse is the

case. During the third stage, legality is once more set free and the explanation has to follow the outlines of fact ; finally, during the fourth stage, there is agreement between the two.

These oscillations mean—and this is the second remark, which will supply us with a working hypothesis for the rest of our book—that between legality and explanation there is partial independence, but also increasingly close collaboration. Thus sometimes, experience and observation break up the established framework and impose new laws which contradict past explanations (this happens in particular when the third stage follows on the second) ; here legality is something very different from causality. Sometimes, the observed law and the resulting prediction contain implicitly the explanation which will eventually spring up in the mind ; here legality already implies causality.

The last point deserves attention. In what does the correct, i.e. the fourth stage explanation of floating consist ? It is, as always, in a deduction of the phenomenon. Beneath the chaos of pure observation the child dimly discerns the existence of density and of a weight relative to volume, and he substitutes these new objects of thought in place of the complex objects given in immediate sensory experience. But how does this deduction take place ? By means of an operation which logicians call " abstraction ". In other words, out of all the relations he has observed the child draws a new notion or idea which serves to support the deduction. Thus the explanation is drawn from the law itself.

During the early stages, explanation by deduction or, as M. Meyerson calls it, by " identification ", leads only to a crude form of realism : the child pictures a force or impetus (élan) behind the phenomenon. During these stages, causality is opposed to legality. But later, as experience and observation become finer, explanation and law merge more and more into one another : the one is simply drawn from the other by means of the logic of relations. Deduction becomes a logical construction, but a construction operated by the " multiplication of relations " or, as the logicians say, by " abstraction ".

If, now, we seek to characterise the various explanations noted in the course of our investigations we shall find a very definite principle of evolution : the moral dynamism of the earliest stages gives way before an integral dynamism, which, in its turn, gives way before a mechanistic explanation introducing relations rather than forces. Dynamism to mechanism might be the formula adopted.

Note the analogy of this process with that which we established in connection with the suspension of clouds and of the heavenly bodies. In this case too, the youngest children began by introducing a dynamism of a moral order. Then (disregarding the details peculiar to the second stage in the explanations of suspension) the child says that the wind keeps up the clouds and the heavenly bodies just as the water current was said to keep up the boats. Or, again, he says that the clouds and the heavenly bodies keep up in virtue of their own impetus (*élan*), just as the boats do in virtue of their movement. Finally, the questions of relative weight appear upon the scene.

The power of a body to float is thus the function of the specific weight or density of its material on the one hand, and on the other it is the relation subsisting between its form or total volume and its weight. Let us try, from this point of view, to establish the laws of evolution governing our four stages.

According to our material, three phases may be distinguished in the evolution of the idea of specific weight. During the first, weight and volume are always equal : big things are heavy and little things are light. Bodies do not therefore differ in their specific weights. Thus the youngest of our children always think that a small piece of wood is necessarily heavier than a pebble of slightly less volume.

During the second phase, the child has discovered that bulky objects are not necessarily the heaviest. Henceforward, he distinguishes between weight and volume. But he has not yet discovered the specific weight of bodies : all he does is to regard different objects as made up of more or less condensed (or rarefied) material. A typical case of this kind is Falq (5 ; 7) who regards the pebble as " full and heavy " in contrast to the wood, but who regards the wood as " much heavier" than an equal volume of water, because the wood is "packed", whereas the water is " liquid ". Weight, during this second phase, is therefore relative to condensation. We have here a way of looking at things analogous to that of which traces may be found in Anaximenes or Empedocles.

During the third stage, which begins at about 9–10 years, the child attains to a clear conception of specific weight, at least in the case of water, wood, and stone. An equal volume of water is henceforward pronounced to be heavier than wood and lighter than stone, in spite of the fact that water is liquid and wood is compact.

To these three phases correspond three types of explanation concerning floating bodies. During the first (which corresponds to the first two of our stages), boats float because they are heavy. During the second, they float because they are light in the absolute sense, or because they are " lighter than the water ", *i.e.* lighter than the total mass of the water of the lake, etc. Finally, during a third phase (fourth stage), the boats float because they are " lighter than the water ", this expression meaning lighter at equal volumes.

We find that the relation of the floating body's weight to its own volume undergoes a very similar process of evolution. During a first phase (which lasts up to the end of the third stage), the weight of the boats is estimated only in terms of absolute weight, relative weight not entering into the calculation at all. During a second phase, the child looks upon things as losing their weight as they grow in bulk : thus the pellet grows lighter in becoming a bowl. But relative weight then constitutes a new absolute entity, in the sense that the child believes the body to have really lost some of its absolute weight. The principle of the conservation of weight is thus completely absent. Finally, during a third phase, relative weight is clearly distinguished from absolute weight : the latter remains constant so long as a body keeps its material, whereas relative weight varies with the form taken on by the same body.

This dual evolution is extraordinarily significant from the point of view of logic. It constitutes a new aspect of a general law to which we have already drawn attention (*J.R.*, Chaps. II and III), and according to which childish ideas proceed from absolute to relative in their development. Every idea begins by being grasped in an absolute sense, and is only gradually and laboriously understood by means of relations.

We have tried to show—and the fresh data dealt with here seem to confirm this view—that such a process is intimately dependent upon the socialisation of thought. In proportion as things are conceived from the personal point of view, realism holds the field, and in proportion as a child frees himself from egocentricity, he acquires a progressive realisation of the relativity of qualities. Thus, heavy in the absolute sense means what the child finds it hard to lift, light means the opposite. We have here two absolutes, because the human point of view is the only one conceived to be possible. Then the terms light and heavy take on a meaning in relation to things conceived as substitutes for human activity. As Lev says at 6 years old, a pebble " is not heavy for our hands but it is heavy for water ". A remarkable discovery which, in making the structure of ideas more relative, turns them into a game. This relativity is restricted at first : the boat is regarded as light, simply in relation to the total mass of water in the lake. But once the way for it is cleared, progress is soon made : wood becomes light in relation to the corresponding volume of water, bodies become light by growing in bulk, and so on. Finally, the child succeeds in avoiding the use of any kind of absolute entity, and in thinking of weight only as a function of the many conditions which determine it.

The discovery of this meeting-ground of child logic and child physics shows that it might be useful to attempt a thorough analysis of the evolution of the child's idea of weight, independently of the special point of view we have taken up in this chapter. This subject will be dealt with on some future occasion, when the experiments which we are engaged upon now are concluded.

CHAPTER VII

THE LEVEL OF WATER

NOTHING is better suited to throw light on the dynamic significance attributed to weight by very young children, and on the difficulty which they have in taking volume into account, than the immersion of a pebble in a glass of water. ·

The problem we are going to set the children is extremely simple, and that is its great advantage over the problem of the floating boats. The child is shown a glass three-quarters full of water and a pebble. We say : " I am going to put this pebble into the water, right in. What will happen ? What will the water do ? " If the child does not immediately say : " The water will go up," we add : " Will the water stay at the same place or not ? " Once the child has given his answer, the experiment is done, the child is asked to note that the level of the water has risen, and is asked to explain this phenomenon. The youngest children always answer that the water has risen because the pebble is heavy and weighs on it. The child is then given a much bulkier, but lighter object, and is asked whether it, too, will make the water rise, and why. The experiment can be varied with nails, with shot, with wood, etc.

It goes without saying that this interrogatory must be made before the children have been questioned on the subject of the boats, so as to avoid perseveration. The children whose answers we are going to quote were questioned first about the present subject and only afterwards about the boats.

Three stages may be distinguished in the explanations

of the displacement of the water-level. During a first stage (under 7-8), the water is supposed to rise because the pebble is heavy. From the point of view of prediction, the child is consistent : a large pebble will make the water rise less high than a collection of very heavy grains of lead. During a second stage (7 to 9 years), the prediction is correct : the child knows that the submerged bodies will make the water rise in proportion to their bulk. But in spite of this correct prediction the child continues, oblivious to the constant self-contradictions which he becomes involved in, to explain the phenomenon by weight and not by volume : the submerged body, he says, makes the water rise in proportion to its weight. Finally, during a third stage (from 10-11 onwards), the correct explanation is found.

§ 1. FIRST STAGE : THE WATER RISES BECAUSE OF THE WEIGHT OF THE SUBMERGED BODY.—Let us start with an observation taken from ordinary life. A little girl of 9, in her own home, who has never been questioned on the present subject, is on the point of putting a large bunch of flowers into a vase full of water. She is stopped : " Take care ! It will run over ! " The child answers : " *No, because it isn't heavy.*" Thus to her mind it is not the volume of the body that matters but simply its weight : the bunch of flowers, not being heavy, can enter the water without exercising pressure and consequently without raising its level.

This little piece of everyday observation will be found to tally with the more general results which characterise our first stage. Children of this stage think that submerged bodies make the water rise in virtue of their weight : a small, heavy body will bring about a greater rise in the level than a large body of lesser weight.

What is the meaning of this statement ? At first sight, it looks as though the child simply confused volume with weight, and designated volume by the word " heavy ". It might also appear as though, in the child's eyes, heavy bodies made the level rise owing to their bulk. Above all, it looks as though, when the child speaks of weight, all he wanted to say was that heavy objects went completely inside the water and in that way raised its level. In point of fact, children of this stage do confuse weight and volume. But these children are not thinking of the displaced volume when they say that heavy objects make the water rise because they are heavy. They think that the submerged body exercises a continuous pressure in the water and thus raises its level, not because it occupies space, but because it sets up a current which runs from the bottom upwards like a wave. Here are some examples :

KEN (7) predicts that the water will not rise. We slip in the pebble, but without making a ripple on the surface (which is important) : " Will that make the water rise ? —*Yes.*—Why ?—*Because it hit.*—Where did it hit ?— *At the bottom.*—Why does the water rise ?—*Because it hit at the bottom.*—But why does that make it rise ?—*Because there is a wind* ! [It will be remembered that for many children a " current " of water is identified with a " current " of air, in other words the wind.] (See Chap. IV, § 2).—If I put this pebble [a larger pebble] very gently ?—*It will rise.*—Why ?—*Because it hits.* [We make the experiment.]—Why does it rise ?—*It makes a wind.*—Where ?—*In the water.*" " Which will make the water rise higher, this pebble or this one ?—*This one* [the larger].—Why ?—*It's bigger.*—Then why will it make the water rise higher ?—*Because it is stronger.*" It will be seen that the thought of volume does not enter in, and that the child is concerned solely with factors of a dynamic order.

ZWA (8 ; 3) immediately foresees the phenomenon. The water " *will go up because the pebble made it go up by falling.*" It seems, then, that Zwa perceives clearly the rôle of volume. Nothing of the kind : " Then why does the pebble make it rise ?—*It rises because the pebble is heavy.* [We make the experiment with a small pebble.]— *It didn't go up much because the pebble went gently.*—What must you do to make it go up ?—*You must put the pebble in hard.* [We make the experiment, but without throwing the pebble or producing ripples.]—*The water has risen a lot because the pebble went in a little harder than before.*—

Why has the water risen ?—*Because it went down ; it went rather hard and the water has risen.*—But why does the pebble make the water rise ?—*Because the pebble is a bit stronger than the water. So that makes the water lift up.*— Why is the pebble strong ?—*Because the pebble is big and the water is light.*" ["Big" here evidently means "heavy" or "condensed."] In front of Zwa we place a piece of wood on the water and the water rises moderately. We then show to Zwa a small pebble and a piece of wood, the pebble is heavier, although smaller, than the wood : " Which will make the water rise most ?—*The pebble because it is stronger.*—Why will it make it rise more ?— *Because the pebble is smaller, but bigger* [=condensed], *heavier.*" Zwa then discovers, to his astonishment, that it is the wood which produces the largest rise in the level of the water. "*The wood made the most because it stayed on the top, and then it's rather heavy,, and then as soon as it touches the water it is strong* [!] *and that makes it rise.*" We then show to Zwa some nails and a pebble of the same weight ; the nails have a much smaller volume. Zwa says : " *They are both the same heaviness, they will both make it rise the same.*" It will be seen that Zwa never thinks of volume. He only speaks of weight, strength, and the current.

MAI (8½) not only does not foresee that the water will rise, but also predicts that the level will sink : " *It will go down.*—Why ?—*Because the pebble is heavy.*—And if I put two pebbles ?—*It will go down.*—More or less than with one pebble ?—*More.*" Thus Mai is of opinion that the pebble compresses the water. We make the experiment. Mai cries : "*Ooh ! It's gone up !*—Why ?— *Because the pebbles are heavy.*" We insist : " Why does the pebble make the water rise ?—*Because the pebble is heavy, and then it is hard, and then . . . when it's at the bottom it makes little balls* [air bubbles—but Mai takes them to be bubbles of water], *and then they go up and come to bits.*" In other words, the water comes out of the bubbles and raises the level. " Why are there these balls ?—*Because the pebble is at the bottom. . . .*—Why does that make balls ?—*Because it is heavy.*"

PERE (11) : " Will the water rise or not ?—*It will rise just a little because the pebble is heavy and then that makes the water rise.*—Why ?—*Because it has a lot of weight.*" Peré predicts that a piece of wood will not make the water rise. He is afterwards very astonished to observe the contrary. " Why has it risen ?—*Because the water is not stronger than the wood.*—Why does it rise then ?—*Because there is no air inside* [Peré means to say that the water, having no current, is unable to resist the pressure of the wood], *because that always makes it rise when you put things inside. That makes it rise.*—Why ?—*Because it makes a weight.*—Is this piece of wood heavy ?—*No, but there's already a stone inside. That makes it rise.*" In other words, the stone continues to make the water rise, when in addition a piece of wood is placed on the top. We show to Peré a little bag containing small shot, and a large pebble, the shot being the heavier : Peré predicts that the bag will raise the level much higher than the pebble " *because the bag is heavier.*"

MIE (10) : " Will the water rise if I put this pebble in ? —*Yes, a little, because it is heavy at the bottom.*"

WENG (8½) : " *It weighs on the water, that makes it go up.*"

MOUL (8½) : " *It will overflow* [although the tumbler is only three-quarters full and the pebble is not large].— —Why ?—*Because it is heavy.* [We make the experiment.]—*The pebble has fallen and the water stays inside !*—Why did it not overflow ?—*Because the pebble is not heavy enough.*" So Moul takes no account of volume.

GESS (9½) predicts that the water will rise. " Why ?—*Because the pebble is heavy.*—Why does that make the water rise ?—*Because the water is light and when you put a pebble in it is a bit heavier, so it rises.*" Thus the water is supposed to expand in becoming heavier, or under pressure.

CESS (12) says that a small pebble will make the water rise higher than a large piece of wood " *because the pebble is bigger, not bigger, but stronger, and that will make the water rise higher.*"

These cases are all clear and definite. But there is an experiment which shows conclusively that when the child explains the rise in the water-level by the weight of the submerged body, he is really thinking of an upward thrust or current and not in any way of volume. When the child says that the water rises because the pebble " knocks the bottom," we simply ask him whether a pebble held by a thread halfway down the column of water would also raise the level. Children of this stage generally answer that it would not, for a pebble that is held by something no longer weighs on the water. Here is an example :

GEN (6 ; 8) predicts that the pebble will make the water rise " *because it is heavy in the water. So it rises.*" " You see the pebble hanging on this thread : if I put it in the water as far as this [half-way], will it make the water rise ? —*No, because it is not heavy enough.*" It is, however, the same pebble.

Weight, according to Gen, is the capacity for exercising a real activity : it is the action of expanding the water, of " making a current." This, it would seem, is the belief universally held at this stage.

In a word, although nearly all the children were able to foretell that the water-level would rise with the immersion of the pebble, not one of them brought the fact of volume into his explanation. They all appealed to weight, with the idea that the pressure of the pebble produces a current, bubbles, an expansion of the water, and so on.

Tendencies of two sorts existing in the child's mind serve to explain the phenomenon. In our analysis of the suspension of clouds and of boats we saw how much more dynamic than mechanistic are the schemas existing in the child's mind. The same tendency is at work here. The explanations we have just quoted even furnish an additional clue to the understanding of those curious statements made by the children about clouds staying in the air or boats floating in the water because they were heavy and big. This means that clouds and boats, by weighing on the air or the water, liberate a current sufficiently strong to keep them in place. This is probably a fresh version of the schema of " reaction of the surrounding medium " which was studied in an earlier chapter.

The very constancy of the phenomena of this stage is due also to a tendency which makes all very young children identify weight and volume. To children who regard weight as always, or nearly always, proportional to volume, heavy objects are sure to be those that raise the level of the water. Their observation of fact is roughly correct. But their interpretation is defective, owing to the dynamic turn of mind of which we have been reminding the reader, and which entirely neglects the factor of weight in favour of the factor of volume.

§ 2. SECOND AND THIRD STAGES : THE RÔLE OF VOLUME IS FELT AND MADE EXPLICIT.—Nothing is so well designed to show the child's difficulty in overcoming his spontaneous dynamism than the existence of this second stage. For during this period the child bases all his predictions on volume, and he will roundly declare that a bulky but light piece of wood will make the water rise higher than a heavy but small pebble. The interesting thing, however, is that the child is not conscious of this choice : he persists in explaining the rise by appealing only to the weight of the submerged body, ignoring the while the incessant contradictions in which he is involved by systematically taking up this attitude. A circumstance of this kind is of the utmost interest in the psychology of childish reasoning. The difficulty of bringing all the relevant factors into consciousness, the difficulty of performing logical demonstration, the part played by motor intelligence as opposed to that of conceptual or verbal intelligence — all these important questions converge on this one point of physics.

Here are some examples :

MEY (10 ; 8) : The water rises when the pebble is put in *" because it weighs on it.*—Why has the pebble made the water rise ?—*Because it is heavy.*—Which is the heavier, this wood [bulky] or this pebble [small] ?—*The pebble is heavier.*—Which will make the water rise higher ? —*The wood.*—Why ?—*Because it is lighter."* We again show a small pebble and a large piece of wood : " Which will make the water rise higher ?—*The wood.*—Why ?— *Because it is lighter.*—Is it because it is light that it makes the water rise ?—*Yes.*—Why ?—*Because it* [the wood] *weighs a very little. It weighs and so that makes the water go up.*—But why does the wood make the water rise more than the pebble ?—*Because the wood is lighter than the*

pebble. It weighs on the water and then the water rises."
The explanation consists in saying that the wood makes
the water rise because it is rather heavy. We put another
pebble in the water. Mey declares that it makes the
water rise *" because it weighs at the bottom.*—If I hold the
pebble on a thread so that it does not lie on the bottom ?
*—It will not make it rise because it doesn't weigh on the
bottom.*—Why not ?—*Because it doesn't weigh,"* etc.

This case is exceptionally clear. Mey foresees everything in terms of volume : a big piece of wood will make
the water go higher than a small pebble. But he explains
everything in terms of weight, even the fact that the
wood raises the water-level. Thus the pebble raises the
level of the water because it lies heavily at the bottom,
and the wood because it lies heavily on the surface. If
the two statements contradict one another, that cannot
be helped ! It would be impossible to find a clearer case
of dissociation between the predicting activity of motor
intelligence and the explanatory function of verbal intelligence.

A. To (7½) says that a large pebble will make the water
rise because it is heavy : " If I put in these three little
pebbles, will the water rise ?—*A little.*—Why ?—*Because
they are fairly heavy."* But pellets of lead, says To, will
make the water rise less than a pebble, although they are
heavier. Thus To foresees phenomena in terms of volume.
In the same way, says To, a large piece of wood will make
the water rise more than a small pebble would, although
the wood is lighter. But To affirms that it is because the
wood is *" a bit heavy."*

MÜLL (8½) : " Will this pebble make the water rise ?—
Yes. It's heavy : it will make the water rise.—And this
one [a small pebble] ?—*No.*—Why ?—*It is light.* [We
make the experiment.]—Why has the water risen ?—
*Because there are a lot, there are a lot of pebbles which are
heavy.*—Will this wood make the water rise ?—*Yes.*—
Why ?—*Because it is not heavy.* [The contradiction, due
to the fact that Müll does not think of volume, can be
clearly seen.]—Which will make the water rise the most ?
—*The wood.*—Why ?—*Because it is bigger.* [Thus Müll
arrives momentarily at the correct explanation.]—Then
why did the pebbles make the water rise just now ?—

Because they are heavy." A moment later, we place a certain quantity of aluminium in the water and the water overflows, conformably to Müll's prediction. " Why did that make the water rise ?—*Because it's light."*

Ro (6½, very advanced in every way) also predicts that the pieces of wood will make the water rise better than the pebble, but he adds that it is because they are " heavy." However, he has weighed them and observed that they were lighter than the pebbles. At a given moment Ro speaks of volume, and when asked what will happen says, " *You must see if they are the same size,"* but at the same time he weighs the objects to be compared as though the size were estimated by the weight.

Thus even in children who are on the threshold of the third stage, like Müll and Ro (though incidentally Müll and Ro talk about volume), explanation by weight is still extraordinarily persistent.

Let us turn to the analysis of the third stage which begins about the age of 9-10. This stage is marked by the appearance of explanation by volume. Thus explanation links up with prediction.

Here are some examples :

Biz (10 ; 3) : " What will the water do when I put this pebble in it ?—*It will rise.*—Why ?—*Because the pebble takes up space.*—If I put this wood, what will happen ?—*It will lie on the water.*—And what will the water do ?—*It will rise because the wood also takes up space.*—Which is the heavier, this pebble [small] or this wood [large] ?—*The pebble.*—Which will make the water rise the most ?—*The pebble takes up less space, it will make the water rise less."*

Pern (10 ; 11) : " *The water will rise because the pebble will take up room.*' The wood will make the water rise more than the pebble does " *because it takes up more space."*

Kim (11) : " *The water will rise because the pebble takes up space at the bottom."*

Men (12) : The water rises " *because the pebble is rather heavy, so it goes a little to the bottom, and that takes up space.*—And the wood ?—*The water rises a little because you can see a little wood go down, and that takes up space.*— Which will make the water rise most, the wood, which

is light, or this pebble, which is heavy ?—*The wood, because
it is bigger.*"

One is almost surprised at the simplicity of these
answers after the complexity of those of the earlier stages.
Weight no longer comes in at all, except to explain how
the object becomes submerged. And at no point is the
submerged body supposed to produce a current from below
upwards. The displacement of volume alone explains
why the level of the water has risen.

§ 3. CONCLUSIONS.—From the point of view of causality,
the foregoing explanations evolve according to a very
definite law which is the same as in the case of the floating
boats : the child proceeds from dynamic to mechanical
causality.   According to the youngest children, the pebble
is active : it makes " wind ", " bubbles ", " a current ",
etc. According to the older ones, weight accounts only
for the immersion of the body, and the rise of the water-
level is due to the displacement of volume.

Such a principle of evolution as this accounts not only
for the curious explanations, according to which clouds
and boats keep themselves up by means of their weight,
but also for the difficulty which children find in taking
account of the volume of a floating body in their explanations.

It might be of interest in this connection to try and
determine whether there exists any relation between the
third stage regarding the rise in the water-level and the
fourth stage regarding the floating of boats. For both
are characterised by the fact that for the first time
attention is paid to volume. In the case of floating
bodies, the fourth stage child discovers the existence of
the respective density of water and wood (*i.e.* in relation
to volume), and also the existence of the relation of the
weight of the moving body to its total volume. In the case
of the water-level the third stage child discovers the rôle
of volume in the rise of the level. Is there any correlation
between these two sets of discoveries ?

We made our calculations by means of the Yule formula (*four group method*),[1] and the result turned out to be $q = 0.78$, which shows that in practice the correlation is fairly pronounced.

This result has a certain degree of interest from the point of view of the psychology of child reasoning. For it is not in virtue of any explicit process of reasoning that the child introduces volume into his explanations of the rising water-level and of the floating boat. In his eyes, there is no connection whatever between the two questions. The correlation merely indicates that the child has discovered a schema which he automatically applies whenever it is possible to do so. We have here a process of assimilation which is independent of conscious and voluntary reflection.

This hypothesis finds definite confirmation in the answers of the second stage regarding the water-level. Children of this stage have the remarkable and paradoxical characteristic of giving, *à propos* of some definite phenomenon, an explanation which bears no relation to the unconscious motives which had guided the prediction of this same phenomenon. The given explanation may even be incompatible with the lines followed in the prediction ; the causality appealed to contradicts the law that has been recognised.

A fact such as this brings out very clearly the difference and even the opposition existing between practical or, as one might say, " motor " intelligence (which combines and predicts events in virtue of muscular experience or of condensed mental experience), and verbal or logical intelligence which systematises as best it can the conquests of the first. Motor intelligence comes before logical intelligence and makes its discoveries independently of it. The work of logical intelligence on the contrary begins with a conscious realisation of the results implicit in motor intelligence. Now, as we have often had occasion to point out, this conscious realisation is no simple

[1] See Claparède, *Psychologie de l'Enfant*, 8th ed., pp. 380-1.

operation (*J.R.*, Chap. IX, § 1 and § 2). It presupposes a process of elaboration which in this case shows
up very clearly, since we are able to see this conscious
realisation distort and change the findings of the motor
intelligence. And this process of elaboration presupposes
a change of perspective by which old difficulties are
shifted on to a new plane of thought. In the present
example, the difficulty of disentangling the respective
parts played by weight and volume in the rise of the
water-level—a difficulty already overcome on the plane
of motor intelligence—reappears in full force on the plane
of verbal reflection. We have here a fresh example of
that law of " shifting " to which we have drawn attention
elsewhere (*J.R.*, Chap. V, § 2).

Further, the existence of this second stage shows us
how ideas actually take shape in the child's mind. The
process takes place, not by association of new data, but
by dissociation of confused and syncretistic ideas. During
the first of our stages, weight and volume are still confused : they make up two aspects of a whole that is as yet
incompletely defined, and each of these aspects for want
of being contrasted with the other is still burdened with
characteristics that do not really belong to it. During the
second stage, these two aspects are in process of dissociation, and during the third stage, they are entirely
dissociated from one another. If one wanted to establish
the origin of these first confused ideas, it would not be
difficult to show, with regard to weight as we did with
regard to force, that they result from the assimilation of
reality to muscular schemas. But since the idea of weight
is closely akin to that of force, we may spare ourselves
the trouble of dealing with the question over again.

Finally, the existence of the second of the stages just
described bears striking witness to the hiatus which
separates the prediction of phenomena from their explanation, or, as M. Meyerson would say, legal science
from deductive or causal science. The relation existing
between the second and third of our stages, however, will

enable us to return to the problem of the relations between legality and deduction, a problem which we touched upon in connection with the floating of boats on water. (See Chap. VI, § 4.)

In the case of the water-level, as in that of the floating boats, two kinds of explanation may be distinguished. The earliest explanations are definitely opposed to legality : they are explanations by physical force, explanations which the child draws from his own imagination and imposes as best he can on the facts and laws which he observes. The later explanations, on the contrary, especially that of the third stage, or explanation by volume, are simply deduced from the observed law by means of the logic of relations and in particular by the operation called " abstraction ". For how does the child come to explain the rise in the water-level by the displaced volume ? Simply by becoming conscious of the factors which really determined his prediction of phenomena during the second stage. The law already contains the explanation implicitly. The latter is, no doubt, a deduction from the former, but a deduction based only upon such relations as have served to establish the former. Explanation is a logical structure based on law, but there is not a logic of law and a logic of explanation, a logic of induction and a logic of deduction. As M. Goblot has pointed out, there is only one logic, but the constructions peculiar to deduction are at first free from any fixed rule and directed only by action (and this is what induction consists in) ; they are subsequently regulated by purely mental operations (and this is what deduction consists in).

§ 4. PREDICTION AND EXPLANATION OF THE PHENO-MENON OF COMMUNICATING VESSELS IN CHILDREN FROM 8 TO 12 YEARS OLD.—The question of the water-level may be connected with that of communicating vessels for reasons which will be given later on. The phenomenon of communicating vases can be foreseen and even partially

explained by children from 8 to 12 years of age, and it
will therefore be interesting to make a brief investigation
of the subject. In order not to make the experiment too
complicated, it is best to use a tube of constant diameter
having the shape ⎣_⎦. The child is then asked to say
how high the water will go in one of the branches if the
other is filled half-way up. We carry out the experiment
and ask the child for an explanation of the phenomenon.
After this, we announce that we are going to tip the tube
over the edge of the table, and we ask what the water will
do : whether it will rise in one of the branches, and if so,
in which, etc.

We discovered three stages between 8 and 12. During
the first, the child predicts that the water will stop at the
bottom of the second branch, because, as he says, the
water can't go up. (We shall call the branch into which
the water is poured half-way up, branch I, and the branch
in which the water rises to a corresponding level, branch
II.) We then hide branch I behind a screen and fill it
half-way up : the child then sees that, in spite of what
he predicted, the water rises in branch II. He explains
this by saying that the water had enough impetus (*élan*)
to rise. We then ask how far the water has gone in
branch II : the child answers that the water has stopped
at the foot of this branch because it had not enough
impetus to come back and go up. Thus everything is
explained in terms of impetus (*élan*) and force. During
the third stage, the phenomenon is correctly predicted
and explained. Between these two, a transitional stage
may be distinguished, during which the prediction is
correct, but not the explanation, the latter still resembling
that of the first stage.

Here are some answers of the first stage :

L. DUP (14, backward) says that the water will not rise
in branch II " *because there is not enough pressure.*—Look
at what happens.—*The water has risen.*—Why ?—*Because
there is a lot of pressure.* [Dup then affirms that there is
no more water in branch I, which is hidden behind a

screen.]—Why?—*Because the water cannot go up again once it is there* [in branch II].—Why not?—*Because there is no pressure.*—Why is there no pressure?—*Because there is no air in the pipe.*" As for the experiment with the sloping tube, Dup predicts the contrary of what takes place, and when confronted with the fact, concludes: "*It makes a force to pull the water in the tube to the bottom.*" Thus Dup understands nothing of the matter, and explains everything he sees by "forces", which he invents as he goes on.

BIZ (10 ; 3) : Same predictions. "*The water will run and will come to the corner* [foot of branch II] *because it can't go up. There would have to be pressure.*—What does that mean?—*It would have to go quickly.*" Observing that the water has risen in branch II, Biz thinks that it has stopped at the foot of branch I "*because there is more pressure than is necessary.*" Thus the impetus is able to make the water rise in branch I, but the water cannot come back with the same impetus.

CHAL (8½) : Same predictions. "Why?—*Because the water cannot rise. There is no current. If there were a big current, the water would rise. The force would make it rise.*" Chal finds, after the experiment, that the level is the same in the two branches. "*It is the same height.*" But he explains this by saying : "*The current makes it rise. It* [the water] *follows the pipe. It can't go anywhere else.*"

The answers of this first stage are interesting in that they show the child's tendency to explain everything dynamically and to leave out any static consideration.

Here is an example of the second stage, namely, one in which the explanation is still analogous to that of the first stage, though the prediction is correct.

BLAN (11 ; 7) : The prediction is good : "*It will go to the other end, to the same level.*—Why?—*It will be the same thing on both sides.*" We make the experiment. "And if I add some water again on one side?—*It will make the water rise on the other side.*" "Why does it move the water when there is more on one side?—*Because the air* (!) *pushes the water from the other side.*—If one slopes the apparatus?—*The water will empty itself from one side and then it will fill the other.*—Why?—*Because it* [the water] *is sloping.*"

The prediction, it will be noticed, is correct. Moreover, the idea that the water of column I " pushes " on the water, or " presses on " the other until a balance is found, seems very good. But as soon as we go below the surface, we find that the child still conceives everything in terms of pure dynamism : the movement of the water is explained by the " air " (*i.e.* the current), by the slope of the tubes, and so on.

Finally, in the third stage, the explanation has the same value as the prediction :

LAED (10 ; 2) : " *If you put a little more on one side, it will also come on the other side. There* [in the middle of the horizontal tube which joins the branches I and II] *it* [the water] *can rise the same on either side. If you pour in on each side, it will make the water go back to the same level.* —Why ?—*Because it will go as far as half-way* [to the same point as before], *one part to the left, one part to the right.*"

This explanation is remarkable. It appeals solely to the principle of sufficient reason : the water goes to the middle of the tube that unites the two branches, and from there it can rise " the same on either side." Thus the equality of level is brought back to a question of equilibrium.

This brief survey will help to confirm our view that there is a universal process in the evolution of children which leads them from a dynamic to a mechanistic way of thinking. In addition, we can see how quickly, once he has discovered an empirical law, the child will look for its explanation. Finally, we realise that we are faced with the same principle as was dealt with in connection with the experiment outlined at the beginning of this chapter : the discovery of a law, of a correct prediction does not entail the discovery of a correct explanation. There is a stage during which the child can predict with truth while retaining the explanations of the previous stage. But correct explanation is based on relations which are already implicit in the operation through which events are foreseen and predicted.

CHAPTER VIII

THE PROBLEM OF SHADOWS

In studying the explanations which children give of the origin of night (*C.W.*, Chap. IX, § 2), we drew attention to the substantialism which makes the child " reify " phenomena (as Sully said long ago). In this particular case it consisted in conceiving of night as a great black cloud which filled the atmosphere, or which sent out its dark rays from the sky. This particular mental orientation deserves further study, and in more concrete conditions. The prediction and explanation of shadows supply first-rate material for analysis in this respect. For it is very easy to ask on which side the shadow of an object will fall when the object is placed on a table opposite a window. It is easy to produce a play of shadows on a screen with the help of lamps or lighted matches and to make the child say in what direction these shadows will fall. It is easy again to question the child as to the " why " of these predictions and, after the experiment, as to the " why " of the observed phenomenon. This enquiry will enable us to study afresh the relation between prediction and explanation ; and this will be all the more useful for our purpose since the explanation of shadows presupposes a necessary " interference " between child logic (especially the logic of relations) and child physics.

We discovered four stages in the explanation of the phenomenon of shadows. During the first, of which the average age is 5 years, shadows are conceived as due to the collaboration or participation of two sources, the one, internal (the shadow emanates from the object), the other, external (shadows come from trees, from night, from the corner of the room, etc.). This participation is exactly analogous to that between the wind and the air produced by moving objects, by means of which the youngest children try to explain the formation of an air current in a closed room (see Chap. I, §§ 1-2). During the second stage (average age, 6-7 years), shadows are believed to be produced by the object alone. They are a substance emanating from the object, but in no particular direction : at this stage, the child is not yet able to say on which side the shadow will fall when the screen is placed in front of the source of light. After he has reached the third stage, however, of which the average age is 8 years, the child is able to predict the orientation of shadows. He can even say that shadows will be formed where there is no light, no sun, and so on. But under this apparently correct explanation we can still trace the substantialism of the earlier stages : the child still believes that a shadow is an emanation of the object, but he thinks it is an emanation that drives away the light and is therefore obliged to dispose itself on the side opposite to that of the source of light. Finally, during a fourth stage (of which the average age is 9 years), the correct explanation is found.

§ 1. FIRST STAGE : SHADOW IS A SUBSTANCE EMANATING FROM THE OBJECT AND PARTICIPATING WITH NIGHT.— Children of this stage are naturally unable to say on which side shadows will fall. They explain shadows by saying both that they come out of the objects, and that they come from outside ; as soon as we place an object on the table, night or the darkness under the trees, etc., produce an emanation which issues from the object itself. Thus shadows have a dual origin—a circumstance which in no way worries the child. Here are some examples :

GALL (5) : " Why is there a shadow here ? [We make a shadow with the hand.]—*Because there is a hand*.—Why is this shadow black?—*Because . . . because you have bones.*—You see this paper, why is it black here? [the shadow of the paper].—*Because there is a hand.* [Gall clings to the idea that the shadow comes from the hand, although there is now only a piece of paper in question.] How is this shadow made?—*Because there are trees."* [Gall looks out of the window and shows us some trees, a hundred yards away, beneath which there is an abundant shadow.] We make a shadow with a book: " Why is the shadow on this side and not on that?—*Because it is daylight.* [Gall points to the side out of the shadow.]— But why is it on this side?—*Because it is night.*—Why is it not night over there.—*Because there is daylight."* " What makes this shadow?—*The sky.*—How?—*Because it is night.* [Gall points to the shadow.]—But where does this shadow come from?—*From the book.*—And how is the shadow of the book made?—*From the sky.*—Why does the shadow of the book come from the sky?—*Because it is night in the sky.*—Which way does the shadow from the sky come here?—*It is black."* In addition, Gall fails to predict the direction the shadows will take: his forecasts are quite arbitrary.

Roc (6 ; 6) also believes in the participation of two origins: " Look [the shadow of our hand on the table.] What makes this shadow?—*The trees.*—How is that?— *When they are quite close* [some trees] *to the others.*—But why does that make it dark here?—*Because there is something on top* [because the hand is on the table.]—Then why does that make it black?—*Because there are things on the ground.*—What?—*Trees sometimes."* It will be seen by these last answers that Roc is hesitating between two attitudes: on one hand, she is only inclined to draw an analogy between the shadow of the hands and that of the trees; on the other, she is inclined to say (as at the beginning of the interrogation) that the shadow of the hands comes directly from the trees. We then make a shadow with a pocket-book. "Where does this shadow come from?—*It comes from the sky.*—Is there shadow there [in our open hand]?—*No.*—And there? [under the hand and putting the hand on the table.]—*Yes.*—Where does it come from?—*From the sky."* " What is the shadow made of?—*Of the trees."* Shadows exist even in the night: " Look, I am making a shadow with my hand. If it were night, would it still make a shadow?—*Yes.*— Why?—*Because it is low down* [the hand is near the table.]—

Would you see it ?—*No.*—Why not ?—*Because it would be night in the rooms.*—But would my hand still make a shadow, or not ?—*Yes, it would.*" As for the direction of shadows, Roc is naturally unable to predict it, but she gives an explanation after consideration. "Why is the shadow on this side ?—*Because the note-book is leaning towards that side.*" The note-book is placed on end and half open. But Roc thinks that the slope of the side which she sees the most clearly determines the position of the shadow on that same side.

MOR (5½) : "Why is it dark there ? [shadow of an exercise-book].—*Because you put that* [book].—Then what makes that shadow ?—*Sky.*—Sky ?—*No, because it's black up there.* [Mor points to the ceiling of the room.] Thus the shadow of the book is produced both by the book, and by the invasion of sòme substance coming from the sky or the ceiling.

TAB (7) : "Why is it dark there ?—*Because it's light there* [shows the other side of the object]. Where does this darkness come from ?—*From the shadow.*—And the shadow ?—*From there.* [Tab points to the end of the room, which is dark, and which is two yards distant from the object.]—Why does the shadow come from there ?—*Because it is black.*—Where ?—There [the end of the room].—Why ?—*It's dark.*" We try to make Tab calculate on which side of a given object the shadow will fall in relation to the window, but his calculations are guess-work. "And this shadow [the shadow of a black leather case], what has made it ?—*The night.*—What night ?—*In the evening.*—How did that make the shadow ?—*Out of the sky.*"

RE (7 ; 10, backward) : "Make a shadow with your hand.—*You must put a tree.*—Why ?— . . . —[We make a shadow with the hand.]—Where does this shadow come from ?—*It comes to hide. . . . It comes from over there.* [Re points to a corner of the room which is in shadow.]—*It is hidden there.*—And the shadow over there, where does that come from ?—*It is going away further still.*—Where to ?—*Behind the other trees.*" "Can I take your shadow when you are out for a walk ?—*No. . . . Yes.*—You're sure of that ?—*Yes.* [We make the attempt. Re walks about the room and we try to hold the shadow by poking it with an umbrella.]—Well ?—*You can't do it.*—Why ?—*There's another shadow* [=a shadow reforms itself elsewhere when the first is held back].

STEI (5) : " You know what a shadow is ?—*Yes, it's the trees that make them, under the tree.*—Why is there a shadow under the tree ?—*Because there are a lot of leaves. The leaves make it.*—How do they do it ?—*Because they are pink.*—What does that do ?—*It makes a shadow.*—Why ?—*Because inside* [the leaves] *it is night, inside.*—Why ?—*Because it's day on top. The leaves are big and it is night inside them.*" We show Stei his shadow on the ground : " There is a shadow there ?—*Yes, the chair does it.*—Why does the chair make a shadow ?—*Because it's black underneath. It's dark.*—Why ?—*Why, because it is dark under the chair, because it's a chair and there is the edge and that keeps the shadow under the chair.* [Thus the frame of the chair " keeps " the shadow, which it holds by means of its edges.]—Why does that keep the shadow ? —*Because the chair is low, because it is the chair that makes a shadow.*" It will be seen how the shadow is identified with a sort of vapour which clings on to objects. At other times Stei conceives the shadow to be the mere reflection of the objects : a box of matches, for instance, makes a shadow " *because it is yellow and there is some black* " [letters printed on the yellow paper], a leather case " *is black and makes things black,*" etc. Also the shadow is sometimes thought of as emanating from the objects, and sometimes as though it hooked itself on to them (the night in the trees, or the darkness in the frame of the chair). Stei, therefore, brings in two simultaneous origins for each particular shadow, one internal, the other external : the chair " makes " a shadow and " keeps " the shadow, etc. Naturally his prediction as to the direction the shadow will take, is quite fanciful.

Cases of the first stage are highly interesting because of the analogies they present with the examples of participation which we examined in connection with air. When we make a current of air with our hands, children of 4-6 assert that the air is made by our hands ; but they also maintain that the wind has come in from outside, in spite of the closed windows, and that it is the cause of the air current produced by the hands. For the child, there is identity between the wind and the current of air coming from the hands, so that this air current has two causes which participate with each other. The wind of the hands is a sort of emanation, at once near and distant, of the wind outside. Exactly the same thing holds good of shadows. The child sees and openly declares that the shadow of a hand is produced by the hand. He goes so far as to say that the shadow comes out of the hand, that there is shadow contained " in " objects, and so on. But at the same time, and without sensing any contradiction, he regards this very shadow as emanating from the sky, from under the trees, or from the corners of the room. The two causes are superposed, but do not mutually exclude each other. There is participation between them.

The cases we have analysed are so numerous as to enable us to reach at once an interpretation, to which we shall return later on. One child, for instance, is inclined at times to conceive of this participation no longer as identity, but as mere analogy : the shadow of the hand is produced by the hand *just as* the shadow of the trees is produced by the trees. Now such cases, where the child seems inclined to translate participation into the language of analogy, are among the most advanced, the least primitive. The younger children, on the contrary, say outright that the shadow of the hands comes from under the trees, that the trees make the shadow of the hands, and so on. In other words, childish participation is probably nothing but a primitive way of feeling analogies, but such that the relation is conceived as identity. The shadow of the hands calls forth a comparison with the shadow of the trees, but the two terms of comparison cannot be conceived as two instances of a general law, because at this age the child is not yet able to generalise and establish laws. The two terms are therefore not compared as they would be in our minds ; they are simply identified, *i.e.* conceived as acting directly upon one another.

To make use of a cruder image, one might compare this phenomenon to what happens in language. Expressive language does not compare, it identifies. We do not say : " That man is as brave as a lion." We say " He's a lion." The same thing happens in the mind of the child, but here this method of comparing is not merely a matter of words : it is a matter of logical structure. For childish reasoning proceeds neither by successive generalisations, nor by syllogisms, but by a passage from particular to particular (transduction). Such a logical structure as this shuts out the possibility of any genuine analogical reasoning or, in other words, of any comparison in which the terms are kept discrete. It leads, on the contrary, to an identification of singular terms, *i.e.* to the idea of an immediate and substantial participation.

§ 2. SECOND STAGE : SHADOW IS A SUBSTANCE EMANATING FROM THE OBJECT ALONE.—During the second stage, participation is done away with. The shadow is produced entirely by the object itself. But this shadow is still conceived as a substance, and the child is not always able to foresee on which side the shadow will be in relation to the source of light. Here are some examples, beginning with a case that is transitional between the first and the second stage :

LÉO (7) tells us, as soon as we ask him what is a shadow : "*The shadow comes from under the trees.*" But this affirmation has little effect on what follows. We point out to Léo the shadow of a man walking in the street : "*Yes. It's everywhere where you walk, it makes the person on the ground and it makes the shadow.*—Why is it black at the back ?—*Because it makes the same shape as the person.*—Why ?—*Because it makes the person on the ground.*" "Where does it come from ?—*It comes from the steps you make.*—How is that ?—*It's the person who does it on the ground. He walks and that makes the shape on the ground.*—How is that ?—*It is because all the steps that you make, the person on the ground always follows your feet.*—Why ?—*Because it is the model of the person.*" "Where does it come from ?—*From the person.*—How does the person do that ?—*When he walks.*—How ?—*The more you walk, the longer that* [the shadow] *becomes.*—And when you are not walking, is there a shadow ?—*When you don't walk and you are under a tree, there's a shadow all the same.*" "Where does this model come from ?—*From the person.*—How ?—*When he walks.*—Where does this shadow come from ?—*From us.*—How is it made ?—*It is made when he walks.*—

When it is night, does he make one too ?—*He makes one,
then* [but] *you don't see it because it's night.*—How do we
make one ?—*You make it when you walk, because every step
you make, it follows us behind.*—Why does it follow us ?—
Because it is the person who makes it on the ground." " But
how can the person do that ?—*He walks.*—Where does
the shadow come from ?—*It comes out of the person, we
have a shadow inside us.*—What does that mean, ' It comes
out of the person ' ?—*It falls on to the ground."*

GILL (7) fails to predict on which side the shadow of a
book will appear. " *On this side* [wrong]. *It can also be
there* " [the opposite]. Either side is equally probable.
Gill says that our shadow is our " *portrait."* " *It can be
behind us. If you turn, it's in front !*—Why ?—*Because
you've turned round.*—Where does it come from ?—*From
us.*—When you are in a room at night, is the shadow still
beside you, or not ?—*No, because it is night. It's there,
but you don't see it, because it is night.*—How do you know
that the portrait is beside you in the night ?—*Because you
can see it in the day. In the night you can't see it, but it's
beside you all the same.*

MART (8) fails to predict on which side the shadow will
appear. After the experiment : " Why is it on this side ?
—*It likes best to be on this side."*

This stage is thus simply the prolongation of the preceding stage, *minus* the idea of participation.

§ 3. THIRD STAGE : SHADOW IS A SUBSTANCE WHICH
FLEES FROM LIGHT.—Children of this stage unite with a
true prediction of the phenomenon, an explanation which
is analogous to that of the preceding stages. The criterion
of the appearance of this stage is, therefore, the circumstance that the child can foresee that the shadow will
come on the side opposite the window or opposite the
source of light. The child has made the implicit discovery
of a relation existing between shade and light. But—
and this is the significant thing—he still believes that at
night objects go on producing shadows. And, in any
case, he persists in his belief that shade emanates from
the object itself, thus showing his ignorance of the part
played by the source of light in the genesis of shade. If
a shadow falls upon the side opposite to that of light, this

is simply because day drives the shadows away before it. Thus, although the prediction is right, the corresponding explanation is still erroneous.

Here are some examples :

CAUD (9) : The shadow " *comes from anything at all.*" —Where does the shadow of the chair come from ?— *From the chair.*" At night the chair still casts a shadow, but it cannot be seen " *because it is dark and the shadow is dark, so you can't see it.* Caud predicts correctly the position of the shadows, but he explains this position in the following manner. The shadow of a book will not come on this side of the window " *because over there* [Caud points to the side near the end of the room] *it's darker than it is towards the window.*—Then why is the shadow there ?—*Because it is lighter there* [side near window], *because there* [opposite side] *it's dark, and the shadow is dark and goes there.*" Thus the shadow is attracted by the darkness and cast out by the light. We point out a man and his shadow, and ask Caud to indicate on which side the sun should be. Caud replies correctly. " Why is the shadow on this side when the sun is there ?— *Because it is lighter here* [side where the sun is]. Caud also realises that if a match is lit in front of an object, the shadow will be on the other side. " Why ?—*Because it is darker* [on this side]. Thus the prediction is excellent, but the explanation remains substantialist : the shadow emanates from the object and turns to the side where there is no daylight. The proof of the correctness of this interpretation is that Caud continues to admit that objects throw shadows even in the night.

BAB (8 ; 11) seems at first to be nearer the truth : " How is it that there is a shadow under the trees ?— *Because you can see a little bit of dark.*—Why ?—*Because there are leaves, that stops you seeing the daylight.*" Bab also knows, apart from a momentary mistake, how to decide on which side the shadow will appear. But he cannot explain the reason for the observed facts : " Why is the shadow on this side ?—*Because it ought to be on this side and not on the other.*" " *Because it can't be on the other side.*—Why ?—*Can't be on the other side.*—Why ?—*It can't be on the other side.*" On the other hand, objects throw a shadow during the night, but on both sides ! " *It always makes them, but the other side makes them too.*—Why does it make a shadow in the night ?—*Because it has to.*—

Would you see it ?—*Oh no, because it is quite dark, you couldn't see it."* Thus the shadow is thought to be an emanation from the object, although Bab is capable of correct prediction.

ROY (7 ; 1) : " How did you make a shadow with your hand ?—*Because I put my hand on top of the paper.*—Why was it dark underneath ?—*Because when you put your hand, it doesn't make it white.*—Why ?—*Because it is a shadow, it hides the white.*—What do you mean by ' hides ' ?—*That there is a shadow."* Roy predicts correctly on which side will appear the shadows of various objects. But to explain the facts, Roy can only arrive at this : the shadow cannot be on the side by the window *" because there's already daylight there."* This expression, " already daylight," shows clearly that Roy considers a shadow to be a substance that is incapable of occupying a space which is already taken by the daylight. The proof is that Roy can find no sort of explanation of the shadow as resulting from an obstruction of the light. When Roy says " it hides the white," he does not mean that the object hides the daylight, but that the shadow made by the object hides the paper.

This shows the clearly defined character of the third stage. The child knows that the shadow will come on the side opposite to that which is the source of light, but he has not yet understood the true cause of shadows : a shadow is still thought to be a substance issuing from the object and occurring even at night. If the shadow turns towards the side opposite that of light, this is simply because it goes to the side of darkness, and because it flies from the day. Besides, it is being driven out by the light of day since, as Roy says, it cannot occupy the space where " there's already daylight."

This stage is therefore entirely analogous to the stages we examined in connection with the floating boats and the rising water-level, stages during which the law is discovered but the explanation is still the same as it was in the early stages. The prediction has been shifted on to a different level from that on which the explanation takes place.

§ 4. FOURTH STAGE : THE CORRECT EXPLANATION IS FOUND.—The explanation of the fourth stage is correct, and this appears chiefly in the fact that the child denies that objects cast shadows at night. Here are some examples :

VEIL (9½) tells us that the shadows are made by the sun. Then we agree to call a box of matches " a house ": " There is a house. The shadow is here. Where is the sun ?—*Here* [correct prediction].—Why ?—*The sun comes from here. The house hides. It is dark behind : The sun can't go any further.*—Why ?—*Because the house is large. It hides the sun."* " At night," says Veil, " *the shadow can't come. The shadow is black and in the darkness it can't show."* This formula is still equivocal, but a moment later Veil says spontaneously of an object which we put in the shade : " *It doesn't make a shadow because it is already in the shadow.*—It makes no shadow, or it does make it and we don't see it ?—*It doesn't make any."*

MEY (10) predicts that the shadow of a note-book will be on the opposite side to that of the window. " Why will the shadow be there ?—*Because the light comes from there.*—Why is there a shadow here ?—*Because there's the note-book.* — What is the shadow ? — *It is a place where there's no light."*

ZWA (9½) : " You know what a shadow is ?—*Yes. It is when there's the sunlight, there is something that makes a shadow.*—Why is the shadow black ?—*Because it's behind the white* [=the daylight]. *There is white, and it* [the shadow] *is always behind.*—Why is it black ?—*Because the sun isn't behind.*—But why is it black ?—*Because there is no light."* Zwa adds : " *I thought that the light can't go behind* [behind the object], *I thought it made a shadow because the light can't go behind."*

DELED (7, advanced) : " How is a shadow made ?—*Because it is hidden.*—What is hidden ?—*The daylight."*

Thus shadow is no longer thought of as a substance that is chased away by light. It simply becomes synonymous with absence of light.

§ 5. CONCLUSIONS.—The evolution undergone by the explanations we have been analysing is interesting from two points of view. In the first place, it confirms the law previously established, according to which child physics proceed from a substantialist dynamism to explanations of a more static order. For during the early stages shadow is held to be a substance which travels about, which accumulates at certain points, and which is often thought to be alive and conscious. During the subsequent stages shadow is still regarded as a fluid which emanates from the objects themselves. It is only once the necessity for a luminous source has been noticed that the substantialist explanation, having become useless, is replaced by the correct explanation.

But this process of evolution is interesting chiefly from the point of view of child reasoning. As in the case of the floating boats and of the water-level, the child is able to predict the law at work before he can give a correct explanation of the phenomenon. In addition, we can observe, with regard to shadows, just as we did with regard to boats and pebbles dropped into a glass of water, a stage (the third), during which the explanation given is, if not contradictory to, at least without any relation to the observed law: the child can foretell the direction of the shadow in relation to the source of light, but continues to believe that the shadow emanates from the object. Now, we have maintained that although correct explanation comes later in the day than correct prediction, it can nevertheless be derived from the latter by simple deduction. When he finds the correct explanation the subject has merely become conscious of the schemas which guided him implicitly in his predictions of the law, and has also become capable of constructions operated by means of these schemas. Does the study of the answers concerning shadows tend to confirm this view or not ?

It would seem that it did. For to explain the phenomenon of shadows is, at bottom, to rely upon judgments of geometrical relations ; it is to place oneself in imagination behind the object which acts as a screen and to grasp the fact that from that position the light is hidden. As soon as you have succeeded in handling these relations of perspective, you will understand why shadows vary in shape and orientation according to the position of the source of light, and in this way alone the substantialist explanation will be rendered useless. To explain a shadow is therefore to ascertain by means of the logic of spatial relations to what extent you can or cannot see the light if you walk round the object which acts as a screen. The explanation of shadows is purely geometrical.

Now the beginning of this logical process is precisely what is presupposed by the discovery of the law of the orientation of shadows, a discovery which characterises the third of our stages. In order that the child may be able to foresee what direction a shadow will fall in, he must have understood that a shadow is not directed in function of itself, so to speak. Thus a shadow practically ceases to be regarded as a living fluid which goes where it wants to ; there is a beginning of relativity by means of which shadows are thought of for the first time as conditioned by daylight. The proof of this is that children of the third stage begin to say that " the shadow hides " the table, or even the daylight. During the earlier stages the child was incapable of this notion. But from the third stage onwards we are always meeting with such remarks as the following. Bab tells us : the shadow " stops you seeing the daylight " [on the ground, under a tree], or " you can see a little bit of dark." Roy says : " It hides the white " (meaning : the shadow prevents us from seeing the paper). These expressions are, it is true, still relative to our point of view : the child simply means that the shadow prevents us from seeing clearly, or prevents us from seeing the table, the copy-book, etc. But a mere change in the point of view will suffice for the words " the shadow hides the table " to take on a much deeper significance, and to mean : " From the point of view of the ray of light, the object forms a screen and hides part of the table."

This change of view-point occurs in the most advanced children of the third stage and in the most backward of the fourth stage. It consists in saying that the shadow hides the table, not from any chance observer, but from the daylight itself. Here are examples :

Xy (intermediate between the 3rd and 4th stage) : " Why is it black ?—*It is hidden* [the table].—What does that mean ?—*That means that you don't see it.*—But you do see it !—*Yes, we do, but the light doesn't see it.*"
PAT (10, 4th stage) : " Why is the shadow of this portfolio on this side ?—*Because the clouds* [Pat thinks that the clouds give light] *do not see on this side.*"

These children think, moreover, that the sun, the clouds, the daylight " see " by the mere fact that they give us light. But this does not interfere with the significance of this change in their point of view. And it is this very change that marks the transition to the fourth stage.

As to the children who no longer attribute the capacity of seeing to light, these place themselves at the point of view which is reciprocal to that of the light, namely, at the point of view, not of any chance of observer, but of the observer placed behind the object that is screening the light : for such an observer, it is the light itself that is hidden.

This shows us that there is complete continuity between the correct explanation and the logical processes that have been set going by the discovery of the law. The discovery of the law is marked by the fact that the child can say : the shadow hides the daylight. After that, it will be sufficient for the child to continue reasoning by means of geometrical relations for him to say : the shadow hides the table, not only from us, but above all, from the light itself ; and at last, reciprocally : the object hides the daylight. Once these consequences of the primitive relation have been liberated, the correct explanation is found. If the child of the third stage clings to a substantialist explanation in spite of this correct prediction, it is because the judgments of relation implied in the prediction have not yet given rise to those changes in the point of view which we have been describing, they have not brought about the inversions and multiplications of the relations in question. As soon as this construction of relations is possible, the correct explanation follows.

In conclusion, in spite of the difference of level between the discovery of the law and its correct explanation, the latter is in direct continuity with the observed law. Thus explanation results from a deduction starting with law and operating without the introduction of any new elements. What is new is the possibility of deduction, the possibility, that is to say, of changes of point of view which will condition the establishment of new relations. During the early stages, up to the end of the third stage, explanation and legality are opposed to one another ; it is during this period that the child, in order to explain the laws or the facts he has observed, invents the principle of a shadow in accordance with an ontology that is foreign to the pure observation of phenomena. But as soon as he begins to reason about the observed law and to draw from it all its possible conclusions by means of the logic of relations, the law grows by natural extension into the correct explanation. In this particular case, the correct explanation is, like the correct prediction, due to the appearance of relational logic, whereas the substantialist ontology of the earlier stages could only lead to an exclusive use of conceptional imagination. These new facts therefore conspire with those brought forward in the last chapter to show that the hiatus between legality and causality is far greater in the earlier than in the more evolved stages, and that it decreases in the measure that ontology is replaced by relativism.

EXPLANATION OF MACHINES

THE artificialist turn of mind, of which we have seen so many manifestations, may certainly be expected to go hand in hand with a systematic interest in industry and adult handicraft. Everyone will have had occasion to notice this. All workmen and especially mechanics excite the greatest interest in boys, and even in little girls, before their more feminine tastes have begun to predominate. Interest in machines, in particular, combined with interest in everything that moves, provokes in the child a universal curiosity about all the means of locomotion—motor-cars, boats, trains, aeroplanes, etc. Considering the persistence with which the children of the *Maison des Petits de l'Institut J.-J. Rousseau* draw trains, boats, and aeroplanes, model them in clay, or build them with bricks and sticks, it seems as though this tendency were at root nothing but a variant of that joy in being a cause of which K. Groos has spoken—the joy of being a cause of movement.

But whatever may be the affective components of this interest, the important thing for us is to try and analyse the explanations which children give of how machines work. Are these explanations pre-causal or are they mechanistic in tendency ? Does the correct explanation of machines come before the correct explanation of natural movements, or is the reverse the case ? What are the relations between *homo faber* and *homo sapiens*? This is the last problem we have to solve, but it is the most fundamental of all.

It will perhaps be objected that the problem is one to

be eliminated, since the spectacle of machinery has been imposed upon children by quite a recent civilisation, and that the explanations given cannot supply us with results of any value for the psychology of the child in general. But this would be a strange objection to raise, for new as machines are, they nevertheless call forth, at least in the very young child, mental reactions which have always existed, if not always at the same age. It is well known that M. Lévy-Bruhl in his recent work on *Primitive Mentality* has not hesitated to devote several chapters to the ideas of negroes on the white man's art of medicine, on fire-arms, on printed books, etc. We may with equal right question the child about the most modern inventions of adult industry. In both cases what one wants to detect is the mental orientation, and nothing else.

CHAPTER IX

THE MECHANISM OF BICYCLES

ONE of the results that show most clearly the interest felt by boys for machines and the original mental reaction of any child when questioned on the subject, is the synchronism of ages marking the correct explanation of a bicycle in the various towns where we collected our material. In Paris and Geneva in particular, 8 is the average age of the boys who can give a complete explanation of this mechanism, supported by a spontaneous drawing. Little girls are naturally two or three years behind in this domain, for lack of interest in the question, and we shall therefore not mention them in the following pages.

A bicycle is an excellent subject for questions. Every boy has observed its mechanism. All the pieces of this mechanism are visible. And above all, the combined use of drawing and speech enables the child who has been questioned to show all he has understood.

The technique to be adopted is as follows :

We say to the child : " Do you like looking at bicycles in the street ? Very well then, draw me a bicycle on this piece of paper." The boy will often protest : " But I can't draw," etc. But we insist. " Do it as well as you can. I know it is difficult, but go ahead, your friends can do it and you'll be able to too." Care should be taken not to let the drawing be too small (7 centimetres at least). If necessary, one can outline the two wheels for the youngest children (it is a question of explanation not of drawing !) and wait for them to finish the rest. Then we ask : " Well, and how does a bicycle go ? " If the child answers " With wheels ", we go on, " yes, but how, what happens when the gentleman sits there ? " and so on, not suggesting the answer to the question one has set, but trying to get at everything that the child knows already. Finally, as a counter evidence we point to the parts that have been drawn, the pedals, the chain, the cog-wheels, and ask about each in turn : " What is that for ? " In this way we obtain a complete and unsuggested explanation, for we confine ourselves to such indications as are given by the drawing.

Thus the drawing is a perpetual and extremely valuable safeguard. Often even after 7 or 8 years it is sufficient to show the quality of the explanation. It is rare for a drawing to be complete without the corresponding under-standing of the mechanism. I call complete a drawing that has, 1° the two wheels of the bicycle ; 2° one cog-wheel correctly placed, i.e. interposed between these two wheels ; 3° one cog-wheel situated in the centre of the back wheel ; 4° a chain surrounding the two cog-wheels in correct fashion ; 5° the pedals fixed to the large cog-wheel. The details as to the insertion of the frame, the saddle and the handle-bars do not enter into this test of explanation (see Figs. 1 and 2).

With very young children it is as well to make use of a sort of puzzle game. You cut out of cardboard a bicycle frame, wheels and cog-wheel, and lay beside them a piece of string which represents the chain. The pieces are explained to the child in detail, and he is required to put them in order. But the best way of all is, of course, to show the youngsters a real bicycle and ask for their explanation on the spot.

The stages we discovered are four in number. During the first stage, the cause of movement is entirely synthetic (global) : sometimes the child says that what makes the bicycle is " the mechanism ", sometimes " the lamp ", " the light ", etc. ; but in neither case is the " how " of the movement in any way analysed. The average age of this stage is 4–5 years. During a second stage (5–6), the pieces are examined in detail, each piece is mentally isolated and thought of as necessary. But the cause of the movement is still synthetic, for the action of the pieces upon one another is in no way made clear, and

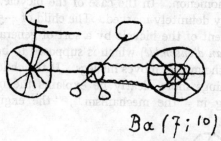

Ba (7; 10)

FIG. 1.

when the child is asked to make it more definite, he takes refuge in a series of vicious circles which do not trouble him in the least. During the third stage, the action of the pieces is sought for, but the correct explanation has not been completely discovered. Finally, during a fourth stage (after 8 years) the complete explanation is given.

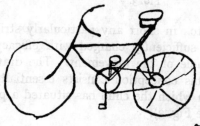

Ju (8; 3)

FIG. 2.

§ 1. FIRST STAGE: THE CAUSE OF THE MOVEMENT IS SYNTHETIC.—As Claparède has pointed out, perception in the very young child is syncretistic, that is to say, synthetic (*global*), confused, proceeding from the whole to the part. As far as causality is concerned, this synthetic perception tends to find together all the elements of a given whole, but does not bring out the analysis of particular sequences. The child has the impression that each element " goes with " all the others or is " made for " all the others but does not enquire as to the " how " of the phenomenon. In the case of the bicycle, this first stage is very definitely marked. The child of 4–5 explains the movement of the bicycle by a sort of general forward impetus (*élan d'ensemble*) which is supposed to be released as soon as the cyclist moves his legs. If the child is asked to state things more clearly he explains the movement by bringing in " the mechanism ", " the engine ", the

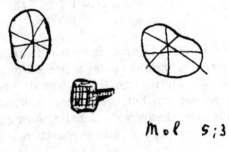

Fig. 3.

lamp, the pump, etc., in short any particularly striking piece which seems sufficiently charged with efficacy to account for the whole of the movement. The drawing corresponding to this conception consists essentially in two wheels between which the child has situated a pedal or anything else (see Fig. 3).

Here are examples :

SCHNEI (4 ; 5) : " How does this bicycle work ? [a man's bicycle that we prop against a chair in front of Schnei].— *When you pedal*—What happens ?—*It turns and then it goes.*—Why ?—*Because the wheels turn.*—Why do the wheels turn ?—*Because there's an engine.*—Where ?—*In the bike.*—Where ?—*In a spoke.*—What is a spoke ?—*A wire.* [Schnei does actually show us a spoke and not the chain].—What does the engine do ?—*When you pedal it makes it turn.*—How ?—*When you turn the wheel.* [Shows

the back wheel].—How does it make the wheel go ?—
When you push the pedal.—And then ?—*It turns.*—Why ?
—*It goes.*—Why ?—*If you lift up* [the pedal] *you push
hard and then it goes.*—If there were no chain, would it go ?
—*Yes.*—Why is there a chain ?—*Because you can pedal
nicely.*—Why can you pedal nicely ?—*Because if there
wasn't a chain you couldn't pedal.*—Why not ?—*Because
that* [showing the bar of the pedals] *couldn't turn."* The
chain, therefore, is merely a support for the pedals and
plays no part in the movement of the wheels : it is the
turning of the pedals which directly causes the wheels to
turn. And further, in connection with the pedals, Schnei
says : " What happens when you pedal ?—*It makes the
wheels turn.*—Why ?—*When the thing is lit.*—What thing ? "
[Schnei shows us the red light, *i.e.* the rear lamp]. Thus
the cause of the movement of the wheels is entirely
synthetic, in that the movement of the pedals suffices, in
the child's eyes, to explain that of the wheels, without
the need for any intermediate links.

PIG (4) : " How does this bicycle go ? [The same man's
bicycle].—*With wheels.*—And the wheels ?—*They are
round.*—How do they turn ?—*It's the bicycle that makes
them turn.*—How ?—*With the handle-bar.*—How does the
handle-bar make the bicycle go ?—*With the wheels.*—And
what makes the wheels turn ?—*The bicycle."* The synthetic character of the explanation is obvious. " Why
do the wheels turn ?—*For it to go.*—Why ?—*To go quickly.*
—How ?—*When you arrange the bicycle it goes.*—What
has to be done ?—*Take off the rubber and then put it back.*
—What does one put in the rubber ?—*Water, so as to go
quicker."* [Pig has seen that the inner tube is put into
water when it is punctured : he concludes from this that
it contains a flow of water which is intended to turn the
wheels !] " What must you do to make the bicycle go ?—
Must put your feet on the pedals.—And then ?—*It goes.*
[We make the experiment].—Why does it go ?—*Because
there's that* [the cog-wheel].—What ?—*A little wheel.*—
What is it for ?—*For the bike.*—Why ?—*To make it go.*—
If there were no little wheel, would it work ?—*No.*—
Why ?—*It would take away the pedal if there wasn't a little
wheel."* It will be seen that the cog-wheel is **only** thought
to be of use as a support. Naturally, Pig still has the
bicycle in front of him. As for the chain, which we
point out to him, its only use is also thought to be to
hold the pedals.

AUB (4) : " How does this bicycle move along ?—*It's that*. [He points to the pedals.]—What does that do ?— *You turn with your feet.*—How does it go?—*That. You put your feet on.*—And then ?—*It goes.*—Why ?—*It turns.* —How ?—*That* [the pedals]." Through failing to understand our questions on the relation of the pedals to the wheels, Aub ends by saying that " wind " is put into the tyres " *to make the bicycle go. Then you get on top. That makes the wheel go.*" In other words, the bicycle moves along as soon as the pedals are turned, the connection between the pedals and the wheels being entirely synthetic ; he adds that the wheels contain " wind " which makes them turn more rapidly.

PAQ (4 ; 3) : " How does this bicycle go ?—*With the wheels.*—And what makes the wheels go ?—*They turn by themselves. It's when you are on top of the bicycle. It's the street that makes the bicycle go* (!) [We mount the bicycle, but without moving]." " *You put your feet on there* [on the pedals]. *That is what you move with.*—How is it that it turns when I put my feet there ?—*Because it couldn't go if it doesn't turn.*" We turn the pedals backwards and ask Paq why it does not move forward. Paq replies : " *Because it doesn't want to go when you turn it.*" Then we work the pedals and make the wheel move : " How does that make the wheel go ?—*Because it must* [!] *go.*—[We remove the chain].—Why does the wheel not turn any more ?—*Because the chain is taken away, must put it back.*—[We put it back]. How does the pedal make the wheel turn ?— . . . —What is the chain for ?— *Because it must go.*" It is evident that in spite of our explanations, made by means of a man's bicycle, Paq has not passed the stage of synthetic explanation : it is even a moral, and not a physical determinism which, for Paq, explains the movement of the machine. It goes without saying that, even after these demonstrations, Paq is incapable of putting in order the pieces of the cardboard bicycle puzzle, although he is extremely interested in the game : he places anyhow the pedals, the cog-wheels and the chain, without troubling about the connection between them.

As for the children to whom we do not show a real bicycle, and from whom we merely ask for an explanation and a drawing from memory, they naturally give even less precise replies :

MOL (5 ; 3) says among other things : " *You must turn the pedals with your feet.*" But he claims that the pedals make the wheels go. " How do the pedals make the wheels go ?--*They can, no, they can't make the wheels go. It's very hard to say. When you want them* [the wheels] *to go quickly, you turn your feet very fast.*" Mol, therefore, has quite realised a connection between the movement of the feet and that of the bicycle, but the " how " escapes him completely, and he does not trouble about it. The details of the mechanism are not at all necessary. " If you don't turn the pedals, can the bicycle go ?—*Yes, you can do that.*—Uphill as well ?—*Yes.*" In short, everything is possible.

CROT (backward) : " *You pedal, you hold the handle-bar and that's all.*—But how does it make it move along when you pedal ?—*You turn the pedals and then it goes.*" Like Mol, Crot draws a pedal between the two wheels, without either chain or cog-wheel. We ask him if there is not something missing. He can find nothing to add : the movement of the pedals only is enough for him, as it was for Mol, to explain the turning of the wheel.

The drawing gives a very good schematic representation of the first stage. It consists of two wheels, and a pedal, a thread or a little wheel, etc., situated between the wheels without showing any attempt to insert or connect the pieces.

Added to these synthetic explanations, we often find remarks such as have been quoted in the cases of Schnei An, and Pig, according to whom efficacy belongs to the lamp, or the air in the tyres, etc.

PER (delicate) can see no link between the pedals and the wheels. He says that in the bicycle there is a " *force, when the rider opens a thing and puts with a pump* [when the tyres are blown up]. *That makes the wheel turn when you pedal.*—Without this force, would it be possible to make the bicycle move by pedalling ?—*No, sir.*"

DES (8, backward) : " *You put a current in the tyres.*"

The rôle assigned to lamps, to air, etc., is highly interesting, and shows how swiftly the child will establish relations between a given movement to be explained and some feature that happens to be particularly striking to immediate observation.

The few features essential to this stage may be summarised as follows.

In the first place these children are in no way concerned as to " how " the mechanism works. Essential parts like the cog-wheel or the chain are not kept in mind by children who speak from memory. Those who have a real bicycle before them certainly make a note of the parts and they incorporate what they notice into their conception of the machine's motion by saying that these parts serve " to make it go " to " bike with " and so on. But in point of fact, nothing is changed. For, 1° these parts are thought to be adjuvants to, not links in the movement. The rôle of the pedals is never even suspected of as being connected with that of the wheels. 2° Some children regard these parts as unnecessary : Schnei, for example, says that the bicycle would go without a chain. 3° Others think that they are necessary, but only as supports : Pig believes that the cog-wheel and the chain help to keep the pedals in place. 4° Others, finally—and this leads us on to the second stage where the phenomenon will become more pronounced—think that the parts are necessary, but merely because they are there : Paq, for instance, says that there must be a chain, but does not know what purpose it serves.

Of the positive features of this stage we may signal out the following three. The first is explanation by moral determinism. Paq, for example, is always saying : " It must go." The wheel may resist (" it doesn't want to go ") but it is obliged to : " it must go ". We have here a conception analogous to that which we emphasised in connection with the movements of the sun and moon and of the clouds.

The second positive feature is explanation without spatial contact : movement of the feet or of the pedals brings about that of the wheels, directly and without any contact. What conception does the child form of this relation ?

It seems as though the child thought that the mere movement of the feet was sufficient to set the bicycle going, just as though the cyclist were swimming or flying and used the bicycle only as a support to carry him over the ground. The cyclist is supposed to travel by himself, while the bicycle merely follows his movements. The wheels, in this case, are certainly bound to go round when the pedals go round, not because the pedals act by contact on the wheels but because both are carried along with the advancing cyclist.

Our reason for thinking this interpretation the most probable is that throughout the second stage we shall see this schema take more definite shape and give rise to explanations by reaction of the surrounding medium which recall the explanations of the movements of the heavenly bodies and of the clouds.

This is why expressions chiefly of a moral character come to be used in characterising the movements of the various parts of the machine. When, for example, Paq declares that : " It's the street that makes the bicycle go, what he means is obviously that the bicycle is forced to move along, whereas in a room it can resist. It was a conception analogous to this which made the children say that the stones make the river flow (by calling forth its impetus), or that the sun or night set the clouds in motion (by driving them away or by attracting them).

Finally, a third feature should be noted : the participation of " forces " or of a " current " shows that there exists in the child a form of causality compounded of phenomenism and dynamism. The lamp, the air in the tyres, the spokes—all these are given without reason at the same time as the wheels, etc. : they are therefore efficacious in bringing about the movement.

§ 2. SECOND STAGE : THE VARIOUS PARTS ARE NECESSARY BUT UNRELATED.—The second stage begins from the moment when the child spontaneously draws chains, cogwheels, etc., or mentions their existence, and from the moment when he thinks of these parts as necessary to the bicycle's forward movement. This stage is distinguished from that which follows it by the fact that the action of one part on another is not supposed to follow any causal order properly so-called, *i.e.* one which assumes regular antecedents and consequents. The bicycle's motion is still explained by means of syncretistic or synthetic relations, and when the child is pressed to enter into details, he only takes refuge in a series of vicious circles. The drawing at this stage is characterised by juxtaposition of the parts without correct insertions, often without even any connection between them.

Here are examples, beginning with some cases that are transitional between the first and the second stage :

GRIM (5½) : " How does the bicycle move along ?— *With the brakes on top of the bike.*—What is the brake for ? —*To make it go because you push.*—What do you push with ?—*With your feet.*—What does that do ?—*It makes it go.*—How ?—*With the brakes.*—What are the pedals for ?—*To make it go at the back.*" As Grim has noticed a chain, but without being able to explain its use, we show him a man's bicycle. Grim then says that the pedal makes the back wheel go, " *because you push like that* [on the pedal] *and it makes that* [the chain] *work.*—What is that chain for ?—*It's to turn that wheel* [the cog-wheel. Grim thus inverts the order] *and that makes the big one* [wheel] *turn with it.*—If there were no chain, would it go with the brakes ?—*No.*—And if there were no brakes, would the bicycle move ?—*No.*" Grim then makes a drawing from memory analogous to that of Fig. 4, *i.e.* a drawing in which all the parts are indicated, but in simple juxtaposition. " What makes the chain turn ?—*The wheels.*—Which ones ?—*That one* [the back wheel].— What makes that wheel turn ?—*The wires* [the brakes]. —What makes the cog-wheel turn ?—*The chain.*—What is the cog-wheel for ?—*To make it go.*—And the chain ?— *Also.*—And the pedals ?—*To make this wheel go* [cog-wheel].—And what does the cog-wheel do ?—*It makes the wires work* [the brakes].—And the wires ?—*They move and make the bicycle go.*—How do the wires make the bicycle go ?—*At the same time as you make the wires go,*

you push with your feet.—How do you make the wires
work ?—*With the brakes.*"

RU (9, backward) is a good case of " synthetic incapacity." His drawing (Fig. 4) shows the two wheels
of the bicycle joined correctly by a bar which serves as
a frame, but between the two wheels are placed in a row,
the chain, the cog-wheel and one pedal, without any
relation between them. Questioning elicits the following :
the pedals serve " *to make the back wheel go* ", the chains
" *to make that go* " [the cog-wheel], etc.

DEC (6½) observes the existence of a chain between the
pedals and the wheels. " What is this chain for ?—*For
moving along.*—What makes the chain turn ?—*The wheels*

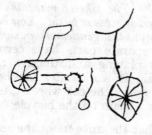

Ru

FIG. 4.

[back and front]." As for the wheels, it is the pedals which
turn them.

AL (6) : The bicycle goes with the wheels and " *the
gentleman makes them work.*—How ?—*When he's riding.
He pedals with his feet. That makes the wheels work.*—
What is the chain for ?—*To hold the wheels, no, the pedals.
The handle-bar makes the wheels and the pedals go.*—What
is the chain for ?—*To hold the pedals.*—And the pedals ?
—*To make the wheels go.*—And the wheels ?—*To make the
bicycle go.*"

BERN (7 ; 10) and FONT (8 ; 6) each places the pedals,
in his drawing, on the actual framework of the bicycle,
stretches a chain between the two wheels and indicates
the cog-wheel, but without inserting them correctly. Yet
they both explain the propulsion of the bicycle by a
concerted movement. Bern : " How does the bicycle
go ?—*With the wheels and the pedals.*—How do the pedals
make the wheels go ?—*It's as he* [the man] *makes the bicycle*

move, that makes the wheels turn.—Do the pedals make the wheels turn ?—*No, because the pedals are to put your feet on.*—And how do you make the wheels work ?—*By making the bicycle go.*—And how do you make the bicycle go ?—*With his hands. He pushes the bicycle. . . . He puts wind in the wheels and that swells the rubber and the bicycle goes better.*—What do your feet do ?—*Make the pedals turn.*—Why ?—*I don't know* [he laughs]. *It is because it makes the wheels turn. When you push the handle-bar it makes them go even quicker. It makes the front wheel go.*"

FONT, similarly : " *The pedals make the wheels go. The bicycle goes because of the wheels, and the pedals are to put our feet on, to hold us up. The person on top makes the pedals go. The pedals pushes the wheels. It's us that pushes it* [the wheels]. *The wheels make the bicycle go. When you move your feet it gives a push. You have to push first* [before mounting] : *the gentleman pushes first and then gets on.*" The separate parts have certainly been observed, but not as playing a distinctive rôle. Bern believes that the chain is worked by the back wheel, while the chain itself works the cog-wheel. As for Font, he denies that there is a chain on the bicycle

It will be noticed that the answers of the second stage are on certain points a continuation of those of the first, whilst on others they clearly introduce fresh features.

The chief residue of the first stage is the idea of a synthetic causality, the belief that the movement of a pedalling cyclist taken as a whole will be sufficient to make the wheels move along. For we do not find a single example at this stage of an intermediary link between the movement of the pedals and that of the wheels. The pedal makes the wheels go, not by a series of causes and effects, but directly. The intermediary factors are certainly seen to be there—the chain, the cog-wheels, etc. But their movement is as much the effect as the cause of the movement of the wheels : here is no series taking place in time, but a syncretistic relation.

In some cases, this immediate action of the pedalling is made more definite. This can happen in the most interesting fashion, as with Font and Bern, and perhaps even with Grim. These children think much as follows :

the cyclist who gives the bicycle a start before jumping on to it, once he is seated on the saddle, pushes the handle-bars (or the brakes, which according to Grim, comes to the same thing) and in this way accelerates the impetus (*l'élan*). Besides this, he "moves his feet," which also gives an impetus. In short, the cyclist pushes himself by pushing the handle-bars and moving his feet. He takes a start before mounting, and adds to it by pushing the handle-bars. We are probably faced here with a new form of the schema of reaction of the surrounding medium, which we met with in connection with the movements of clouds and of water, etc. : the bicycle pushes itself by means of the start it has taken. This interpretation is forced upon us by the cases of Bern and Font, since these children go so far as to say that the pedals are simply there for " the gentleman " to rest his feet on, so that he can " keep up " to push the handle-bars or get a start by moving his legs.

Obviously, it is the same schema that lies at the back of the minds of the first stage children and enables them to be so easily satisfied with the idea that the pedals make the wheels go round without any intermediary factor.

It should be noted, moreover, that as in the first stage the child brings in helping forces :

BE (8) : " *There's a current in the tyres, because they are pumped up.—Why do you pedal ?—To make the wheels go. —And the current ?—It also makes them go when it* [the bicycle] *is started. It makes it go downhill, and along a straight road, but not uphill.*"

BOT (8 ; backward) : The bicycle goes round " *because the light* [the lamp] *is there.*"

The fresh feature of this stage, as compared to the preceding one, is the presence of a certain analysis of detail. The child remembers the existence of the cog-wheels and of the chain, and declares these parts to be necessary. If they did not exist, says the child, the bicycle would not go. It is interesting to note that this feeling of necessity comes long before any understanding of the " how ", and consequently before causality properly so-called. For at this stage, although the child declares the separate pieces to be necessary, he does not know what they are for. Sometimes he assigns to them the rôle of support, sometimes that of motor, but actually, this rôle is always added afterwards. The child says to himself quite simply : " They are necessary since they are there," and this is sufficient to make him feel very strongly the necessity of their existence. But this necessity is uniform, as it were, or always of the same degree : Kar (6 ; 8), for example, is of opinion that the tyres are just as necessary as the pedals, although he is not thinking of the " current " which we spoke of earlier.

This absence of any concern about the " how " of things leads naturally to a complete absence of order in the relations subsisting between the parts. The same child will say at one time that the chain makes the cog-wheel go round, and at another that the reverse is the case ; at one time that the back wheel makes the chain go round, at another that the reverse is the case. There is, as yet, no irreversible succession.

Finally, the drawings show a mere juxtaposition of the parts, since the mind has not yet grasped their relations. We have here a very good example of correlation between what M. Luquet has called " synthetic incapacity " in the child's drawing, and what we have called " juxta-position " in the child's mind. And this is yet another example of the necessary bond existing between juxta-position and syncretism (see *J.R.*, Chap. I, Conclus.) : it is because the cause of movement is synthetic that the pieces are simply juxtaposed, and it is because the pieces are simply juxtaposed that the explanation of the move-ment is still synthetic or syncretistic.

§ 3. THIRD AND FOURTH STAGES : THE SEARCH FOR CONTACTS AND MECHANICAL EXPLANATION.—It is at about the age of 7 that the child passes from the second stage and sets out to find an irreversible order in the actio··

of the parts upon each other. But, naturally, the correct explanation is not found straight away, and it is necessary to distinguish a third stage before reaching that of complete explanation. The third stage is therefore characterised by the fact that the child gives up synthetic explanation and looks for an irreversible sequence of cause and effect in the detailed interaction of the parts.

Here are examples :

JOR (7 ; 9) : " *There's a high seat. It's made to join the pedals. When the pedal turns, I believe there are some little round things hidden away . . . when the pedal turns, the seat turns, and then comes down.*"

DHER (8 ; 1) : " *The gentleman makes the pedals turn. The wheels turn with them. There is a chain that is joined to the pedals and the wheels.*" But Dher draws the chain as in Fig. 5, *i.e.* joining it directly to the tyres and the pedals.

GE (9) similarly imagines a chain joined to the tyres, on which the pedals would work directly (see also Fig. 5).

This shows a great advance on the preceding stages in so far as the contact is definitely sought for and leads to an irreversible causal sequence. But most of these children go no further than rudimentary explanations such as imagining that chains or bars are attached to the tyres, and they are quite unperturbed by the unlikelihood of such suppositions. This fact alone shows how far removed were the subjects of the earlier stages from mechanical explanations, since the present subjects, who are far more advanced, still cling to schemas of such obvious absurdity.

It is only fair to add that this third stage is of short duration and serves chiefly as a transition to the next. Boys over 8 are able, as a rule, to give a correct explanation of the bicycle. Here are three examples :

IN (8 ; 3) : " *You pedal and it makes a wheel* [the cogwheel] *go round. There's a chain, and it makes the back wheel go round* " (see Ju's drawing from memory, Fig. 2).

STER (10 ; 1) : " *When you pedal, there's a chain, two* [cog-] *wheels and a cog-wheel that makes the* [back] *wheel go.*"

LIV (10) : " How do the pedals make the wheels go round ?—*With a chain.. It goes round at the same time as the pedals. There's a thing like a cog-wheel that makes the chain go round. The chain makes the* [back] *wheel go round.* How many cog-wheels are there ?—*Two.*"

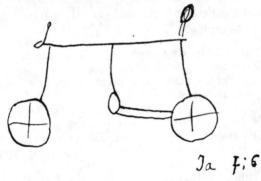

Ja 7:6

FIG. 5.

Here we have the first truly mechanical explanation that has occurred so far between the years of 8 and 9. To conclude, the evolution of answers about the bicycle shows a gradual progression from irrational dynamism to dynamism of the ἀντιπερίστασις type, and from this more intelligible dynamism to a genuinely mechanistic view of causality.

CHAPTER X

THE STEAM-ENGINE

EVERY boy is interested in engines. Later on, we shall have occasion to examine the explanations which they give of its mechanism. But to start straight away with the analysis of these explanations would be to run the risk of misunderstanding them, since the child is speaking from memory and has nothing concrete before him. Let us begin, therefore, by questioning the children about a little toy engine which will be made to work in front of them. We have chosen one of those little engines which most boys play with, and of which the working can be almost entirely seen from outside. It consists of a vertical boiler, with a small spirit-lamp under it, from which, when it is lit, the steam escapes through a little pipe that can be seen from outside to run into the cylinder. The piston contained in the cylinder is invisible, but the connecting-rods come out at the bottom of the cylinder and work, by means of a metal bar, the big wheel outside on which a belt can be attached so as to utilise the force (see Fig. 6). The fire is, of course, lit in front of the child. Sometimes we tell him beforehand that there is water in the boiler, sometimes we let him find this out by himself. The latter is the best course to take, for we shall see that the younger children do not feel the need for any mediating factor between the fire and the wheel, whereas the older ones immediately look for such a factor. This is a valuable index to the mental orientation characteristic of each stage.

As will appear, moreover, most of the boys we questioned already possessed an engine of this kind or had seen one at their friends' houses. But whether they were already acquainted with such an engine or not, the children all gave answers which it was possible to compare with one another, and we noticed a remarkable continuity between the most primitive answers and those that were more advanced. In spite of the fairly marked differences which roughly separate the three stages we

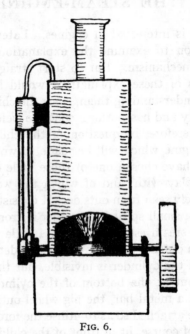

FIG. 6.

are about to describe, our children could be ranked in successive classes closely akin to one another, and showing how imperceptibly explanation develops with the mental stature of the child. The continuity, together with the progress, add greatly to the value of the reactions we observed.

We were, therefore, able to discover three definite stages. The first extends from about 4 to 6 years, and yields as an average age $5\frac{1}{2}$. During this stage, the fire or heat is believed to produce directly the movements of the wheel (which is external to the cage in which the fire is enclosed). The second stage extends from 6 to 8 years, and yields the average age of 7 years and 5 months. During this stage the need for intermediaries appears : thus the child announces simultaneously that there must be water in the boiler and that the pipe must be able to conduct the water to the wheel. During a first sub-stage of this second stage, the fire is thought of as actually pushing the water, by entering into it, and the water as pushing the wheel. During a second sub-stage, the child only thinks that the fire heats the water and that the water creates a current which pushes the wheel. A third stage sets in at about 8–9 years, and is characterised by the discovery of the part played by steam : when the water is heated by the fire, it evaporates, and the steam goes directly to the wheels, which it pushes by means of the connecting-rods which are still thought to be tubes ; or else, the steam pushes the piston, and the piston pushes the connecting-rods. Thus at the beginning of this stage the force of the steam is likened purely to an impetus (*élan*) or current, regardless of volume or expansion. Later on, the child acquires a certain understanding of the nature of this pressure.

§ 1. FIRST STAGE : THE WHEEL TURNS BECAUSE OF THE FIRE.—The explanations of this first stage are very curious, and present us once more with all the beliefs based on participation which we learned to know through the more primitive of the explanations regarding the movement of air, clouds, etc., or regarding the formation of shadows. For at this stage, the mental orientation of the child is directed entirely to immediate relations, conceived without intermediaries, and dwells not for a moment on the " how " of the process in question. The older children begin by examining the pipes and the connecting-rods, and look for factors intermediate between the fire and the wheel. In this way they are led to notice the existence of the cylinder and of the pipe that connects it with the boiler. But the little ones look only at the fire and at the wheel, they do not attempt to find any connections, and they give their explanations straight away. Thus in the very attitude of the child there is already a differentiating factor. As to the explanation that is given, it is of the simplest : the fire has acted directly on the wheel. If we ask the child how this can be, he brings in either direct action through the walls of the furnace (the wheel is, in point of fact, separated from the fire by a metal wall that presents no opening) or else action issuing from the opening of the furnace and travelling through the air. It is chiefly in this second type of explanation that one can see participations at work : the fire produces wind, which attracts the wind from outside, etc., and this complexus is offered as an explanation of the wheel's movement.

Here are some examples :

SCHNEI (4) : " What makes the wheel turn ?—*When the thing* [the lamp] *is alight.*" We turn out the lamp and the wheel stops : " What does that do ?—*You've turned out the light.*—Why ?—*Because the wheel wasn't turning quickly.*" [1] We remove the lamp and place it at 10 centimetres distance from the wheel, on the table : " And if I light it here, will the engine go or not ?—*That makes it go too.*—Why ?—*Because there's light too* [=because it's lit].—And here [at 30 centimetres], I am going to light up, will it go or not ?—*It will go.* [We light it.]—Does it go ? —*No.*—Why ?—*Because you didn't put it inside* [=we did not put the lamp in the boiler].—And if I put the lamp here [outside, but near the wheel] ?—*It will go* " . . ., etc. We put the lamp under the boiler again and the wheel begins to turn once more. Schnei says that it is " *the light* " which makes it go. "How?—*Because there's a hole inside* [Schnei points to a metal partition which separates the lamp from the wheel, at the point where a screw makes a mark.]—If I put the lamp outside, will it go ?—*Yes.* [We make the experiment.]—Why does it stop ?—*Because it must be inside.*—Why ?—*Because it's*

---

[1] Here the child reverses the causal relation, although he knows the true relation, as can be seen by his previous remarks. Cf. *J.R.* Chap. I, § 3.

open in front." Schnei is referring to the opening which is in front of the fire, and believes that the " light " can come out of there and go to the wheel by travelling round the walls of the furnace !

ROY (6) : " What makes the wheel turn ?—*The fire.—* Why ?—*Because it's good at making it go.*—If I put the fire here [under the connecting-rods], will it go or not ?—*Yes.* —Why?—*Because the fire will touch the wheel.*—And why will it go ?—*Because it's good at making it go.*—And there [20 centimetres] ?—*No.*—And here [10 centimetres] ?— *Yes.*—Why ?—*Because it's nearer.* [We light the lamp, 10 centimetres away from the wheel].—Does it go ?—*No, but it's going to go.*—Is it going ?—*No, but it's going to go, it's not going yet.*—How long will we have to wait ?—*Just a minute.*—It will go ?—*Yes.*—Why is it not going ?— *Because we must wait.*"

DON (5½) : The fire " *will go to there* [the wheel] *and it will make that turn.*—How ?—*The fire is quite near there* [Don indicates the distance between the fire and the wheel, by marking the course on the outside of the boiler]. —But how does the fire make that work ?—*It will burn on this side and that will make that turn.*" " But how does the fire make the wheel turn ?—*It's the fire. It burns on this side and that makes it turn.*—But how ?—*It comes there, it moves along.*"

We shall now give some more subtle cases, which will explain how this action at a distance is possible. For the action invoked by the children we have just quoted is very curious. These children know perfectly well that the fire does not come out of the furnace and " go " towards the wheel. Something must have emanated from the fire and gone to push the wheel. What is it ? According to the children we are now going to examine, this something is air :

BLAN (6½) : " Why does that turn ?—*Because you light it there.*—What does that do ?—*It heats.*—And then ?— *It makes it turn.*—Why ?—*It makes air.*—What ?—*The fire.*—Is this air used for something ?—*Yes, to make it turn.* — What ? — *The wheels.* — Which wheels ? — *Those* [Blan indicates the wheel and the base of the connecting-rods].—How does that make them turn ?—*Because it* [the air] *blows.*" Blan then explains to us that the air comes out of the funnel: "*It* [the air] *comes under the wheel and all the time there is more coming.*—Show me how.— *By this pipe* [the funnel], *and afterwards it* [the air] *turns right round.*" [Blan indicates the journey from the top of the funnel to the wheel.] "But how does this air get on to the wheel?—*Because the window is open* [the window of the room] —But is it the air from the fire or the air from the window that makes the wheel turn, or both?— *Both.* [We shut the window.] [The wheel turns] *because it* [the air] *comes in by the other window.*" In short, Blan believes that the fire makes air and that this air, by participating with the air from the window, makes the wheel of the engine turn, by merely blowing against it.

DEB (8½ ; backward): "How does this wheel go?— *With the heat.*—How?—*It will push the wheel. When you turn the wheel* [with the hand, as we are doing] *it turns, and the heat pushes it some more.*—What is that [the boiler]?—*It's the thing where it's lit. It's there that the smoke goes up.* [Deb points to the funnel.]—Where does the smoke come from?—*It comes from the furnace.*—But here?—*That comes from the lamp.*—How does this wheel go?—*It goes with the smoke.*—Why?—*Because the smoke is made of air.*—How is that?—*Because it makes just a little wind.*—What does the wind do?—*It pushes the wheel. It does that and that makes it turn.*—Where does it come from, this wind that makes the wheel turn?—*It comes from the sky. If the wind comes like that* [Deb indicates the orientation of the wheel], *it comes from the North.*— But where does this wind come from?—*It comes to where the wheel is.*—What does this wind do?—*The smoke* [Deb indicates the funnel] *goes up and that makes clouds.*— And the clouds?—*They make rain.*—Is it the smoke that makes the wind which pushes the wheel?—*Yes.*—How? —*Because the smoke goes up to the sky and that makes a wind.*" Thus, the fire produces the smoke, which in its turn produces wind, which wind comes at the same time from the sky and from the clouds, and the whole pushes the wheel of the engine.

These few first stage cases enable us to reach the following conclusions. In the first place, very young children give proof of a remarkable lack of interest as to "how" the phenomenon takes place. The two terms, *fire* and *movement of the wheel* are related immediately, without any intermediate links, and the child pays no attention whatever to the pipe or even to the connecting-rods whose movement should certainly strike the eye.

Then the question arises as to what these explanations by immediate relation mean from the point of view of action at a distance. A strong metal wall separates the furnace from the wheel, and, on the face of it, the fire seems to be rising towards the boiler rather than in the direction of the wheel. But this does not matter: the child says that the fire goes through the separating wall, or goes round it by the opening of the furnace. It looks, therefore, as though the child admitted action at a distance. It would be nearer the truth to say that the fire is believed to send an invisible " current " or force, which goes to the wheel and pushes it. This relation is brought out very clearly by the older children who introduce the air or even the smoke produced by the fire.

Such a schema as this presupposes two implicit tendencies, which in some cases come very clearly to the surface. First, animism: fire and air must be able to direct themselves, to go to the wheel with intention and intelligence, etc. Then, finalism of an artificialist kind: the fire is " good at " making the wheel go, says Roy, and in his eyes this goodness has a causal value and is sufficient to explain why the fire sets the wheel in motion.

Finally, note should be taken of the interesting beliefs held by Blan and Deb, according to which there is participation between the air produced by the fire and the wind outside, and which thus give additional confirmation to what we pointed out in connection with the air and the shadows.

According to Blan and Deb, smoke or fire make wind, and this wind is at the same time an emanation of the wind external to the room. The case of Deb is particularly illuminating because of the unmistakable syncretism of his reasoning. For in reasoning about the engine, he does not succeed in distinguishing the particular case of wind produced by the smoke of the engine from the general case of the clouds of the atmosphere. Questioned about one, he will answer about the other. This shows that there is no conscious generalisation and application of a general law, but immediate fusion of a new and incompletely observed fact with an old and incompletely generalised schema. Deb does not say, " Here is smoke, smoke always makes clouds, and clouds always makes wind," which would lead him to conclude : " It's the wind produced by this smoke that pushes the wheel." On the contrary, he starts more or less as follows : " Here is smoke. That's the same thing as the clouds in the sky. They both make wind," and concludes, " The wind that pushes the wheel comes both from the clouds and from the smoke." Participation as a mode of explanation is therefore closely allied to syncretism and transduction as a mode of reasoning. The problem of the actual relations between participation and transduction is one that will occupy us later. For the moment, we shall only draw attention to the interest which these beliefs of the first stage possess from this particular point of view. Deb can thus be compared to certain children like Roy who think that the sun grows bigger " because we are getting bigger." For these children, comparison means identity of essence, and analogy supplies the efficient cause.

§ 2. SECOND STAGE : THE WHEEL TURNS BECAUSE OF THE WATER.—Children of the second stage discover that there is water in the boiler. This is no fortuitous circumstance. Some, it is true, knew it beforehand, but the majority looked for and discovered it, and these refused to admit that the fire could push the wheel without any intermediaries. They postulated contacts, took note of the tubes and the connecting-rods, and finally, when they saw small droplets escaping from the cylinder, they concluded that the boiler was full of water. These children's ages, moreover, showed very clearly that the discovery of the water does not happen by chance but is a function of the mental age of the child.

We shall distinguish two sub-stages. During the first

of these, the fire is believed to enter into the water and in this way give it the current necessary for setting the wheel going. Here are examples :

LEO (7) himself possesses an engine. " What will make the wheel turn ?—*Water with fire.*—How ?—*Because it's fire and water.*—How ?—*The fire goes up with the water, and that makes the wheel turn.*" Leo then contends that the boiler is full of water and that the fire rises almost to the top of this boiler. " What is that [the connecting-rods] ?—*That is for turning the wheel.*—What makes them go ?—*The water and the fire.*—How ?—*It goes through the pipes and that makes them go . . . because they* [the water and the fire] *go down, they go inside there* [in the connecting-rods, imagined to be pipes], *and that makes it go.*" " What makes the water go down ?—*It's the air.*—How ? What air ?—*From beneath* [the fire].—What makes this air ?—*It's the fire.*—What pushes the water here [in the pipes] ?—*It's the fire that pushes it. . . . It pushes the water* [movement of pushing upwards].—Is there air in the water ?—*It is only when it moves that there is air.*" In short, the fire pushes the water by making a current of air which goes through the water and lifts it up.

JUG (6½) believes, like Leo, that the fire comes into direct contact with the water, and does not understand that they are separated by a metal partition. " How is it able to turn ?—*There is heat. That will make the wheel turn.*—Why ?—*Because it* [the heat] *makes it express.*—How is that ?—*It makes it go express.*—How ?—*It makes zigzags.*—Where ?—*In the boiler.*" This express or these zigzags go into the connecting-rods and make the wheel go : " *That makes the wheel turn.*—How ?—*Because it gives heat.*" Therefore, that which Jug calls heat, is a sort of current which issues from the fire and which is able to put things in motion.

ROUL (7 ; 9) : " *The fire comes there* [to the bottom of the connecting-rods].—How ?—*The fire goes up through this pipe* [the pipe and the cylinder] *and the water runs.*—How ?—*When that* [the fire] *goes, there is water which comes and that pushes this* [the connecting-rods].—Why does the water push ?—*Because there is some water that must go to its place.*—What does that mean ?—*It wants to run*—Why ?—*Because it's going up.*—Why ?—*It's the fire that makes it go up.*—Why ?—*The fire pushes it.*—Why ?—*Because that makes it go up with the flames.*—Why ?—

Because the fire goes into the air." In brief, the fire pushes the water into the connecting-rods and thus the water pushes the wheel.

FALQ (8 ; 2) also explains the movement of the wheel by that of the connecting-rods, and the latter by the current of the water, which in its turn is due to the fire : " What makes that [the connecting-rods] go ?—*The water, because it has force.*—Why ?—*Because it is mixed with coal* [with smoke, as is shown by the context], *that makes it go, that gives force."* The smoke is used *" to put speed into it."*

All the children of the first sub-stage have thus discovered that the connecting-rods and the axle are necessary to the movement of the wheel. But they explain the movement of the connecting-rods by the impetus of the water and believe the latter to be due to the fact that the wind, or smoke, or air produced by the fire enter into the water and push it along.

Children of the second sub-stage are more exact. In their view the fire simply heats the water (which can be separated from the fire by a metal partition), and the water, having come to the boil, acquires enough impetus by its actual heat to set the connecting-rods in motion :

BER (8 ; 9) : " How does this go ?—*It's the two pistons* [the connecting-rods] *that make it go.*—Do they go by themselves ?—*No, it's the water. It turns because of the force of the water.*—What is the force of the water ?—*Because it's hot."* The water goes to the big wheel through the connecting-rods, which are thought to be pipes : " Why does the wheel turn ?—*Because the water is boiling."*

REYB (9 ; 2) similarly supposes that the water *" is boiling because it goes in the pipe. It will force itself into the piston.*—Why ?—*Because it can move about. It has force, it can go up in the pipe.*—Could it go with cold water ? —*No, it would have no force, because it is* [=would not be] *hot, it can't move* [when it is not hot].—Why is the water strong here ?—*Because it is heated by the fire.*—What does the water do, when it is strong ?—*It rises."*

During the second sub-stage the movements of the connecting-rods and of the wheel are explained by the force of the water when it has been brought to the boil.

Steam has not yet been noticed, or if it has, it is not regarded as serving any useful purpose.

The interest of these answers resides on the whole in the following facts. In the first place, some concern is shown as to the "how" of things, and this leads to the discovery that the connecting-rods and the pipes are necessary, whatever may be the rôle assigned to them by the child. Since the average age of this stage is 7 years, we have here a confirmation of the view that genuine physical explanations appear between the ages of 7 and 8.

Now, another very general feature of these early physical explanations is that they are dynamic and not mechanical: everything is explained by the movement of the water. Sometimes the fire goes into the water and pushes it, sometimes the fire simply heats the water, which then "goes up." Thus in both cases things are explained by a push or impetus. As to the details of the process, these have naturally not begun to excite the child's interest or attention.

§ 3. THIRD STAGE: THE WHEEL TURNS BECAUSE OF THE STEAM.—During the preceding stage, the steam was often noticed by the child, but it was not regarded as having any efficacy. During a third stage, however, (after 9–10 years) steam is believed to play the rôle which up till then had been played by the water, namely, it is supposed to push the connecting-rods and the wheel. Thus at the beginning of the stage, the general structure of the explanation remains exactly what it was—steam has force because it has movement. Neither quantity nor expansion come into play: impetus alone is what counts. This impetus is often called "pressure", but this is on the analogy of the impetus of kitchen taps. The word does not yet contain the idea of pressure due to accumulation. This idea seems to appear, however, after the age of 10–11.

LUC (10): The steam goes into the cylinder, the connecting-rods and the axle, to the wheel: "*The steam*

has force. . . . It makes it turn."—" Why must there be
water ?—*To make the steam.*—If there were only a very
little steam, would it go ?—*Yes, it would move just a
little."*

SANT (10 ; 1) : The steam makes the piston and the
connecting-rods work : " *It's heavy* [= the steam has
force], *and it presses on top.*—Why ?—*It is strong. . . .*—
And so ?—*It moves, and then . . . it goes quickly, so that
makes the thing go down"* [the piston].

MART (10 ; 11) : " *The steam flies away.*—And then ?—
It gives force.—Why ?—*By pushing against something."*
The steam has force " *because it makes air."* " When has
it got force ?—*Because it must have force, so as to push.
It must go at a pretty good rate."*

AUD (10) : The piston pushes the connecting-rods
" *because the steam has gone on top.*—Why ?—*All the
steam, when the boiler was full, it pressed on the top* [of the
piston].—Why ?—*Because it was heavier* [than the piston]
and that made it go down.—Why heavier ?—*Because that*
[connecting-rods] *was lighter than the steam.*—Why ?—
*Of course it must go down, because when it's quite full,
there's a good pressure.*—What does that mean ?—*That
means that it goes very quickly.*—Why ?—*Because the steam
goes quickly and it goes on top."*

The reader will note how strongly the explanation by
impetus persists, even in Aud, who has already begun to
introduce the volume of steam into his explanation.
Attention should also be paid to the part played by air
in Mart's explanation : the steam makes air, and this air
pushes the piston.

But the chief interest attaches to the notion of weight
held by Aud and Sant. Steam is " heavier " than the
connecting-rods and the piston, etc. Here, again, we have
an example of the dynamic sense given to the word
" heavy." This is strictly analogous to what we showed
in connection with the pebble that made the water rise
because it was heavy. Weight is pressure implying
impetus and movement.

In conclusion, this short enquiry into the explanations
of engines has taught us nothing new, but it has supplied
us with a certain amount of useful counter-evidence. On

the one hand, we can see quite clearly how these explanations evolve from a stage that is characterised by lack of interest in the " how " of things to stages marked by a growing understanding of the function of intermediaries. And on the other hand, we can see causality evolving from the idea of a sort of action at a distance to the idea of force-activity, and from this idea to more mechanical conceptions.

In addition, we have found numerous examples of the importance of the rôle assigned to air in child physics and of the supposed transmutation of substances : fire, smoke, water, etc., all change into air. A child of 8 spoke to us as follows : " What is steam made of ?—*Water.*—And smoke ?—*Of fire.*—And fire ?—*Of wood.*—Can the air make fire ?—*Yes.*—How ?—*Because when the fire is going out, you blow and then it kindles again.*"

In a word, the experiment with the engine, artificial though it is, has enabled us to observe once again the spontaneous mental tendencies of the child, tendencies which we had occasion to notice before in connection with the explanation of natural phenomena.

CHAPTER XI

TRAINS, MOTOR-CARS, AND AEROPLANES

THE results we have obtained so far will enable us to understand the explanations which children give of the movement of mechanical means of transport. These will not teach us much that is new, but it is worth while making a rapid survey of these explanations, as they correspond with a very active " centre of interest " in children.

One cannot fail to be struck by the spontaneous interest in vehicles evinced by the children of the *Maison des Petits de l'Institut, J.-J. Rousseau*, and manifesting itself anew each school year. Not only do these children make and draw boats, trains, motors, and aeroplanes in preference to all other objects, but they are constantly asking questions about the origin and manufacture of vehicles and about the details of their mechanism. But the curious thing is that, in asking these questions, the younger children, at any rate, show little concern as to the " how " of the mechanism, as though the cause of the movement were perfectly clear to them. It is only among the older children that questions of description, name, or origin tend to be replaced by those of a more definitely causal order. The reason for this evolution will strike the reader at once.

§ I. STEAM-ENGINES AND MOTOR-BOATS.—The explanations of all steam-engines naturally do not obey so simple a law of evolution as that which we found to be at work in the case of the toy engine in the last chapter. Roughly speaking, however, the schema of development is the same. During a first stage, the child takes some vaguely conceived force as being responsible for the movement of steam-engines or motor-boats and does not trouble to find the intermediaries between the origin of this force and the wheels : the fire, the smoke, etc., work directly upon the wheels and make them go round. During a second stage, the search for intermediaries sets in, and during a third stage, an explanation is found which is in the main correct.

Here are examples of the first stage :

CHA (3½) : " How does a train go ?—*With the wheels.*— What makes the wheels turn ?—*From the stuff* (Fr. fabrique).—What is the stuff ?—*Heat, smoke.*—Where does it come from, the heat that makes the wheels turn ?—*To the sky* [=from the sky ?].—Where does the heat of the engine come from ?—*In the tunnel, on the ground.*—Where does the heat of the tunnel come from ?—*It comes out of the funnel. It's heat, smoke.*—What makes the smoke ?— *The funnel. It comes out.*" " Where does this smoke come from ?—*To the sky. It goes through the holes in the station.*—Is there smoke in the sky ?—*Yes, over there* [points to a cloud].—What is it ?—*Heat.*—Are the clouds made of heat ?—*Yes, of smoke.*—Where do the clouds come from ?—*From the heat.*—Where does the smoke of the train come from ?—*It goes out of the funnel.*—Where does it come from ?—*In the tunnel, in the holes of the station.*—Where does it come from ?—*Right up high.*" It seems that Cha cannot distinguish the question " where does it come from " from the question " where is it going ". But whether he distinguishes or confuses them, it seems that, for him, there is a connection between the clouds and the smoke of the train. Thus the clouds would make the train move along as the train would make the clouds. Or, rather, it is smoke in general which makes the train move along, and this smoke comes at the same time from the train itself and from the clouds.—It goes without saying, that the interpretation which we give of the case of Cha is hypothetical, having regard to the extremely equivocal language of children of 3 years old. If we include it, it is above all, for comparison with the cases of Blan and Deb (Chap. X, § 1) and with the following case of Dan.

Dan, a child of 14 years of age, told us that he remembered very clearly that he used to think that it was the smoke which made the engine move along, but in the following manner : the smoke, when coming out of the funnel, was pushed by the wind, and it was the movement of the wind which pulled the engine along. The analogy with the case of Cha is clear.

AL (4) : " What makes the engine go ?—*The smoke.*— What smoke ?—*The smoke from the funnel.*

BI (6½) : " *It's when you put coal inside* [the engine]. *The smoke makes the coal light. The coal has force. So that makes the engine move along.*"

BEN (7) : The smoke " *gives a current.*—What is the current ?—*It's what makes everything go.*—How does it make things go ?—*It's steam, smoke, then it's hot.*"

At other times, it is the fire that acts as motive power.

LÉO (7) : " *It goes with the fire. The fire makes the wheels go, by heating.*" Léo draws us an engine, quite empty, in which the fire can be seen to be advancing towards the wheels without any intermediary. Léo adds : " *The fire heats it inside and that makes the wheels turn.*"

MA (7) : " *The coal burns and that makes the train go. It's the heat that makes the train go.*—What makes the wheels turn ?—*It's the train.*—And the train ?—*The heat pushes the train.*"

FONT (7) : " *The fire pushes the machine* [=the whole of the engine. Font does not imagine that there is anything inside].—What makes the wheels turn ?—*The machine.*—What makes the machine go ?—*The fire.*"

ZUM (8) : " *It's the fire that gives force to the wheels.*"

Finally, others assume that it is merely a crank or a " handle-bar " which makes the train go, thanks to the strength of the engine-driver :

DON (5½) : " *When you turn the thing* [a crank, which can be seen in Don's drawing], *it turns the wheels.*"

The first stage presents certain general features which confirm the conclusions we came to regarding the bicycle and the little engine. In the first place, there is an absence of any preoccupation as to " how " things happen. For these children there are no intermediaries between the fire or smoke and the wheels. There is nothing in the body of the engine. The connecting-rods do not serve as supports to the wheels. The fire acts through its own efficacy.

In the earlier cases, the engine seems to move, owing to a sort of wholesale or general movement which forces the wheels to go round, and not owing to the movement of the wheels themselves. According to Cha and Dan the smoke pushes the whole engine along. According to Font and Ma, the fire " pushes the train," but not the wheels, so that the train makes the wheels move along, and not the wheels the train ! This is the same schema as that observed in the case of the bicycle, where movement was explained by the youngest children by a general impetus and not by a detailed action exercised upon the wheels.

During a second stage, the child begins to look for intermediate links. The connecting-rods take on a necessary function. Here are some examples :

PETA (8) : " *There's a big fire. The fire makes a bit of iron go, that's sort of bent* [connecting-rods], *and that makes the wheels turn.*"

ASS (8) : " *Round the wheels there's a big bit of iron that makes, and the wheels go with it.*—What makes the bit of iron go ?—*A little wheel inside.*—And the little wheel ?—*The steam*" [by blowing on it].

Finally, the third marks the appearance of the complete explanation (between 10 and 11 years) :

BLAN (12 ; 1) : " How does an engine go ?—*With steam. That makes the wheels turn. There's a piston which has two little holes. The steam comes out under pressure, it presses on the piston, that makes the wheels turn.*—How does it press on the piston ?—*Because it has a lot of force.* —How ?—*Because the piston is free. There must be pipes that are arranged. There must be a lot of it* [of steam] *so that there is more pressure.*—Why ?—*The more there is, the faster it can escape.*"

As for steamships, the explanations naturally pass through the same stages. It is unnecessary to enumerate them again. Let us merely take note of an interesting fact which can be fairly frequently observed : it is that, for certain children, the boat is pushed by the waves that it produces itself. This is a new form of explanation by the "reaction of the surrounding medium":

DEBR (8) : The boat "*makes waves. That makes the boat go.*"

TAI (7) also says that the boats go "*with the waves*," and later states precisely that the waves are made by the boat.

It can be seen how varied in its application is the schema of the reaction of the surrounding medium, which we have already come up against so often.

§ 2. MOTOR-CARS AND AEROPLANES.—The explanations relating to motor-cars yielded results fairly similar to the preceding. Three stages can be distinguished. Here are examples of the first :

DON (5½) : "How does a motor go ?—*When you turn the steering-wheel.*" We can obtain no more from him.

DUC (7) : "*You turn a crank and that makes it go.*" No special force intervenes.

There is here no thought as to "why." The first explanatory example appeals, curiously enough, to the air :

PÉC (7) tells us that motors have a current : "Where does this current come from ?—*From the engine.*—And that of the engine ?—*From the air.*—Does one put air into the engine ?—*No.*—Then where is the air ?—*The air that makes the motor.*"

BER (9) : "*It makes a wind and it goes.*—How ? Where does this wind blow ?—*In the engine, then it goes into the wheels and makes them turn.*"

DEBR (8) appeals to the petrol. "How does the petrol make the wheels turn ?—*Because the petrol does like the strong wind does, then it turns.*"

But, generally, the petrol is appealed to merely as a "force", which has no need of contact in order to act :

DEC (6½) : "*You put petrol in the motor. Petrol gives force.*—What is force ?—*It means that it goes well.*—Have we got force ?—*Yes. Got to eat lots of soup.*"

Thus all children dissociate themselves completely from questions of contacts and intermediaries. The second stage marks, on the contrary, the appearance of a need for spatial explanation (about 9–11 years) :

BLAN (12 ; 1) : " How does a motor go ?—*With an engine.*—What is it ?—*There is a boiler, a valve, two cylinders, some pipes.*—How does the engine make the wheels go ?—*You put some petrol.*—What is that for ?— *To make the engine go.*—How ?—*It makes a wheel turn, and the wheel makes a belt go. There is a cog-wheel that makes the two back wheels go.*—How does the petrol make this wheel go ?—*Perhaps it's the force that makes it turn.*— What is it ?—*Enough pressure to make it turn.*—What is pressure ?—*It is something strong. It pushes. It makes things turn.*—Has petrol got pressure ?—*It must have, since you put it in the engine.*"

The explanation is crude, but after the age of 7–8 one can observe the formation of these spatial series which connect the petrol with the wheels of the motor-car.

The third stage is marked by the appearance of correct explanations, but as they are all directly inspired by adults, they need not be mentioned here.

In the case of aeroplanes the ideas about the engine are naturally the same, but they are supplemented during the first two stages by an interesting phenomenon. This is once again the " all round " or synthetic explanation by reaction of the surrounding medium, that is to say, by the air which is (quite literally) produced by the propeller as it turns :

REYB (9 ; 1) : The propeller " *turns so hard, it makes it move along.*" In empty space, says Reyb, " *it would go quicker.*—Why ?—*Because it wouldn't be stopped.*—Why ? —*When there's wind, it stops it.*" In other words, the aeroplane is pushed by the air that it produces itself, but stopped by the wind or the air of the atmosphere.

KENN (7½) tells us, that in a room without air, the aeroplane would fly " *the same way.*" The propeller " *makes a wind.*—If there were no air in the room, would the propeller make a wind ?—*Yes.*"

CHAL (9) : " *The propeller turns fast. That makes a wind, and that makes the aeroplane go up in the air.*" In space it's the same, because the propeller " *as it turns and turns, makes air.*"

The first chapter supplied us with a sufficient number of cases where the children believed that in a closed and even airless room air can be produced by moving the hands. We need not dwell on the point any longer. The explanation is perfectly clear : the propeller makes wind by turning round, and this wind is what pushes the aeroplane along.

During the third stage, on the other hand, the child sees that for the aeroplane to move forward it must have a supporting medium, and that that medium is the air.

DEN (7, advanced) : " *An engine makes the propeller go. The aeroplane is like the sea-gulls, like the swans, which divide the water* [motion of swimming]. *The aeroplane is the contrary, it drives the air away.*—And if there were no air ?—*It couldn't go.*—Why not ?—*Because in doing this movement* [gesture] *it wouldn't drive the air away and couldn't move along."*

§ 3. CONCLUSIONS.—We have sounded as briefly as possible the child's mind at work on the subject of machines. The question now confronts us as to the relations existing between children's explanations of movements in nature and their explanations of mechanical processes. Does progress in the former involve progress in the latter, or vice versa ?

At a first glance, the child's ideas about machines seem singularly poor and rudimentary. But we ourselves, unless we are engineers or possess a car and garage, understand very little of the subject. We know that petrol and steam are necessary. We know that they can do nothing without intermediaries, such as pistons, cog-wheels, chains, connecting-rods, and so on. We know the part played by these intermediaries, but cannot account for their action in detail. And this much, if one comes to think of it, is precisely what the child of 8, or thereabouts, is beginning to discover.

With regard to bicycles, there can be no room for doubt. After the age of about 7, the connection between the parts is sought-for, and after 8, the correct explanation is found, to the extent even of doing a very accurate drawing from memory. Thus, although in their views about the origin of things these children are still entirely mythological, although they are still animistic, and explain the movement of bodies by means of conscious and internal forces, on the subject of a bicycle, they can attain to the conscious grasp of a purely mechanical explanation.

In the case of steam-engines there is naturally a certain shifting of the mental level. But after 6 or 8 years, the search for contacts supplies the initial data for the correct explanation, which begins to appear from about 8–9. The need for contacts is at any rate quite definitely felt with regard to machines from about the age of 7–8.

Now, it is precisely after 7–8 that *mythological artificialism* begins to decrease and make way for *technical artificialism* (see *C.W.*, Chap. XI). This is the period when the purely moral and pre-causal explanation of natural movements makes way for a physical explanation, the latter being marked at about the age of 10 with genuinely mechanical tendencies. There would therefore seem to be a synchronism at about the age of 7–8 between the appearance of correct explanations of machines and a general change of mentality concerning nature, and it would seem that progress made in the sphere of machines preceded progress in explanations of natural events. Can we then say that the first form of progress is the cause of the second ?

One factor in favour of this hypothesis is the obvious disproportion between the interest which boys take in nature and that which they take in machines. The latter, as we reminded the reader at the opening of this chapter, is quite remarkable. Interest in nature certainly exists, but it is far less active. In their conversations, children are almost silent about nature, but they are full of remarks about machines. It may be objected that with girls the opposite is the case. But at about 4–5 years, little girls like observing and occupying themselves with machines as much as boys do. Moreover, at the age when girls become definitely different from boys, they are behind-hand as compared to boys, both in the domain of the explanations of nature and in the technical world.

The strongest argument in our favour, however, seems to us to be the existence of child artificialism. Since in the eyes of the youngest children everything in nature is manufactured, it is highly probable that progress in the knowledge of human technique will lead the child to correct his view of nature himself. Mere observation of nature is far too strongly coloured with pre-relations to account for the decline in artificialism. It is in making things and in seeing them made that the child will learn the resistance of external objects and the necessity of mechanical pro-cesses. Thus the understanding of machines would seem to be the factor which brought about the mechanisation of natural causality and the decline of artificialism in the child.

We have hardly any definite facts to quote in support of this hypothesis, unless it be the personal recollections of one of our number, recollections which show to what extent the interest in machines precedes and directs the interest in nature. At an age which through various coincidences he can place at exactly between 8 and 9, one of us remembers having played a great deal with machines. He actually invented a new means of loco-motion, which he christened the " auto-steam " (Fr. *autovap*), and which consisted in applying to motor-cars the principle of the steam-engine—boiler, piston, con-necting -rods. The inventor of the autovap even published his discovery in an illustrated work, which, incidentally, was written in pencil. Thus machines constituted for this child his first systematic and lasting centre of interest. He liked at this period of his life to collect catalogues of motor-cars, etc., and he dreamt of nothing but factories and machines. He was conscious, however, of a certain clumsiness, and this, together with the numerous failures which attended his attempts at mechanical construction, gradually discouraged this budding vocation, so that from the age of 9–10 onwards he took up geology and zoology. He can remember very well the effort which he made at this time to understand the natural formation of mountains and the distribution of fossils of sea origin : it was after a walk, during which someone had pointed out to him some nerinea in the limestone. His naturalist's mentality had been fashioned by his games with machines, which had developed in him the desire to understand by means of mechanical schemas, and this desire, though diverted from its original object, had remained identical throughout the child's subsequent hobbies.

We may, therefore, venture to conjecture that without the spectacle of modern civilisation the children we examined would have stayed much longer in the primitive mythological stages. The modern child moves in an atmosphere of mechanism and scientific explanation. It is not that adults bring any pressure to bear upon the children's minds, but simply that nowadays to walk down a street imposes a whole conception of the world.

It would be highly desirable in this connection to resume some of our enquiries in a remote country district. Two main points would have to be submitted to control. First, one would have to see whether, as we have maintained (*C.W.*, Chap. VIII), artificialism would really be the same, if not in its actual contents (since each child makes his own immediate observation) at least in its orientation. Secondly, one would have to see whether, as we have just been suggesting, the primitive conceptions of movements in nature were more persistent, owing to the absence of mechanical education.

THE CHILD'S CONCEPTION OF REALITY AND CAUSALITY

SUMMARY AND CONCLUSION

WE propose in this final section.[1] to enquire into the relations existing between the mind of the child and the external world. This should lead us into the very heart of the Problem of Knowledge. But we intend to approach the matter from an angle, and to formulate the problem so as to keep within the bounds of Psychology and not encroach upon the domain of Epistemology.

If we examine the intellectual development of the individual or of the whole of humanity, we shall find that the human spirit goes through a certain number of stages, each different from the other, but such that during each, the mind believes itself to be apprehending an external reality that is independent of the thinking subject. The content of this reality varies according to the stages : for the young child it is alive and permeated with finality, intentions, etc., whereas for the scientist, reality is characterised by its physical determinism. But the ontological function, so to speak, remains identical : each in his own way thinks that he has found the outer world in himself.

This being so, two points of view are possible in the study of intellectual evolution.

The first of these is to choose a system of reference and agree to call " external reality ", reality such as it is conceived to be during one of the stages of mental

---

[1] We shall summarise in this section the conclusions reached in the present volume and in our last book *The Child's Conception of the World*.

evolution. Thus it would be agreed upon to regard as the external world reality as it is postulated by contemporary science, or contemporary common-sense. From this point of view, the relations of child thought to the external world would, in fact, be its relations to the universe of our existing scientific thought taken as the norm. In each explanation given by a child it would be possible to determine the part played by the activity of the subject and the part played by the pressure of objects, the latter being, by definition, objects as we now conceive them to be. And this would be Psychology, for the statements which this method led to would not claim to have any decisive bearing upon the Critical Problem in general.

Or else, the attempt to regard any system of reference as absolute can be abandoned. Contemporary common-sense or even contemporary science may be regarded as stages among other stages, and the question as to the true nature of external reality left open. And this would be Theory of Knowledge : this would be to place oneself above all the types of mentality that characterise the various stages of human development, and to seek to define the relations of the mind to reality without any preconceived notions as to what is mind and what is reality.

For our part, we shall confine ourselves to psychology, to the search, that is, for the relations between child thought and reality as the scientific thought of our time conceives it. And this point of view, narrow and question-begging though it appear, will enable us to formulate very clearly several outstanding problems. Does the external world (and by this we shall in future mean the world as it is viewed by science) impress itself directly on the child's mind, or are childish ideas the product of the subject's own mentality ? If the child's mind is active in the process of knowing, how is the collaboration effected between his thought and the data of the external world ? What are the laws which this collaboration will obey? All these are the traditional problems of the Theory of Knowledge, which we shall be able to transpose into the particular sphere which we have just defined.

More exactly, the problems we are about to study are biological problems. Reality, such as our science imagines and postulates, is what the biologists call Environment. The child's intelligence and activity, on the other hand, are the fruit of organic life (interest, movement, imitation, assimilation). The problem of the relation between thought and things, once it has been narrowed down in this way, becomes the problem of the relation of an organism to its environment. Is the organism entirely moulded by its environment in so far as intelligence is concerned? If so, then we have, in terms of cognition, what may be called the empirical solution of the problem. Or does the organism assimilate the actions to its environment in accordance with a structure that is independent of these actions and that resists the pressure of all modifications coming from outside? If so, then we have in terms of cognition what may be called the a priori solution. Or is it not rather the case that there is interaction between the two—organism assimilating the environment to itself, but the environment reacting upon the structure of the organism? Such is the solution which, in the domain of cognition, would imply a capacity for transformation in the categories of thought and an increasingly delicate adaptation of thought to things or of things to thought.

These, then, are the terms in which we set the problem. And if, in describing the results we have obtained in child psychology, we occasionally use words like empiricism, apriorism, etc., it must be remembered that we are not giving to these terms their strictly epistemological meaning, but are using them in a restricted and, as it were, in a purely psychological sense.

But, be it said in passing, it might perhaps be possible to make use in the Theory of Knowledge of the results acquired by our restricted method. Let us suppose, for the sake of brevity, that intellectual growth takes place along a straight line, in a linear series such that the stages A, B, C, . . . N follow one another without either interferences or changes from one level to another. We shall take the external world corresponding to stage G as absolute, and compare to it the external world corresponding to stages C, D, E, . . . etc. Such a comparison is without any epistemological bearing, since there is nothing to prove that G is decisive. But if, now, we take into account this very possibility of variation and regard the series C, D, E . . . G as capable of being extended, on the one hand, backwards, by the supposition of stages A and B, and, on the other hand, forwards, thanks to the future stages H, I, K . . . N, we shall discover the following : there will obviously exist a relation between the comparison of C, D, E to G and the comparison of G to H, I, etc. ; and the fragmentary conclusions obtained by the comparison of C, D, E to G will become a particular case of the general conclusions obtained by comparison of all possible stages.

To put things more concretely, it may very well be that the psychological laws arrived at by means of our restricted method can be extended into epistemological laws arrived at by the analysis of the history of the sciences : the elimination of realism, of substantialism, of dynamism, the growth of relativism, etc., all these are evolutionary laws which appear to be common both to the development of the child and to that of scientific thought.

We are in no way suggesting, it need hardly be said, that our psychological results will admit straight away of being generalised into epistemological laws. All we expect is that with the co-operation of methods more powerful than our own (historical, sociological methods, etc.), it will be possible to establish between our conclusions and those of epistemological analysis a relation of particular case to general law, or rather of infinitesimal variation to the whole of a curve.[1]

[1] The reader who wishes to pursue this subject further may be referred to a critical study which appeared under the heading " L'ex-

§ 1. THE CHILD'S REALITY.—How does the idea of reality constitute itself in the child's mind ? Any direct analysis of its origin is beyond our power ; the earliest stages precede language or are contemporaneous with the first spoken words, and any effort to reach the child's consciousness during these stages is fruitless, if one claims to go beyond mere hypothesis. But if we can content ourselves with conjecture, then it is best to try and extricate the laws according to which the idea of reality develops between the ages of 3 and 11, and to extrapolate the guiding lines thus obtained so as to reconstruct the earliest stages. Moreover, as soon as we put this method into practice, we find that we can learn enough from the laws of evolution between 3 and 11 years, and that there is no need to attach any special importance to the original stage.

Three complementary processes seem to be at work in directing the evolution of reality as it is conceived by the child between the ages of 3 and 11. Child thought moves simultaneously : 1° *from realism to objectivity*, 2° *from realism to reciprocity*, and 3° *from realism to relativity*. By *objectivity* we mean the mental attitude of persons who are able to distinguish what comes from themselves and what forms part of external reality as it can be observed by everybody. We say that there is *reciprocity* when the same value is attributed to the point of view of other people as to one's own, and when the correspondence can be found between these two points of view. We say that there is *relativity* when no object and no quality or character is posited in the subject's mind with the claim to being an independent substance or attribute.

Let us examine these processes more closely. In order to be objective, one must have become conscious of one's " I ". Objective knowledge can only be conceived in relation to subjective, and a mind that was ignorant

périence humaine et la Causalité physique de L. Brunschvicg, *Journ. de Psychol.*, Vol. XXI (1924), p 586.

of itself would inevitably tend to put into things its own pre-notions and prejudices, whether in the domain of reasoning, of immediate judgment, or even of perception. An objective intelligence in no way escapes from this law, but, being conscious of its own " I ", it will be on its guard, it will be able to hold back and criticise, in short it will be able to say what, roughly, is fact and what is interpretation.

So that in stating that the child proceeds from realism to objectivity, all we are saying is that originally the child puts the whole content of consciousness on the same plane and draws no distinction between the " I " and the external world. Above all we mean that the constitution of the idea of reality presupposes a progressive splitting-up of this protoplasmic consciousness into two complementary universes—the objective universe and the subjective.

We have met with many examples of this realism of the first kind and of its progressive reduction. Children's ideas about thought may be taken as a first illustration of the phenomenon in question. The feeling of subjectivity and inwardness felt by the adult is, to a great extent, connected with the conviction of being the owner of a thought that is distinct from the things thought about, distinct from the physical world in general, and more internal and intimate than the body itself. This conviction only comes late in the child's development. During the earliest stages, the child believes that he thinks with his mouth, that thought consists in articulating words, and that these words themselves form part of the external things. The voice, being thus identified with thought itself, is regarded as a breath which participates with the surrounding air, and some children go so far as to say that it is identical with the wind in the trees, and that dreams are made of " wind ". They are quite incapable of distinguishing between thought and the things thought about. To use the expression chosen by M. H. Delacroix. the sign " adheres " to the thing signified.

Later on, the child gives up this realism and localises thought inside his mouth, then in a little voice placed in the head ; he then gives up materialising thought and makes of it something *sui generis* which characterises the self as spirit (*C.W.*, Chap. I).

The evolution of ideas about names is particularly suggestive from this same point of view. Word and name are about all that the child knows of thought, since he identifies thought with the voice. Now, names are, to begin with, situated in objects. They form part of things in the same way as do colour or form. Things have always had their names. It has always been sufficient to look at things in order to know their names. In some cases, this realism actually turns to magic : to deform the name is to deform the thing. Later on, names are situated in the adjoining air where the voice has uttered them, then in the voice, and finally in thought itself.

Dreams give rise to an equally definite realism. At first, they are thought to be pictures of air or light which come before our eyes from outside. At the earliest stage, the child thinks, naturally enough, that anyone could see the dream come into the room and go out again. Later on, the dream is believed to have an internal origin, but is conceived as coming out of the head or the stomach before appearing before the child. Finally, the child learns to distinguish between " being " and " seeming ", and localises the dream, first in the eyes, then in the head.

All these facts show that the localisation of the objects of thought is not inborn. It is through a progressive differentiation that the internal world comes into being and is contrasted with the external. Neither of these two terms is given at the start. The initial realism is not due simply to ignorance of the internal world, it is due to confusion and absence of objectivity.

Consequently, during the gradual and slow differentiation of the initial protoplasmic reality into objective and subjective reality, it is clear that each of the two terms in process of differentiation will evolve in accordance with its own structure. In the case of every object there will be a displacement of values which will modify the character of the object. Take, for example, the notion of "air", or of "wind". During the earliest stages, air is conceived as participating with thought : the voice is air, and, in return, the wind takes notice of us, obeys us, is "good at making us grow", comes when we move our hands, and so on. When thought proper is localised in the self, and the participations between air and thought are broken, the nature of air changes by virtue of this fact alone. Air becomes independent of men, sufficient to itself, and living its own life. But owing to the fact that it is held to participate with the self, it retains at the very moment when it is severing these bonds, a certain number of purely human aspects : it still has consciousness, of a different kind perhaps than formerly, but its own nevertheless. Only very gradually will it be reduced to a mere thing.

This phenomenon is very general. During the early stages the world and the self are one; neither term is distinguished from the other. But when they become distinct, these two terms begin by remaining very close to each other : the world is still conscious and full of intentions, the self is still material, so to speak, and only slightly interiorised. At each step in the process of dissociation these two terms evolve in the sense of the greatest divergence, but they are never in the child (nor in the adult for that matter) entirely separate. From our present point of view, therefore, there is never complete objectivity : at every stage there remain in the conception of nature what we might call "adherences", fragments of internal experience which still cling to the external world.

We have distinguished at least five varieties of adherences defined in this way. There are, to begin with, during a very early stage, feelings of participation accompanied sometimes by magical beliefs ; the sun and moon follow us, and if we walk, it is enough to make them move along ; things around us notice us and obey us, like the wind, the clouds, the night, etc. ; the moon, the street lamps, etc., send us dreams " to annoy us ", etc., etc. In short, the world is filled with tendencies and intentions which are in participation with our own. This is what we have called dynamic participation, in contrast to substantial participation, to which, however, it may lead.

A second form of adherence, closely allied to the preceding, is that constituted by animism, which makes the child endow things with consciousness and life.

A third form is artificialism (see *C.W.*, Sect. III). The reader should be reminded at this point that artificialism in the child is not a theory which after reflection systematically takes man as the point of departure for everything. The terms must be reversed, and that is why artificialism has the same right to be classed among the adherences as animism. The child begins by thinking of things in terms of his own " I " : the things around him take notice of man and are made for man ; everything about them is willed and intentional, everything is organised for the good of men. If we ask the child, or if the child asks himself how things began, he has recourse to man to explain them. Thus artificialism is based on feelings of participation which constitute a very special and very important class of adherences in the sense that we have defined.

A fourth form is finalism : the starting-point and then the residuum both of animism and of artificialism, the deep and stubborn finalism of the child shows with what difficulty external reality frees itself from schemas due to internal and psychical experience.

A fifth form of adherence is constituted by the notion of force : things make efforts, and their powers imply an internal and substantial energy analogous to our own muscular force.

It is a striking fact that both the area of application and the strength of resistance of these adherences decrease progressively throughout the mental development of the child. And not only do these adherences lose ground little by little in correlation with each other, but their progressive disappearance seems to be proportional to the increasing clarity with which the child becomes conscious of his subjectivity. In other words, the better the child succeeds in dividing off the internal world from the external, the less stubborn are the adherences.

Three groups of facts may be mentioned in this connection. In the first place, as the child comes to notice the existence and the mechanism of his own thought, he separates signs from the things signified : thus, names cease to belong to the things named, thought is interiorised and ceases to participate with wind, dreams are no longer regarded as emanations of objects, and so on. Thus participations are loosened little by little, and even eliminated.

In the second place, in so far as the child discovers the existence and inwardness of his thought, animism, far from being strengthened is, through this alone, compromised and even completely destroyed. The decline of animism brings with it a progressive reduction of child dynamism. For so long as things seem to be alive and consequently active, the forces of nature are multiplied by the child ; and the elimination of life leads to a mechanisation of force which means ultimately an impoverishment of the actual notion of force. This very general process of evolution which leads the child from a dynamic to a mechanical view has been dealt with at sufficient length in connection with the details of children's explanations to render any further comment necessary.

Finally, as the child becomes conscious of his subjectivity, he rids himself of his egocentricity. For, after all, it is in so far as we fail to realise the personal nature of our own point of view that we regard this point of view as absolute and shared by all. Whereas, in so far as we discover this purely individual character, we learn to distinguish our own from the objective point of view.

Egocentricity, in a word, diminishes as we become conscious of our subjectivity. Now the decrease of egocentricity means the decrease of anthropomorphic finalism, and consequently the decrease of all the feelings of participation that are at the bottom of artificialism.

Progressive separation of the outer from the inner world, and progressive reduction of the adherences, such, in brief, are the two fundamental aspects of the first process which we defined as a passage from realism to objectivity. What we have just said about the relations between egocentricity and artificialism takes us on to the analysis of the second process, for it goes without saying that all these processes are closely related to each other, so much so, indeed, that they may be said to be completely indissociable.

The second characteristic process in the evolution of the idea of reality is the passage *from realism to reciprocity*. This formula means that the child, after having regarded his own point of view as absolute, comes to discover the possibility of other points of view and to conceive of reality as constituted, no longer by what is immediately given, but by what is common to all points of view taken together.

One of the first aspects of this process is the passage from realism of perception to interpretation properly so called. All the younger children take their immediate perceptions as true, and then proceed to interpret them according to their egocentric pre-relations, instead of making allowance for their own perspective. The most striking example we have found is that of the clouds and the heavenly bodies, of which children believe that they follow us. The sun and moon are small globes travelling a little way above the level of the roofs of houses and following us about on our walks. Even the child of 6–8 years does not hesitate to take this perception as the expression of truth, and, curiously enough, he never thinks of asking himself whether these heavenly bodies do not also follow other people. When we ask the captious question as to which of two people walking in opposite directions the sun would prefer to follow, the child is taken aback and shows how new the question is to him. Children of 9–10 years, on the other hand, have discovered that the sun follows everybody. From this they conclude that the truth lies in the reciprocity of the points of view : that the sun is very high up, that it follows no one, and that each sees it as just above him.

What we said just now about dreams is also to a certain extent germane to the present process : the child begins by regarding his own dreams as true, without asking himself whether every one dreams the same as he does.

Side by side with this realism of perception and images, there is a logical realism which is far more important. We met with numerous examples of it in the course of our studies on child logic. Before the age of 10, on the average, the child does not know that he is a brother in relation to his own brothers. The ideas of right and left, of dark and fair, of the points of the compass, etc., are all subject to the law which is occupying us at the moment. These conceptions are at first regarded as absolute, so long as the personal point of view is accepted as the only possible one ; after that, the reciprocity of relations gradually begins to make itself felt (*J.R.*, Chaps. II and III). In the present volume (as also in *C.W.*) we have pointed to several fresh examples of this process, examples which were of importance in forming the structure of reality.

Such are, above all, the ideas of weight and density. During the earliest stages, an object is heavy or light according to the immediate judgment implied by the child's own point of view : a pebble is light, a boat is heavy. Later on, other points of view are taken into account, and the child will say, for example, that such and such a pebble is light for him but heavy for the water, and that a boat may be light for the lake while it remains heavy for the child.

These last examples bring us to the third process

which marks the evolution of the child's idea of reality : thought evolves *from realism to relativity*. This process is closely related to the last, and yet differentiates itself from it on certain points. During the early stage, the child tends to think of everything under the form of absolute substance and quality ; after that, bodies and their qualities seem to him more and more dependent upon each other and relative to us. Thus, substances become relations, on the one hand, because the mutual connection of phenomena has been seen, and on the other, because the relativity of our evaluations has been discovered. It would perhaps be as well to distinguish between these two aspects of " relativity ", but the second is, as a matter of fact, nothing but a combination of the first with the " reciprocity " of which we spoke just now. It will therefore be enough to point to this connection without complicating our classification.

The most striking example of this process is undoubtedly the evolution of the conceptions about life and movement. During the early stages, every movement is regarded as singular, as the manifestation, that is, of a substantial and living activity. In other words, there is in every moving object a motor substance : the clouds, the heavenly bodies, water, and machines, etc., move by themselves. Even when the child succeeds in conceiving an external motor, which already takes away from the substantiality of movement, the internal motor continues to be regarded as necessary. Thus a leaf is alive, even though it moves with the wind, *i.e.* it retains its spontaneity even though the wind is needed to set it in motion. Similarly, a cloud or one of the heavenly bodies remains master of its movements, even though the wind is necessary to start it on its path. But later on, the movement of every body becomes the function of external movements, which are regarded no longer as necessary collaborators but as sufficient conditions. Thus the movement of clouds comes to be entirely explained by that of the wind. Then these external motors are conceived as themselves dependent upon other external motors, and so on. In this way there comes into being a universe of relations which takes the place of a universe of independent and spontaneous substances.

Closely analogous to this is the evolution of the idea of force, since it is, as we saw, intimately connected with the idea of life.

The idea of weight supplies us with an excellent example of this advance towards relativity, and the evolution in this particular case is closely bound up with the advance towards reciprocity which we spoke of just now. During the earliest stages, weight is synonymous with strength and activity. A pebble sunk in water weighs on the water, even when the latter is motionless, and produces a current towards the surface. An object floats because, being heavy, it has the strength to keep itself up. Weight is an absolute thing : it is a quality possessed by certain bodies, a variant of that life, or substantial force which we have described. Later on, weight is regarded as relative to the surrounding medium : bodies float because they are lighter than water, the clouds, because they are lighter than air, etc. But the relation is still vague : the child simply means that for the water in the lake, such and such a boat is light, but no comparison has been made which introduces proportional volumes. The wood of the boat is regarded as heavier than an equal volume of water. Finally, between the years of 9 and 10, " lighter than the water " begins to mean that the body in question is, taken at equal volume, lighter than water. Thus do the ideas of density and specific weight make their appearance : absolute weight is succeeded, in part at any rate, by relative weight.

The explanation of shadows and of night also offers an example of the progression from substantialism to an explanation founded on relations. During the earliest stages, night and shade are substances that emanate from clouds and bodies in general, and which come and go more or less intentionally. In the later stages, night and shade are nothing but the effects conditioned by the spatial relations which regulate the diffusion of light.

In every domain the substantialist realism of perception is succeeded by explanation through geometrical and cinematic relations. Running parallel with this growing relativity of phenomena in relation to each other, can be seen a growing relativity of ideas and notions in relation to ourselves and our evaluations. Thus the establishment of relativity between phenomena leads to a relativity between the measurer and what is measured. The evolution of the notion of weight brings out very clearly this double development. On the one hand, as we have just seen, the weight of the body becomes relative to the medium constituted by the other bodies, and presupposes the establishment of a relation between weight and volume. On the other hand, the words " light " and " heavy " lose the absolute meaning they had during the earliest stages, and acquire a meaning that is relative to the units of measurement that have been chosen : the pebble is heavy for the water, light for us, etc. The absolute concept has become a relation. In such cases, the advance towards relativity ends by converging absolutely with the advance towards reciprocity of view-points ; in other words, the second and third processes as we distinguished them, finally merge into one.

Such, then, is the evolution of the notion of reality in the child. Three processes help to make it emerge from its initial realism and to orientate it towards objectivity. In what relation do these three processes stand to one another ? The first is of a purely social nature : the child replaces his own individual and egocentric point of view by the point of view of others and the reciprocity existing between them. The second of these three processes is of a purely intellectual order : substantialism of perception is replaced by the relativism of intelligence. The third process is both social and intellectual in character : in becoming conscious of his " I ", the child clears external reality of all its subjective elements, and thus attains to objectivity; but it is, above all, social life that has forced the child to become conscious of his " ego ". Are we then to conclude that social factors determine the progress in the understanding of reality, or does this progress itself explain the development of social life ? Let us note, in the first place, that the three processes synchronise. All three begin very early, all three are very slow, they remain uncompleted at the close of childhood and survive throughout the intellectual development of the adult. There is therefore every reason to believe that they are interdependent.

As a matter of fact, we have here, as in the case of child logic, to suppose that social life is necessary to ra⁺ional development, but that it is not sufficient to create the power of reasoning. Without collaboration between his own thought and that of others, the child would not become conscious of the divergences which separate his ego from that of others, and he would take each of his perceptions or conceptions as absolute. He would therefore never attain to objectivity, for lack of having ever discovered his own subjectivity. Without social life, he would never succeed in understanding the reciprocity of view-points, and, consequently, the existence of perspectives, whether geometrical or logical. He would never cease to believe that the sun follows him on his walks. He would be ignorant of the reciprocity of the notions of right and left, of dependence, in short, of relations in general. It is therefore highly probable that the relativity of ideas would elude him. This, at least, is what we endeavoured to show in an earlier volume (*J.R.*, Chaps. II and III).

But at the same time, it would seem that reason, while it presupposes a social environment in which to develop, at one point transcends it. Once it has liberated the appearance of the logical norms in the child, the social environment enables him to become " permeable " to experience. And when this faculty has been acquired, the collaboration of logical reason and experience itself suffices to account for the intellectual development that takes place.

With this last remark we are led to analyse the evolution of the idea of reality from the point of view of the influence of environment on intelligence. Here, we are at once confronted with a paradoxical fact : compared with ourselves, the child is both closer to immediate observation and further removed from reality. For, on the one hand, he is often content to adopt in his mind the crude forms of actuality as they are presented in observation : one boat will float because it is light, another, because it is heavy, etc. Logical coherence is entirely sacrificed in such cases to fidelity to fact. The causality which results from phenomenism of this kind is not unlike that which is to be found in primitive races and has been wittily compared by M. Brunschvicg to causality as it was understood by Hume. Anything can produce anything : so long as two facts are given together in raw observation, the one may be considered the cause of the other. We shall give this the name of *phenomenistic causality*. It is the starting-point of a large number of childish notions. The moon that follows us, the clouds that go with the rain, the heaviness or lightness of floating bodies—all these are phenomenistic associations at the start, which later on lead the child to say : the moon moves along because I do, the clouds are the cause of rain, floating is determined either by heaviness or by lightness, etc. When the child is presented with a new and unknown fact, such as a toy engine, this phenomenistic turn of mind comes out very clearly : the child makes associations at random, connecting any one thing with another, and immediately takes these associations as causal.

But, in another sense, the child is far farther away from reality in his thought than we are. Reality, for him, is still overgrown with subjective adherences : it is alive and artificial ; words, dreams, and thought reside in external objects : the world is filled with forces.

Phenomenistic relations themselves take place against a background of dynamism, either magical or animistic. Thus the fact that the moon follows us is immediately interpreted by means of pre-relations, one of which makes the child think that he has power over the moon, the other that the moon is interested in him.

This paradoxical dualism of pure phenomenism on the one hand, and of magical dynamism, animistic or artificial-ist on the other, is a new manifestation of that dualism of juxtaposition and syncretism which we examined in our earlier volumes (*L.T.*, Chap. IV, and *J.R.*, Chap. I). Child thought proceeds by juxtaposition of its elements. There is a synthesis, but the terms juxtaposed in this way are embodied in subjective schemas, syncretism consisting in connecting everything with everything else in accordance with the hazards of a mental orientation that is subjective and egocentric.

The counterpart of this paradoxical dualism of pheno-menism and egocentricity is the following : as it develops, the idea of reality tends to become both desubstantialised and desubjectified. Reality, as the child conceives it, is desubjectified with the years, in the sense that the adherences of animism, of artificialism, and of dynamism are progressively eliminated. But at the same time, reality becomes desubstantialised, in the sense that a universe of relations gradually takes the place of the universe of absolute substances which were assumed by primitive perception. Movement, weight, shadow, and night, force, etc., are all of them notions whose evolution is characteristic in this respect.

In short, from the point of view of the action of the physical environment upon the child, we are faced with a continual paradox : the child is both nearer to and farther from the world of objects than we are, and in evolving an adult mentality he both advances towards reality and recedes from it.

If by empiricism we mean the doctrine according to which intelligence is entirely moulded by its environment, then we must admit that empiricism fails to explain the paradox we have spoken of, and for two reasons. In the first place, the empirical hypothesis is in conflict with the circumstance that the more primitive childish intelligence is, the farther it is removed from what we call reality : the initial confusion between the ego and the external world, the existence of lasting subjective adherences, are sufficient to show that the physical environment does not imprint itself as such upon the mind of the child, but that it is assimilated by means of schemas that are drawn from internal experience. According to the opposite thesis, the most primitive thought would have, on the contrary, to be that which was nearest to external objects : pure phenomenism would have to exist to the exclusion of any adherence of internal origin. It may be objected that these adherences can be explained by the empirical hypothesis, in the sense that the mind first discovers its own internal sensations, and then having associated them together (in the phenomenist manner) proceeds to project the result of those associations into the external world. This projection would seem to account for the paradox mentioned above, but the question remains as to whether the child really discovers his own mind in the same way as he explores by pure phenomenism a new object presented from the external world. Now, obviously, the child does nothing of the kind. For, while the external world is perceived by means of schemas of internal origin, internal phenomena (thought, speech, dreams, memory, etc.) are in their turn conceived only through schemas due to external experience. The child vivifies the external world and materialises the internal universe. Thus at no point is the child mind completely ruled by pure phenomenism. What one observes is a reciprocal digestion of objects by endogenous schemas, and of psychical experience by exogenous schemas. Such phenomenism as exists in the child is never pure, and those who want to revive empiricism in order to explain the point of contact between child thought and the external world will have to complete it by a theory of intellectual assimilation, which means that they will have to abandon empiricism as such.

In the second place, the development of the idea of reality in the child seems to us inexplicable on the empirical hypothesis for the reason, to which logicians have often drawn attention in another sphere, that a false notion does not in itself differ from a true one. Thus the observation that the heavenly bodies follow us about contains nothing incorrect in itself. Only the confrontation of one's own point of view with that of others, and the construction of a world of impersonal relations show the impossibility of the phenomenon. Further, the concepts of weight, of density, of force, of movement, etc., cannot be imposed by any experience : only an act of choice, due to the logical structure characteristic of the particular stage of intellectual development can account for the presence of one particular conception among the collection of possible conceptions. There is no truth without relations, and there can be no concepts without choice ; so there can be no facts without interpretation, and no interpretation without certain dominant mental tendencies. The construction of reality cannot, therefore, be the product of pressure exerted then and there by the physical environment : reality is built up by intelligence, which means that reality, as it appears to the child, is the fruit of a genuine collaboration between the mind and the world around it.

Does this mean that we are to regard knowledge as a free construction of the mind, which would mean admitting a more or less rigid apriorism ? It should be noted that from the point of view of modern biology such a theory is not absurd. According to a contemporary school, the environment does not act upon hereditary mechanisms : acquired characteristics are not transmitted. Thus the reaction of the organism to its environment is conditioned by a structure which is transmitted from germ-cell to germ-cell, without suffering any external change other than chemical influences capable of intoxicating the whole organism. Such a structure is therefore radically in-dependent of its environment and of the influences which this environment may exercise upon the *soma*. From this point of view, intelligence itself might easily be thought to possess a fixed structure, and the sensations by means of which the environment imprints itself upon the mind might be thought to mingle and combine in obedience to laws that were completely foreign to this environment. An a priori theory of knowledge works in perfectly well with a psychological biology. Apart from any question of heredity, moreover, the " Gestalt " psychology of Wertheimer, Köhler, and Koffka,[1] would seem to constitute a revival of apriorism : for if every psychic synthesis implies the appearance of a general feature that is new and not reducible to the sum of its parts, it seems that the structure of knowledge must be irreducible to that of reality. Köhler,[2] it is true, claims to find " structures " in the physical world, which fact seems at variance with our interpretation. But it remains an open question whether the " Naturphilosophie " which at bottom M. Köhler is trying to establish alongside of his experimental psychology would not lose some of its value if the author were to express the problem in terms of Criticism instead of trying to retrace in the physical world the same structures as he finds in the human spirit.

Be that as it may, it is possible to conceive an apriorism defined within the limits of experimental psychology. But the a priori hypothesis is, to say the least of it, unnecessary for the interpretation of our results. In addition, it seems unable to account for two facts, with the second of which it is even in flat contradiction. The first is that, far removed though the child may be in certain respects from pure observation, his docility towards experience is nevertheless sufficient to give rise to a type of causality that is properly phenomenistic. Above all—

---

[1] K. Koffka, *The Growth of the Mind* (International Library of Psychology).
[2] Köhler, *Die physische Gestalten*, 1920.

and this is the second fact—the idea of reality undergoes with age a progressive transformation. This means that the categories of child thought are capable of evolution. Now, apriorism presupposes fixity, whereas every change in the actual structure of thought seems to show that this structure is plastic to the action of external things, whether this action be immediate or remote.

The truth, in short, lies half-way between empiricism and apriorism : intellectual evolution requires that both mind and environment should make their contribution. This combination has, during the primitive stages, the semblance of confusion, but as time goes on, the mind adapts itself to the world, and transforms it in such a way that the world can adapt itself to the mind. What is the mechanism of this adaptation ? This is the question we shall try to answer in § 4. In the meantime, let us make a definite statement of the results of our analyses regarding the ideas of cause and of law.

§ 2. CAUSALITY AND THE CHILD.—The evolution of the idea of causality in the child follows very much the same lines as those we have just been observing in connection with the notion of reality. But it is important at this point to recall the facts in all their complexity. If we decide to do away with any arbitrary simplification, we shall find no less than 17 types of causal relation in child thought. Let us first make an analytical survey of these, and then try to establish the laws which control their evolution.

The first type is that of psychological causality, which is both causal and final ; let us call it the *motivation* type. For example, God or men send us dreams because we have done things that we ought not to have done. This type is, no doubt, the most primitive, but jt is also the one that survives the longest. Its scope is reduced, however, as mental development proceeds, since things in general cease to be thought of as conscious or as specially made by men. But during the primitive stages the motivating relation is omnipresent. Elsewhere we have designated as *pre-causality* this tendency to take a psychological motive as the true cause of everything : there are two Salève mountains, because there must be one for grown-ups and one for children, and so on.

The second type is that of pure *finalism*. This type overlaps with the preceding one to a certain extent, but it gradually separates itself from it. When the child says that the river flows so as to go into the lake, the river is not necessarily endowed with consciousness, nor the makers of things with a motive. There is simply finality, without either the origins or the consequences of this finalism being noticed by the child. It is much the same when we say, in accordance with ordinary common-sense, that ducks have webbed feet so as to swim better. Implicitly, of course, there is present some idea of a divine plan, or of conscious and voluntary effort on the part of the duck. But these links with psychological causality are not perceived or made explicit, which shows that finalism is to be distinguished from motivation.

A third type is constituted by *phenomenistic causality* : two facts given together in perception, and such that no relation subsists between them except that of contiguity in time and space, are regarded as being connected by a relation of causality. A fire lit under an engine or along-side of it is regarded as the cause of movement, long before the child has attempted to find a single inter-mediary between this fire and the wheels of the engine. A child will say that one pebble sinks to the bottom of the water because it is white, that another pebble is light because it is black, that the moon remains suspended in the sky because it is yellow and bright, and so on. Any-thing may produce anything.

This form of causality is undoubtedly independent of the preceding forms, since the connections which it implies are imposed by the external world itself. But we cannot, as Hume would have liked to do, regard phenomenistic causality as the only original form of causality in the child. For phenomenistic causality is

260 CHILD'S CONCEPTION OF CAUSALITY

essentially unstable ; as soon as it is established, a phenomenistic relation transforms itself into one that is animistic, dynamic, magical, etc. Thus the child who thinks
that he is the cause of the movements of the moon always
interprets this relation in a way that goes beyond the
limits set by pure phenomenism. Up to the age of 4–5,
he thinks that he is " forcing " or compelling the moon
to move ; the relation takes on an aspect of dynamic
participation or of magic. From 4 to 5 he is more inclined
to think that the moon is trying to follow him : the
relation is animistic. The child who attributes to the
fire the movement of the engine, immediately lends to
the fire a force, the capacity for making air, etc.

The phenomenistic relation is therefore essentially
vicarious ; it clears the way for the dynamic and other
forms of relations which follow immediately upon it. One
even wonders whether the phenomenistic relation would
exist if there were not other forms of relations to support
it. Rather does it seem that the mind of the very young
child, saturated as it is with dynamism, with finalism,
with animism, with magic, with pre-causality, with artificialism, etc., when it is confronted with new phenomena
establishes at random spatial and temporal contiguities,
and sees relations between any one thing and another.

In short, though it cannot be reduced to causality by
motivation, etc., phenomenistic causality, such as we find
it in the child, would seem to be capable of existing in a
mind already attuned to other forms of relation. Thus
phenomenistic causality is to these other forms what, in
our case, induction is to deduction properly so called : we
make inductions independently of any sort of deduction,
simply by empirical groping, but we do so because we are
perpetually on the lookout for some possible deduction.

A fourth type of relation is *participation*. This type is
more frequent than would at first appear to be the case,
but it disappears after the age of 5–6. Its principle is
the following : two things between which there subsist
relations either of resemblance or of general affinity, are

conceived as having something in common which enables them to act upon one another at a distance, or more precisely, to be regarded one as a source of emanations, the other as the emanation of the first. Thus air or shadows in a room emanate from the air and shadows out of doors. Thus also dreams, which are sent to us by birds " who like the wind " (*C.W.*, Chap. III, § 2).

Closely akin to participation is *magical causality* (a fifth type), magic being in many respects simply participation : the subject regards his gestures, his thoughts, or the objects he handles, as charged with efficacy, thanks to the very participations which he establishes between those gestures, etc., and the things around him. Thus a certain word acts upon a certain thing ; a certain gesture will protect one from a certain danger ; a certain white pebble will bring about the growth of water-lilies, and so on.

In its origins participation is connected with certain conditions of logical structure to which we shall return later. But participation and magic are connected even more closely with psychological causality. For not only does the child regard his desires as efficacious in themselves, but all realism presupposes a realism of thought and gesture, that is, a realism of signs in general. And this realism is the result of that initial confusion between the self and the external world which is the very thing which primitive psychological causality implies.

A sixth type, closely related to the preceding ones, is *moral causality*. The child explains the existence of a given movement or of a given feature by its necessity, but this necessity is purely moral : the clouds " must " advance in order to make night when men go to bed in order to sleep ; boats " have to " float, otherwise they would be of no use, etc.

Closely akin to psychological causality or finalism, but with an added element of necessity, moral causality is also related to that form of participation which we have called dynamic : external objects have intentions which participate with ours, and in this way our desires force them to obey us in accordance with purely moral or psychical laws.

The seventh type of relation is *artificialist causality*. Psychological causality or pre-causality is at the start neither purely moral nor purely physical. A given event is explained straight away by the intention or motive at the back of it, but the child does not ask himself how this intention has worked itself out in action. Since all nature —both matter and consciousness—is nothing but life, the problem does not arise. As soon as the two terms come to be differentiated, artificialist causality appears, at the same time as moral causality and in the nature of its complement : the event or object to be explained is then conceived as the object of human creative activity. This shows the family resemblance to the preceding types which are all capable of growing into artificialism or of finding themselves completed, thanks to this new type of relation.

An eighth type is *animistic causality*, or what might be called causality by realisation of form. The existence of a character or form is explained by an internal biological tendency that is both alive and conscious. The sun is what it is because, after having been made by men, it grows. Mountains have grown, etc. Clouds and the heavenly bodies move along because they are alive. This is the complement of artificial causality ; external motors act on things only if the latter possess an internal motor capable of carrying out the directions and commands received from without.

A ninth type, which is simply left over from the preceding, is constituted by *dynamic causality*. Once animism proper has been eliminated, there still remain in objects forces that are capable of explaining their activity and their movements. Thus, primitively, force is confused with life itself, but dynamism outlives animism, just as finalism outlives pre-causality. Throughout this book we have had occasion to point to the very general character of childish dynamism.

A tenth type of relation is explanation by *reaction of the surrounding medium*. It is, properly speaking, the child's first genuinely physical explanation. For all the preceding forms appeal either to motives or to intentions, either to occult emanations or to mystical manufactures. But reaction of the surrounding medium implies, and, for the first time, the need for defining the " how " of phenomenon, *i.e.* the need for continuity and contact. At first reaction of the surrounding medium still goes hand in hand with animistic dynamism. Only it completes this dynamism with a more exact mechanism. Thus the clouds are regarded as setting themselves in motion, but once this movement is started, the clouds are driven along by the air which they produce by their flight. Later on, reaction of the surrounding medium will serve to explain purely mechanical movements. Thus projectiles which are supposed to be devoid of any spontaneous movement are pushed along by the air which they make in moving. The prime motor is thus the hand that throws the projectile, and not an internal force, as in the case of the clouds. We have seen what universal use children make of explanation by reaction of the surrounding medium. The movement of clouds, of the heavenly bodies, of water, of air, of projectiles, of bicycles, of aeroplanes, of boats, of tops, the effects of centrifugal force—all these are reduced to a schema which up till now was thought to be peculiar to Greek and mediæval physics.

An eleventh type of causality is constituted by *mechanical causality* properly so called, *i.e.* explanation by contact and transference of movement : the wind pushes the clouds, the pedals make the bicycle go, etc. This form of causality appears between the years of 7 and 8. It is always the result of eliminating dynamism. The child who always begins by attributing these movements to the collaboration of two forces, one internal (the object's own force) and the other external, gradually comes to look upon the internal motor as unnecessary. At this point explanation becomes mechanical. Very often the schema of reaction of the surrounding medium serves as a transitional stage between the dynamic character of the early stages and the mechanical character of the later explanations which the child may offer of a given phenomenon.

A twelfth type of relation is what may be called *causality by generation*. The explanation of movement naturally admits much more easily of being reduced to the mechanical type than the explanation of how bodies are actually produced. And at the stage when children bring their ideas of movement in general under the heading of mechanism, they still look to artificialism and animism to explain the origin of things. How, then, will an attempt at a rational explanation of this origin first present itself? We saw that in the matter of the heavenly bodies, of the clouds, etc., as soon as the child has given up the idea that they were made by men, he tries to think of them as being born out of each other. This is the type of relation which we shall call generation. The sun, for example, is regarded as a little living ball that has come out of a fiery cloud ; the clouds themselves have come out of smoke, of air, of fire, etc. This is simply an extension of the animistic idea, with the added notion of a transmutation of substances. The idea of such transmutations is often imposed by relations of dynamic participation : the child feels that there is a relation between rain and clouds long before knowing that the one comes out of the other. He begins by saying that the clouds " come with " the rain, then, from the moment that the rain ceases to be thought of as made by men, he imagines that it comes out of the clouds. Thus a mere participation between intentions and movements (clouds are at first believed to accompany rain, just as the sun and moon accompany us, not for any reason, but because they are made to) gives rise little by little to the idea of generation proper.

From this type of explanation to the thirteenth, namely, to explanation by *substantial identification* there is but a step. We shall say that there is identification when bodies that are born from each other cease to be endowed with the power of growth as it exists in living beings. It is not always easy to draw the line, but it is useful to note the difference. For instance, great progress has been made when the sun is no longer believed to have been born of a cloud, but is regarded as a collection of clouds that have " rolled themselves up into a ball." In the first case, the sun is looked upon as a living being that is very small at first and gradually grows bigger. In the second case, it is regarded merely as matter resulting from the fusion and burning of other inert matters. It will be remembered how frequent were these explanations by identification between the years of 8 and 10.

Once this thirteenth type of explanation has detached itself from the preceding type, it quickly gives rise to the more subtle fourteenth and fifteenth types. The fourteenth is characterised by the schemas of *condensation* and *rarefaction*. For it is not enough for the child to say that the sun has been made by clouds that have rolled themselves up into a ball, or that a stone is formed of earth and sand. The qualitative differences have to be explained, which separate bodies of similar origin. The child then makes the following perfectly natural hypothesis. That the qualities of the sun result from the fact that the clouds have been " well packed " (*serrés*). That the hardness of the stone comes from the fact that the earth is " close " (*serrée*). Thus the matter that makes up bodies is more or less condensed or rarefied. Naturally, the child does not seek, as did the early pre-Socratic thinkers, to reduce all qualitative differences to differences of condensation. Nevertheless, between the ages of 9 and 10, we can see a very general attempt at explanation by condensation. This shows with particular clearness in the evolution of the idea of weight. According to the very young children, bodies are heavy in proportion to their size, and the child has no notion of differences in specific density. The older ones, on the contrary, say that the water is light because it is " thin ", or " liquid ", whereas wood and stone are heavy because they are " big ", " thick ", " full ", and so on. In short, putting aside mistakes in the evolution of weight, water is a rarefied matter, whereas wood and stone are condensed matters.

The fifteenth type of explanation is, in a sense, simply an extension of the last : it is that of *atomistic composition*. From the moment that bodies are regarded as the result of the condensation or rarefaction of original substances, it follows inevitably that sooner or later they will be conceived of as made up of particles tightly or loosely packed together. This is the conclusion which the child comes to with regard to stones : the stone is made of little stones, which are made of grains of earth, etc.

The sixteenth type of explanation is *spatial explanation*. Thus the explanation of the cone-shaped shadow appeals, in the later stages, to principles of perspective. Similarly, the explanation of the rise in the water-level due to the immersion of solid bodies appeals, after the age of 9–10, to the volume of the immersed body. This is rather an advanced form of explanation and consequently only occasionally to be found in children.

Finally, the seventeenth type of explanation, the most subtle, but towards which most of the others tend, is *explanation by logical deduction*. A good example of this was supplied by the experiment of the communicating vessels : the level of the water is the same in both branches, so some of the children told us, because the water can go equally well in one or both directions, and this is what explains the final equilibrium. This is explanation by the principle of sufficient reason. All mechanical explanations, spatial, atomistic, etc., appeal sooner or later to the principle of deduction, and this type of explanation is therefore one of increasing frequency after the age of 10–11. For example, from the laws which he has observed in connection·with the floating of boats, the rise in the water level, the child gradually draws explanations which imply concepts, such as density, specific weight, and so on. These concepts are pure relations ; they are chosen in view of deductions to be made, and are not imposed by facts.

Having distinguished these seventeen types, we can now lay down three main periods in the development of child causality. During the first, all the explanations given are psychological, phenomenistic, finalistic, and magical (types I–VI). During the second stage, the explanations are artificialist, animistic and dynamic (types VII–IX), and the magical forms (III and IV) tend to diminish. Finally, during a third period, the preceding forms of explanation disappear progressively and give place to the more rational forms (X to XVII). Thus the first two periods are characterised by what we have called pre-causality (in the widest sense of the word), *i.e.* by the confusion of relations of a psychological or biological type in general with relations of a mechanical type, and true causality does not appear till about the age of 7–8 (third period).

Three processes seem to us to characterise this evolution : the desubjectification of causality, the formation of series in time, and the progressive reversibility of the systems of cause and effect.

The first process is very definite. Causality, like the whole of reality, is at first teeming with subjective elements. No distinction is drawn between motivation and physical causality (types I, II, VI) or between muscular and manual activity and mechanical action (types VII and IX), or again between the influence of mind on body or of the body on itself, and the influence of external objects on each other (types III, IV and VIII). As to phenomenistic causality, it is, as we saw, essentially vicarious and unstable. In the course of our studies on child psychology we had expected to fix upon 7–8 as the age before which no genuinely physical explanation could be given of natural phenomena. Our present enquiry entirely confirms this expectation. After 7–8 the more positive forms of causality gradually supplant the others, and we can say that at the age of about 11–12 the evolution is completed. There is, therefore, in the domain peculiar to causality a process of evolution exactly similar to that to which we drew attention in speaking of reality : confusion of the self and the universe, then progressive separation with objectification of the causal sequences.

The second process is peculiar to causality : it is the constitution of temporal series. What strikes one most about the child's more primitive forms of causality is the immediate and almost extra-temporal character of the relation. It was the same with participation : the moment we have made a certain movement in a room, the air rushes into our hands through closed windows. As soon as we bring a copy-book up to the table, the shadows of the sky or of the trees come and interpose themselves between our hand and the wood of the table. As soon as we walk along the street, the sun or the moon begin to move. Not a thought is given to the question of distance or of how long the action would have to take in travelling from the cause to the effect. Joined to this relative immediacy, is a remarkable absence of interest as to " how " phenomena occur. Thus, according to the very youngest children, the pedals make the wheels go round without being in any way attached to them, simply by influence. The fire makes the wheel of the engine turn, even 50 centimetres away. There is no contact, during the primitive stages, between cause and effect. Immediacy of relations and absence of intermediaries, such are the two outstanding characteristics of causality round about the age of 4–5. But such features are completely absent from children of 11–12 in subjects of which they know nothing. Thus, it is more or less impossible for a child of 10 to understand how a motor-car works. Nevertheless, the child presupposes pipes, cog-wheels, chains, and belts to act as intermediaries between the petrol and the wheels. From 7–8 onwards, excellent explanations from memory are to be found concerning bicycles, whereas before this age, the various parts were believed to act on one another, but never in the same order. In the sphere of nature, the establishment of contacts and of series in time is also very definite. The step from pre-causality to mechanical causality in the explanation of movement is a good example ; and the explanation by reaction of the surrounding medium—an explanation which serves as a transition between the two extreme types of causality—marks precisely the presence of a need for a chain of intermediate links between cause and effect. There is, therefore, in every sphere a constant progression towards the establishment of series of intermediaries, and series ordered in time.

We shall not go so far as to say, however, that even in the earliest forms of the causal relation there is not a feeling of before and after. Indeed, it may be that although cause and effect are infinitely close, the child still refuses to reverse the terms. This is a special problem, which we hope to take up again with I. Meyerson. All we are saying for the moment is that between cause and effect there is no series properly so called : there is nothing at all, and progress consists precisely in establishing chains of intermediaries such that each should be the effect of the one that precedes it and the cause of the one that comes after it.

A third process in the evolution of causality is the progressive establishment of reversible series. At first sight this aspect of the question seems to be in contradiction with that which we have just been discussing, but it will soon be seen that this is not the case. If we examine a mechanism of any complexity that has been correctly understood by a child of 8–10, we shall always find that it is a reversible mechanism. When the stone has been understood to be composed of little particles of earth, the child admits that the stone can be decomposed into earth. When a child has understood how the pedal of a bicycle makes the wheel move round, he sees that by turning the wheel the pedals can be made to turn. The child believes that the cloud is made of smoke and that this is how it produces fire : from this he concludes, sooner or later, that the cloud can turn itself back into fire and in this way give rise to thunder and to the heavenly bodies. This reversibility does not exclude the existence of a series in time. Only, the series in question is one that can happen in two different directions.

Now, if we really look into the matter, we shall find that all the more advanced forms of explanation in the child are reversible. Mechanical causality is obviously so. So also is causality by substantial identification, *i.e.* by transmutation of the elements. Children, at any rate, have no doubts on this point : air produces fire, and fire, air ; water produces smoke, and smoke, water, etc. Causality by atomic composition follows the same rule, so much so, indeed, that the child always becomes involved in vicious circles when he applies it for the first time : the stone is made of earth, and vice versa. Later on, these vicious circles cover more ground, *i.e.* a greater number of intermediaries are introduced between the extreme terms of the series. But the explanation is still circular. As to spatial and deductive explanations, it goes without saying that they are reversible, since they omit the time element.

The primitive forms of causality, on the contrary, are all irreversible. Take, for example, psychological, magical, finalist causality, etc. : an action or a motive explains a given phenomenon, but the reverse is inconceivable. Artificialism is in the same case : men made the universe, but the universe did not make men. Participation raises a special problem : its immediacy seems to imply reversibility. But in every participation there are emanations and there is the source from which they issue. This is therefore anything but reversibility. Of all the types of causality that come before that of mechanical causality, explanation by reaction of the surrounding medium is the one that points most clearly to a beginning of reversibility. But this is precisely the type that clears the way for the higher forms of explanation.

The progress from irreversibility to reversibility is thus continuous. This process, moreover, seems extremely natural if we bear in mind the manner in which the idea of reality grows up in the child. For the primitive universe is both strewn with subjective adherences and very near to immediate perception. Now, in so far as it is tinged with the child's subjectivity, this universe is irreversible : the flow of consciousness, psychological time, the whims of desires and actions which follow one another without order or repetition—all these things are projected in their entirety into the external world. Similarly, in as much as it is near to immediate perception, the child's universe is irreversible, for perception never shows us the same sun nor the same trajectory, nor the same movements twice. Events cannot happen over again in the same way. It is the mind that builds up reversible sequences underneath perception. To the extent that the child's universe is removed from these constructions and close to the immediately given, it is irreversible. Thus the advance towards reversibility shown by the development of child causality follows exactly the same lines as those underlying the processes defined in connection with the idea of reality.

It is not our business to compare these results with the conception which M. E. Meyerson has so ably defended in his works on explanation in the sciences. Anyone can see the affinity between the three processes we have distinguished and that " identification " to which M. Meyerson has reduced the progress of causality. At the same time, we prefer the word reversibility to the word identity for characterising the causality of the later stages, because, even if it is true that to explain always means in the last resort to deduce, it is not by any means so sure that to deduce means the same as to identify. One can also say that deduction is simply, as Mach and Goblot have shown, a construction, and this view would tend to bring together causality and legality, after having kept these two notions strictly apart.

What conclusion are we to draw from our study of

child causality as regards the influence of physical environment on the growth of intelligence? Here, again, we can only note that the more primitive the ideas of the child, the further removed are they from the physical environment as we know it. All the early forms of causality—magic, finalism, animism, artificialism, and, above all, dynamism, are inexplicable if we do not allow that between environment and consciousness there come to be interposed schemas of internal origin, *i.e.* psycho-physiological schemas. The starting-point of causality is a non-differentiation between inner and outer experience : the world is explained in terms of the self.

Are these facts, then, a confirmation of Maine de Biran's psychological realism ? We have already mentioned, in connection with the idea of force, what seemed to us to be the difficulties of such a doctrine. With regard to causality in general it will therefore be enough to say that if the world is interpreted by the very young child in terms of his own " I ", the " I " in its turn is explained in terms of external experience. We have no more direct cognisance of the self than we have of external objects. Participation and magical causality show, on the contrary, that it is for lack of having discovered his own subjectivity that the young child feels his gestures, his words, and his thoughts, to be bound up with the objects themselves. We do not therefore, as Maine de Biran maintained, begin by discovering internal causality and then proceed to transfer it into objects. Causality is the result of a sort of bodily contact between the organism and the world, which is prior to consciousness of self, and this bodily contact takes us back to the notion of an assimilation of things by thought, a notion to which we shall return later in § 4.

On the other hand, to make causality into an a priori form, fixed once and for all in the structure of the mind, is to raise insuperable difficulties. For, after all, why should not causality appear from the first in its completed form ? Why does it evolve to the extent of giving rise to 17 forms, distinguishable among children alone ? Why is it dependent upon the influence of environment ? If these are, in causality, signs of a structure which eludes empirical explanation, it will have to be admitted that this structure is plastic, and this leads us back once more to the hypothesis of an assimilation of external objects by the organism, such that the objects modify the organism, and such that the organism in its turn adapts things outside to its own peculiar structure.

§ 3. THE CHILD'S IDEA OF LAW.—The notion of law presents in the child, as indeed in the whole history of thought up to modern times, two complementary features —universality and necessity. Law is a constant and necessary relation. M. E. Meyerson has done very useful work in drawing attention to the difficulties of the position, and in distinguishing clearly between legality and causality, legality being simply generality, while causality alone could serve as a foundation for necessity. But from the genetic point of view, the concepts of natural and of social law have always reacted upon each other. For the child, who alone concerns us here, law is inconceivable without necessity. Let us therefore try, without the help of any preconceived ideas, to trace the development of these conceptions.

We can distinguish three periods in the evolution of law in the child. Each of these is characterised by the peculiar relationship in which generality and necessity stand to one another. During the first, generality is non-existent ; as to necessity, it is purely moral, physical determinism not having been separated from the idea of social obligation. During the second period, these two types of necessity are differentiated, and generality comes into being. During the third period, generality is established, and physical determinism is accompanied by logical necessity, which is the last term in the evolution from moral necessity.

The first period lasts till about the age of 7–8. During

this time, there are no natural laws. Physical and moral determinism are completely confused with each other. More exactly, any law observed to hold among external objects is regarded as a social law, and things are believed to behave in accordance with rules that are imposed upon them from outside. This will be recognised as the combination, to which we have so often drawn attention, of animism and artificialism : nature is a society of living beings of whom man is the master and at the same time the creator. All recurring movements are explained primitively in this way. The movements of the sun and the moon, that of the clouds, the return of night, the course of rivers and of waves—all these are subject to the same principle : things have obligations towards us. Before the age of 7–8 we found no example of movement regulated by purely physical laws. There are always two motors which ensure the movement, thanks to their collaboration : an internal motor, which is the obedient will of the moving object, and an external motor, which is at first man himself, and then certain other bodies which play the part of masters or of more vigorous enemies (such as the sun driving away the clouds and the night summoning them).

We saw the counterpart of these facts when we came to analyse childish animism (*C.W.*, Sect. III). When children between 5 and 8 are asked whether the sun could go away if it wanted to, they always answer that it could : if it does not go away, it is because it " has to shine a little longer ", or because " it has to lighten us during the day ". Clouds cannot go because they show us the way, etc. In short, if there are natural laws at work, it is not because the bodies in question are physically determined ; they could perfectly well evade the law if they wished to. It is simply that they are obedient.

This is why for the child, as for Aristotle, the two notions which for us are to characterise the world of laws —violence and chance—come under no law whatsoever. With regard to violence, we cannot claim to have found in children any explicit belief that could be compared to the distinction made by Aristotle. But the whole of the moral conception of law of which we were speaking just now, shows that natural movements are, in the child's eyes, not violent, but harmonious and free. This implicit belief is constantly coming to the surface. Thus a boy of 6 told us that the sun is clever " because he wants to make it warm " ; we are clever " when we don't do what we ought not to do " ; as to clouds, they are " not clever ", because " they try to fight the sun ".

We have dealt at great length elsewhere (*L.T.*, Chap. V) with the question of chance, and shall therefore content ourselves now with recalling our results. Before the age of 7–8 the child seeks, as far as possible, to eliminate chance from nature. The very way in which he formulates his " whys " shows that for him everything has a reason, even when to us it seems fortuitous and contingent. Now, whatever contradicts this conception provokes, by the mere fact of doing so, the maximum of curiosity on the part of the child. And this is why we find the child trying to find the reason or justification for a whole number of facts which for us are inexplicable because they are due to chance : why there is a big and a little Salève mountain, why pigeons are like eagles, why one person has smaller ears than another, etc. In short, law may be arbitrary in the sense that the will of gods or of men may be capricious ; but chance is banished from nature, for everything admits of justification or of motivation, since everything in nature has been willed.

To conclude, during the first period the necessity of law is entirely moral, and physical necessity is simply the lining as it were of this moral necessity, *i.e.* it is simply dependent upon the force and authority of the masters of nature. What is the type of generality that could go hand in hand with such a conception of necessity as this ? History has shown over and over again that to a moral conception of natural law there corresponds a belief in the possibility of numerous exceptions. These exceptions are of two kinds : miracles and the resistance of external things (monsters, etc., conceived by Aristotle as the resistance of matter in relation to form). The child thinks in exactly the same way. Corresponding to the confusion existing between natural and moral law, there is, during this first stage, a complete absence of generality in the laws of nature.

We have repeatedly had occasion to note this absence of generality. First of all, in child physics : according to one and the same child a given boat will float because it is heavy, another, because it is light ; a given body immersed in water will raise the level because it is big, another will fail to do so although it is heavy, and so on. There are certainly laws, but the exceptions are as frequent as the rule. As a rule, the water in rivers flows down, but it might just as well flow upwards. Sometimes the wind drives the clouds before it, sometimes they move by themselves.

The possibility of miracles is, of course, admitted, or rather, miracles form part of the child's conception of the world, since law is a moral thing. Children have been quoted who asked their parents to stop the rain, to turn spinach into potatoes, etc.

During the second period, on the contrary, we see two processes at work which are complementary to each other and take place between the years of 7–8 and 11–12 ; on the one hand, moral necessity and physical determinism become differentiated, and on the other hand, law becomes general.

We have seen numerous examples after 7–8 years of the manifestation of physical determinism. Thus the movements of water and clouds come fairly soon to be attributed to purely mechanical causes : the water cannot do otherwise than go down the slope, the cloud is bound to move forward when there is wind, and so on. At 8 years old on the average, the mechanism of a bicycle is completely understood, and this fact alone points to a mentality that is beginning to bend to the idea of uniform and physically determined causal sequences.

But the clearest index of all is the appearance of the idea of chance. At about 7–8 the child begins to admit that there are things which serve no particular purpose and events due solely to chance encounters. Thus the arbitrary and capricious element, which during the preceding period went hand in hand with the conception of law, has turned into chance, which means that it has lost its moral aspect and has taken on a purely physical character.

It goes without saying that moral necessity is not changed into physical determinism at a stroke. Up to the age of 11–12, many natural laws are still thought of as moral. The movements of the sun and the moon, for example, are those which are interpreted the longest as obeying purely moral laws. Moreover, determinism conquers only the details of events, whereas the body of natural laws taken in their most general aspect remains moral in character. For instance, the child may know that the formation of rain and the movement of clouds are due to purely physical processes, but he continues to believe that if there are clouds it is " for the gardens ". Finalism dies hard.

As to the generality of law, it naturally grows in proportion as moral necessity decreases. As soon as the movement of rivers is interpreted physically, water is considered as always flowing in the same sense, etc. This is the age when the child seeks to avoid contradictions, and when he begins to understand that a law either is general or is not.

Finally comes the third period, which sets in at about 10–11. During this period, the generality of law naturally takes deeper root. But what becomes of necessity ? For a general law is not, as such, necessary. The child may very well discover the absolute regularity of a given physical law (such as that light bodies float, and that heavy ones sink, etc.) but there is no physical necessity that can account in his eyes for this regularity. Apart from cases of apparent constraint (as when the wind pushes the clouds) there is no physical necessity. What makes a law necessary in our eyes is its deducibility : a law is necessary if it can be deduced with a sufficient degree of logical necessity from another law, or from sufficient geometrical reasons. Thus a paradox attends the evolution of law in the child : as the generality of laws increases their necessity grows less (in so far as this necessity, as during the first two periods, is moral). For as the child abandons the idea of moral necessity for justifying laws, he is faced with a mere generality of fact that is, however, devoid of any foundation whatsoever. When we ask the child why water goes down whereas smoke goes up, he can answer that heavy bodies fall whereas light bodies rise, which is certainly a general law ; but when we question him further as to why this is so, he can answer nothing. The younger ones invent a moral reason to get out of the difficulty, but the older ones are nonplussed. Are we then to admit that moral necessity disappears without leaving a trace, or shall we, during this third period, find this necessity reappearing in a new form ? We believe this last solution to be the right one, and that after the age of 10–11, moral necessity becomes logical necessity.

For at about this age various attempts at deduction and logical justification of laws manifest themselves. We recalled just now the attempt to reduce the principle of the communicating vessels to an explanation by sufficient reason. During the same age, we find explanations of floating by the notion of density or by the relation of weight to volume or form, all of which are attempts in the right direction. Questions about shadows, about immersed bodies, etc., also give rise to so many deductions of laws.

But what possible affinity can we allow to exist between moral and logical necessity, two types which at first sight seem so radically distinct ? Let us imagine a universe controlled by moral necessity. Now take. from it all direct influence, all consciousness and will, and also all mystical activity exercised by man upon things. Much will still remain. There will still be the ideas of order, of organisation, of regularity, coherence, and intelligibility. Thus there remains the possibility of explaining one group of phenomena by taking another group as our starting point. All this is characteristic of logical necessity ; for at its root lies the conviction that every law that has been observed empirically must admit of justification by an appeal addressed no longer to the will and the emotions, but to reason.

What conclusions can we draw from our analyses from the point of view of the influence of environment ? We cannot honestly account for the evolution of the idea of law by any direct action of the physical environment. The idea of law, like those of cause and reality, is much more remote from the child than it is from us. From the very first, we see that the feeling of the moral necessity of law comes before any exact knowledge of the law itself. From the first, we can observe a fusion of physical experience and internal feeling. No doubt only " conditioned reflexes " and motor anticipations will supply the contents of the most primitive laws discovered by the child, but this purely empirical attitude in no wise explains the " obligatory " character of law.

This feeling of obligation, thanks to which the child co-ordinates things as they are presented to him, can therefore only be of internal origin. Nothing in nature herself can give the child the idea of necessity. To immediate perception nature is full of whims, and there are no laws that do not admit of numerous exceptions. The child sees this himself when he begins by refusing to allow any generality to the laws of nature. But why does he not stop there ? On the contrary, we are faced with the paradoxical fact that the earliest relations perceived are conceived as morally necessary even before having become intelligible. This strikes one particularly in the explanations given of floating or of movements in general : wood stays on the water because it *must*, the moon follows us because it is *forced* to do so, the river flows because it *must* flow, etc. Sully long ago noted this feeling of a rule, but these primitive rules have a meaning that is far more moral than logical : they imply, not generality, but simply obligation. The same thing strikes one also in the explanations children give of machines : all the parts present *must* be there for the machine to go, says the child, before having understood, or even guessed at the true rôle of these parts ; thus the lamp, or the brake, or the tyres of a bicycle, will seem as necessary to movement of the whole as do the wheels and the pedals.

If, then, the feeling of necessity is not due to the pressure of the physical environment, is it perhaps the outcome of social surrounding ? For one may well wonder how a child would think who was removed from the authority of his parents. Is not the concept of nature simply the outcome of comparisons with family life rather than the result of pre-relations properly so called ?

Only one of the various theories put forward to account for the moral obligation attaching to the idea of law tends to make us subscribe to this hypothesis. We are thinking of the fine work done by M. Bovet on the conditions of obligation in the conscience.[1] There is obligation in so far as the orders are given by persons for whom we feel respect, respect being a *sui generis* mixture of fear and love. There is obligation in the measure that a relation exists, not between person and person, but between the small and the great.

It would therefore be in the relation of the child to its parents that we should have to look for the origins of law. Only, in M. Bovet's view, this relation would go a long way back. And indeed, observation shows the extreme importance and the great precocity of this attitude of mingled fear and love, which according to

[1] " Les conditions de l'obligation de conscience ", *Année Psychol.*, t. XVIII, pp. 55-120.

M. Bovet is precisely what constitutes respect. The child's conceptions about natural law would therefore seem to have their roots in a very universal and a very primitive reaction.

We must not therefore say that the child's concept of nature is based simply on an analogy with family life. What is at work is a genuine pre-relation. Moral obligation forms part of the very structure of the child's mind, if we admit that the feeling of obligation is derived from the earliest contacts of the child's will with that of its parents, for these early contacts condition the whole of the child's mental life.

§ 4. ASSIMILATION AND IMITATION.—In studying the evolution of the idea of reality in the child, we found in the primitive stages a dualism that was little short of paradoxical. On the one hand, the universe of the child is closer to immediate perceptions, closer to external things than the universe of the adult. On the other hand, it is more subjective, more permeated with characters that are, in fact, taken from internal experience. The same phenomenon appears in the evolution of the ideas of cause and law. The most primitive laws which the child lays down take account of every feature and every detail of immediate perception : they are not general, they have exceptions, and the explanations are over-determined. They point to a type of necessity borrowed from inner experience, and the pre-causality which goes with them is marked by a confusion of motivation with physical connections.

The same dualism is to be found in the logical structure of child thought. Child thought proceeds by juxtaposition. Judgments are not interrelated, because each espouses the object in all its detail and takes no account of the judgments that came before it. But there is syncretism, which means that the lack of objective relations is made good by an excess of subjective relations.

In brief, there is dualism everywhere—realism on the

one hand, subjective adherences on the other. It should be noted in passing that the situation is closely analogous to what M. Brunschvicg has so clearly shown to exist in the mentality of primitives. "With regard to relations of causality, the metaphysics of dynamism mingle with the phenomenism of contingency ".[1] We would therefore seem to be in the presence of a very general feature of the evolution of thought. But we shall confine ourselves, in what follows, to the psychology of the child, which we have chosen as our special province.

In order to explain this dualism, we shall be obliged to carry into the sphere of psychology the epistemological distinction between the *form* and the *matter* of knowledge. All we need do is to agree upon the meaning which we wish to give these terms in the domain of practical experience. The line which we proposed to follow at the opening of these general conclusions will supply us, in this connection, with a perfectly natural solution.

If we agree to take as our system of reference, nature as science describes her, then we shall call matter, or content of the child's knowledge all that experience and observation impose upon the child. And we shall name form of the child's knowledge everything that the child adds to this matter, that is the pre-relations and pre-notions which we, as adults, have shed. The choice of system of reference is, we repeat, a convention, but we are making use of this convention quite consciously, and shall not allow it to lead us into epistemological realism of any kind.

In the sphere of biology, moreover, the distinction between form and matter, such as we have just described, has a very definite meaning. The matter of knowledge belongs, as a special case, to the sum of influences which the environment exercises on the organism. These influences are in the main transmitted through the medium of substances that are absorbed as food, as the energy of heat, light, movement, sound, etc. Among these

[1] *L'expérience humaine et la Causalité physique*, p. 102.

energies, some are not accompanied by consciousness, others liberate psychical states and reactions, and thus constitute a collection of pressures exercised by the physical environment on the motor activity of the subject and on the intelligence that is bound up with this activity. The form of consciousness, from the biological point of view, is, on the contrary, a special case of those structures which the organism imposes upon matter and assimilated energies. The organism has a structure which is retained by assimilation and which, moreover, conditions by selection the choice of substances and energies to be absorbed. Thus the influence of the environment can never be pure: every external stimulus presupposes an internal reaction, and what is assimilated by the organism is always and necessarily the result of an external influence and an internal digestion, which process of digestion may equally well be mechanical or motor as chemical.

Actually, indeed, it is impossible even so much as to think of " an environment " and " an organism " without abstraction. There exists between these two terms a complexus of relations, of changes and reactions which implies complete physico-chemical continuity. For it is impossible to mark the boundaries within an organism between what is living, what is functioning, and what is the collection of substances already assimilated or already rejected and hardened into deposits. The environment is being perpetually modified by the organism, and a given reaction which has just taken place will never take place again, as such, because of the fact that this reaction is a perpetual " becoming ".

Psychic life being conditioned by organic life, there seems no reason why it should escape these laws. The origin of knowledge is no doubt fraught with mystery, but however far back we go, we always find sensations and movements. At one time, psychologists laid all the stress on sensations, which led them to believe that knowledge was simply a replica of external reality. But they soon realised that there are no sensations without movements and that knowledge consists to a great extent of accomplished or anticipated movements. Now, once this has been admitted, it will have to be conceded, at least as a hypothesis, that motor schemas have already been formed at the moment when knowledge takes its rise, and that, in relation to knowledge, these schemas play the part of *form* which is independent of matter. There seems no reason why psychological assimilation should consist in reproducing the environment as it is, when we remember that all physiological assimilation is performed as the function of a structure that persists and that conditions every influence coming from the environment. On the contrary, there is a strong presumption in favour of the view that these two kinds of assimilation are partly analogous, both consisting in giving to matter coming from outside a form conditioned by the structure of the organism.

These biological hypotheses, it will be seen, account for the facts we have observed, and are necessary for that purpose. The whole structure of the child's idea of reality rests on a primitive lack of differentiation between the self and the external world, that is on a fusion of organic experience and external experience. External perceptions are moulded into muscular sensations ; the contents of organic consciousness is amalgamated to external things. Sometimes we have complete fusion of the element of muscular sensation with the external element, as in the idea of force. Sometimes we have progressive dissociation between the self and external objects, as in the evolution of the notion of cause. Thus the analogy is clear that exists between this confusion of the self with the world on the one hand, and the continuity of the organism with its setting on the other. In both cases, we have two terms in relation, but each of these terms exists only as a function of the other, and the interchange between them makes it impossible to dissociate them without mental work.

Let us try to define this initial complexus more closely.

Every fresh external influence exercised upon the organism or the mind presupposes two complementary processes. On the one hand, the organism adapts itself to the object which exercises this influence : in this way there is formed a sort of motor schema related to the new object. This is what we shall call, in a very wide sense, *imitation*. On the other hand, this adaptation implies that between the new movements and the old habits there is a certain continuity, *i.e.* that the new movements are partly incorporated into already existing schemas. This incorporation we shall call *assimilation*.

There is no need at this point to dwell upon the importance of imitation in mental development. J. M. Baldwin has done enough to emphasise this importance and to show that imitation transcends the limits usually set by the word. We shall go even further in this direction. Imitation can be by gesture and by movement, as when the child who plays at being its model who is learning to talk, to walk, etc. Drawing is imitation. But imitation can also be of thought, thought being a compressed form of action. In all these imitations there is a motor element, and this is why it is worth while reducing all these processes to imitation by gesture. And this, indeed, is what M. Delacroix has done, showing with his usual penetration that every perception " imitates " the perceived object.[1]

As to assimilation, insufficient attention has been paid to the important part it plays. Assimilation must not be confused with analogy, with that perpetual tendency to reason by analogy which has been taken as the characteristic of elementary intellectual reactions.[2] For even if analogy is derived from assimilation, the latter is quite a different thing at first. There is analogy when two percepts or two concepts of the same order are reduced to one another. Thus when we see what we believe to be a tree, what we actually are perceiving is a green patch, an oblong shape, etc., and by immediate

---

[1] H. Delacroix, *Journal de Psychol.*, Vol. XVIII (1921), p. 97.
[2] A. Cresson, *Les réactions intellectuelles élémentaires*, Paris, 1922.

fusion we identify this perception with other earlier analogous perceptions and in this way are enabled to recognise a tree. In such a case there is analogy because the terms compared are on the same plane of reality, that is, they both are borrowed from external experience. But assimilation takes place when percepts, formless in themselves, and incapable of being completed by elements drawn from the same plane of reality, are worked into schemas taken from another plane of reality, into schemas, that is to say, which *were there before the experience* of the kind in question, and which are conditioned by the structure of the organism.

We have met with typical examples of assimilation in connection with the genesis of the idea of force or of animism in general. Inanimate objects are assimilated to living beings who act with effort and will. Now this assimilation is not the result of a mere judgment of analogy. The feeling of effort is bestowed upon objects in quite a different manner. It is introjected into the object before having been conceived as characterising the self, or at any rate at the same moment. For the internal experience is not more directly accessible than the external. On the contrary, it is only after having assimilated the activity of external bodies to his own muscular activity that the child turns this new-made instrument upon himself and, thanks to it, becomes conscious of his internal experience. Thus the child learns to know the force of external objects through his own, and his own through that of external objects. By which we mean that he does not directly see force anywhere, but conceives it, thanks to the relation existing between a schema which is prior to knowledge and to the contents of this knowledge.

In short, the subjective adherences which we observe during the primitive stages of intellectual evolution cannot be due simply to judgments of analogy, because there are not in this case two separate terms, known separately, which are compared and then identified with one another.

There is fusion which takes place prior to any knowledge of the terms compared. This fusion is what we have called assimilation, and is something which cannot be understood unless one imagines the existence of schemas already formed by action and into which are merged the elements of knowledge in the process of formation.

We are fully aware of all that remains obscure in this notion of assimilation. But our results up to date do not permit of any further analysis of the subject. In order to grasp the mechanism of assimilation one would have to investigate the zone that lies between organic and intellectual life. It is therefore from an analysis of the first two years of the child's life that we may hope for light on the subject. All we can do for the moment is to postulate the existence of this process of assimilation. For the confusion made by the child between the self and the external world seems to us to constitute a *sui generis* relation. It is not a relation between two terms situated on the same plane, because one of the two terms is not an object of cognition but a factor in cognition, in that it imprints its structure upon the other term. One would therefore have to turn to the a priori synthetic relations which Kant has foisted upon the Theory of Knowledge in order to find an adequate comparison. But in Kant's theory, the a priori form is fixed and cannot be modified by experience, whereas the schema of assimilation is plastic. Experience changes it and fresh schemas are constantly emerging under the pressure of facts. This is what M. Brunschvicg has brought out so admirably in dealing with the history of the sciences. Moreover, as indeed M. Brunschvicg himself admits, form and matter are inseparable in epistemology. Form alone is nothing : it can neither be defined nor give rise to a cognition. Only, M. Brunschvicg has intentionally severed the connection between his psychological reflections and biology, whereas we, on the contrary, feel constrained, as psychologists, to look for the continuity between cognition and life. Assimilation in this respect appears to us as the biological equivalent of judgment. It has been said, with truth, that the act of judgment cannot be reduced to any other. But it is none the less legitimate to seek for what may be its biological roots, provided, of course, it be remembered that judgment can only be reduced to assimilation in so far as it is already potentially contained in it.

Having said this, we can now return to the study of the paradox of child thought which necessitated the more detailed account we have given of these various ideas. Child thought is at once more realistic and more subjective than ours. But if we appeal to the concepts of assimilation and imitation, this dualism becomes comprehensible. For assimilation and imitation are at the root of two strictly antagonistic tendencies which arise, when the organism is confronted with something new (a circumstance which is all the more likely to occur when the child is very young). Assimilation consists in adapting the object to oneself by divesting it of all its irreducible characters. Imitation consists in adapting oneself to the object by abandoning attitudes which could obstruct this adaptation and by taking up an attitude that is entirely new.

Le Dantec's deplorable neglect of experimentation in biology is well known, but to him belongs the merit of having discovered certain very general and synthetic formulæ such as are made in thermo-dynamics for lack of any possible analysis of detail. Now, Le Dantec has shown in a very striking manner this contrast between assimilation and imitation with regard to organic life.[1] The organism left to itself tends to assimilate its environment, it tends, that is, to persist exactly as it was before and to deform the environment so as to subject it to this assimilation. But the environment resists and influences the organism. According to the strength of this resistance the organism is forced to change, and each of these variations consists in a sense, in an imitation of the object which is exercising its constraining power. Biology,

[1] Le Dantec, *La Science de la vie*, Chap. II.

concludes Le Dantec, can be summed up as the struggle between assimilation and imitation.

In the psychic life of the child, which is closer to organic life than ours, this antagonism still shows clearly ; that is, if we agree to regard assimilation and imitation in the sense in which we have defined these terms, namely as special cases of the process described by Le Dantec. Assimilation and imitation work in opposite directions, so that each pulls the mind its own way. Any mental attitude during the primitive stages will therefore consist in a compromise between these two tendencies and not in their synthesis.

This situation will serve to explain the paradox which we referred to above. Sometimes the child makes an effort to imitate reality, and then he is servile in his acceptance of the outlines and curves of direct perception. In such cases, one has the impression of a purely empirical, a purely " phenomenistic " mind, which does no more than establish relations between any one thing and another, provided experience has allowed of their being brought together. This is thinking by juxtaposition. For in so far as imitation triumphs, assimilation is repressed. When, on the contrary, assimilation has the upper hand in the thought process, the child seems not to trouble in any way about objective observation, and rushes headlong into dynamism, animism, and participation.

Such a situation as this is not an accident in the history of thought, but a biological necessity. Lacking collaboration, the two tendencies, the imitative and the assimilative, lead to no coherent result. Because he fails to imitate correctly when he is assimilating, the child deforms reality in assimilating it to himself, and because he fails to assimilate when he is imitating, he becomes the victim of direct perception instead of constructing a world of intelligible relations.

But such an equilibrium as this is unstable, and assimilation and imitation soon begin to collaborate. It may even be questioned whether the definition of the whole of thought does not lie precisely in this collaboration.

As imitation and assimilation become complementary to one another, their characters change. Assimilation ceases to deform, *i.e.* to alter reality in terms of the self. The assimilating schemas become more and more flexible in yielding to the demands of external things and of experience. Now a non-deforming assimilation is synonymous with understanding or deduction, which means that it does no more than bend the data of experience to the exigencies of logical structures corresponding to the various stages of development. Under the influence of assimilation, imitation in its turn loses its servility and grows into intelligent adaptation to the external world. Deduction and experience then become the two opposite poles of one and the same effort of thought which synthesises the formerly antagonistic tendencies, assimilation and imitation.

From the point of view of the evolution of the ideas of reality, etc., the effect of the process we have been describing is quite clear, and it would not be difficult to reduce it to these various factors. It would be sufficient to remember that assimilation and imitation are not only reactions to the physical environment, but also to the social environment. From this point of view, the deforming assimilation of the primitive stages is synonymous with egocentricity, and imitation synonymous with social imitation. At first only a compromise is effected between these two tendencies ; but by collaborating progressively throughout the mental development of the child, imitation becomes adaptation to others, and assimilation turns into understanding and a sense of reciprocity. So that we can now see how the processes which transform primitive realism into objectivity, reciprocity, and relativity, are all based upon the progressive collaboration of assimilation and imitation. As to the progressive reversibility of thought, which brings with it the progressive reversibility of causal sequences, we have shown elsewhere in what manner it results from the same tendencies (*J.R.*, Chap. IV, § 4).

§ 5. CHILD LOGIC.—It may be of interest now to see whether our present study confirms the results previously arrived at concerning child logic. In this way we shall be able to establish what are the relations between this logic and the structure of reality, of causality and of legality as these are conceived by the child.

Let us remind the reader once again that in questioning the children about the phenomena of nature we did not reach their spontaneous thought, but a thought that was necessarily systematised and consequently deformed by the very fact of the interrogatory. Further, and this is the fundamental point, the most original and the most important part of the answers which the children gave us had never been communicated to anyone before it was given to us. Children do not talk amongst themselves about their conceptions of nature, and in so far as they put questions to adults upon the subject, these tend to annul the purely childish character of their conceptions. And yet these conceptions are constant in the towns where we were able to question children, and they are to be found amongst nearly all children of the same mental age. Nothing is more striking in this respect than the very simple experiments which are completely removed from anything that the children can have been taught. Such is, for example, the experiment of the pebble placed in a glass of water, so as to make the level of the water rise : all the younger children say that the water rises because the pebble is heavy, and all the older ones say that it rises because the pebble is big. The convergence here is extremely interesting.

This secret and yet constant character of childish views about the world shows very clearly that before the interrogatory the spontaneous thought of the subject must have been made up more of images and motor schemas than of conceptual thought, such as could be formulated in words. We have here a general confirmation of the hypothesis we put forward earlier, and according to which child thought is not social but egocentric, and consequently intermediate between autistic and logical thought. In autistic thought, intellectual work is carried on by means of images and motor schemas. In logical thought, word and concept replace these primitive instruments. These two processes mingle in the child's mind, the first retaining its power in so far as thought is secret and unformulated, the second undergoing development in so far as thought becomes socialised.

This explains why the thought of the children we questioned was so lacking in logic. We were able, within each sphere, to establish special stages, but it would be extremely difficult to establish inclusive stages for the reason that during these early years the child is still very incoherent. At the age when the child is still animistic, artificialist, or dynamic in his way of thinking on some points, he has already ceased to be so on others. He does not reap the benefits of a progress in all the domains where this progress is bound eventually to make itself felt. Corresponding stages are at varying levels, because the influence of one belief upon another takes place unconsciously and not thanks to a conscious and deliberate generalisation. Thus child thought is in no way organised. There are, of course, certain remarkable correlations between one given achievement and another. (We may recall the correlation mentioned in Chap. VII, § 3 of this volume.) But this is not the sign of discursive and reflective logic, it merely indicates the existence of a certain coherence between the warring parts of an organism which is unable as yet to release instantaneously such synergy as may exist. There is therefore not deduction, but juxtaposition, devoid of systematic logical multiplication and addition. The concepts of life, of weight, of force, of movement, etc., are not concepts properly so called, they are not defined by means of exact logical additions or multiplications, but they are those conglomerate concepts of which we have spoken elsewhere (*J.R.*, Chap. IV, §§ 2–3).

But leaving these more general considerations, let us see whether our present results tend to confirm the analysis which we formerly attempted to make of transduction, *i.e.* of the childish method of reasoning (*J.R.*, Chaps. IV and V).

Childish transduction is opposed to adult deduction by the possession of three fundamental characteristics. 1° Transduction is, in the first place, purely a mental experiment, by which we mean that it begins by simply reproducing in imagination events such as they are or could be presented by immediate reality. For instance, having noticed that the presence of stones in a river produces tiny waves, the child explains the movement of the river by appealing to other stones which are supposed to have set it in motion. 2° Transduction is carried on by predicative judgments, or by certain simple judgments of relation. It might be better to say judgments of prerelation, relations being conceived simply as properties : " the stone has force ", etc. For to do no more than combine the data supplied by immediate perception is to forget the part played in perception by the self or by the personal point of view : it is, therefore, to take a false absolute instead of objective relations as a foundation for reasoning. Thus when a child says that a boat floats because it is heavy, he does so because, in his mind, the weight of the boat has not been compared to its volume nor to the weight of the water, but has been evaluated as a function of the subject's own point of view, taken as absolute. In the same way all those instances of reasoning which bear upon the concepts of force, life, and movement, will be found to contain false absolutes, mere pre-relations, simply because the laws of physics have not been desubjectified. 3° Owing to the fact that it does not reason by relations but is a simple combination of judgments, transduction does not attain to the strict generality of deduction but remains an irrational passage from particular to particular. When the child seems to be deducing, that is, to be applying the universal to the particular, or to be drawing the universal from the particular, he does so in appearance only, owing to the indeterminate character of the concepts employed. Here is an example : a boy tells us that large-sized or " big " bodies are heavier than small ones ; yet a moment later he declares that a small pebble is heavier than a large cork. But he does not, for that matter, give up his first affirmation, he only declares that the stone is heavier than the cork " because some stones are bigger than corks ". Thus the character " big " has not at all the same meaning as for us. It does not define a class, it is transmitted by syncretistic communication to analogous objects : since there are big stones, little stones participate in their bigness, and thus acquire weight. At other times, the child reasons only for special cases and does not generalise at all : one boat floats because it is heavy, another because it is light, and so on. In short, either we have a juxta-position of special case reasonings without generalisation, or we have apparent generalisation, but generalisation by syncretism and not by correct logical addition and multi-plication.

Our interpretation of transduction is therefore that it moves from particular to particular, regardless of contra-dictions, because it is ignorant of the logic of relations, and that there is mutual dependence between this ignorance of the logic of relations and the fact that reasoning occurs simply by mental experimentation. This interpretation entails three debatable points which in our former studies we perhaps failed to analyse in sufficient detail, un-acquainted as we were with much of the material which our present study has brought to light. Let us then submit these three points to somewhat closer examination.

The first runs as follows. It may be objected that transduction differs in no way from adult deduction, unless it be by insufficient elaboration of the material dealt with. In other words, between the child and ourselves there is no difference in logical form (the form of reasoning being taken as independent of its contents), but only a difference in the concepts used. It might be maintained, for example, that the fact that in purely mental experiment the reasoning process starts from immediate perceptions is of no value to the analysis of the structure of reasoning, since correct deductions, from the formal point of view, can be made from false or insufficient premises. In our view, on the contrary, this circumstance is of fundamental importance to the actual structure of reasoning, for if the child reasons only from immediate perceptions, it is because he cannot handle the logic of relations. In his eyes, for example, the concept " heavy " is one that qualifies absolutely : a thing is either heavy or not heavy. It is not a relation, such that one object is always heavier than another, and less heavy than a third (*J.R.*, Chaps. II and III).

But it may be argued that the mere fact of not reasoning by relations but by predicative judgments and pre-relations is of no importance from the formal point of view. In other words, syllogistic or deductive reasoning in general may be correctly carried out even by minds that are ignorant of the logic of relations. We shall return to this question later on, and from a different point of view (third point) : we shall then try to show that any correct deduction, even if it rests only on judgments of inherence, presupposes a substructure of relational judgments.

The second point is the following. In our interpretation of childish transduction the fact that the child reasons merely by mental experiment and the fact that he is ignorant of the logic of relations are regarded as inter-dependent. The reader will perhaps wonder why this is so ? For, be it noted, this double character of childish transduction is paradoxical. The child is content, on the one hand, to combine together the facts of direct experience, whilst, on the other, he elaborates such absolute concepts as weight in itself, movement of its own, life, and so on, and thus seems to generalise far more than we do, and to attain to concepts far more abstract, and further removed from immediate experience, than ours. To put the matter differently, a mere combination of particular cases observed directly and without any appeal to general law, goes hand in hand with the use of apparently very universal concepts. (It should be remembered, however, that this generality is only apparent, or at least belongs to a different order from that of our concepts, since it contains a contradiction within itself.)

We are faced here with a particular case of that general paradox which we discussed in the preceding paragraph. Transduction is simply a mental experiment, because the child sticks slavishly to given reality ; but at the same time, the child assimilates the real to his own self and fails only to construct a universe of intellectual relations because he cannot strip the external world of its subjective adherences nor understand the relativity of his own point of view. The double aspect of transduction is therefore only the result of the duality that characterises the child's whole conception of the world.

But these two aspects of transduction are above all closely connected with each other. Why does the child reason with absolute concepts which give an impression of greater generality than our adult concepts ? It is because, judging everything from his own immediate point of view, he takes his perceptions of weight, colour, size, etc., as absolute. But if the child reasons simply by means of mental experiments, content, that is, to " imitate" reality as it is, this again is because the world of logical relations remains foreign to him, so long as his own point of view is not completed by the reciprocal view-points of others. The two characteristics therefore belong together, and each has the same cause, which is the following. The self must necessarily take part in the knowledge of reality, in the sense that all evaluations and perspectives are necessarily relative at first to the subject's own point of view. Now, as soon as we become conscious of this inevitably personal character of our point of view, we rid ourselves of all forms of realism, that is to say, we succeed simultaneously in turning our absolutes into relatives, and in reasoning, no longer from immediate perception, but by means of intellectual relations. And on the contrary, to the extent that we are still ignorant of the personal character of our own point of view, we remain the victims of every form of realism. Realism of immediate perception continues to hold its sway, whilst reasoning is carried on by means of substantialist and absolute concepts which have all the appearance of being very abstract and general.

Finally, the third point which we have left open to doubt is the connection between the logic of relations and the process of generalisation. According to our interpretation of transduction, it is when he has succeeded in handling the logic of relations that the child will be able to make a right use of the logic of classes and judgments of inherence : so that the logic of classes would seem to be subservient, as it were, to the logic of relations, the latter alone rendering generalisation and strict syllogistic deduction possible.

If this be so, we shall have to regard a class as a residuum of relations. Reasoning by classes, in other words, the classical syllogism will become a condensed form of true reasoning which would consist in multiplying relations with each other. One can, of course, reason with perfect correctness by making sole use of classes, as the whole of Aristotle's logic shows, but the classes themselves could only be constructed thanks to relations. Thus the biological classification which is at the root of Aristotle's logic can only be understood as the result of comparisons and relations between the characters peculiar to each species, genus, etc. Further, classes disintegrate under the pressure of intellectual progress which consists in multiplying relations. So that the class is not only a residue, but a provisional and unstable residue : every class implies characters of which the analysis shows that they are neither fixed nor absolute, but in a state of

298 CHILD'S CONCEPTION OF CAUSALITY

perpetual mobility. Thus the zoological classification had an absolute sense for Aristotle and even for Linnæus, Cuvier, Agassiz, and others, whereas nowadays species and genera are regarded as a conventional framework by means of which we make arbitrary divisions in the continuous flux of evolution. The only reality is therefore the sum of the relations between individuals, and, strictly speaking, one should not say : " This animal is a sparrow ", but : " This animal is more (or less) sparrow than this or those animals ", just as we say of an object that is " more (or less) brown than . . .". The evolution of child logic has shown with sufficient clearness that all the ideas that are relative for us (colour, right and left, the points of the compass, etc.) are taken by the child as absolute. Our present research only confirms this result : the ideas of weight, force, movement, etc., also evolve from the absolute to the relative (§ 1). It does seem, then, as though the logic of relations gradually gained the ascendancy over the logic of classes. In any case, classes only play a vicarious part : they are snapshots which it is possible to take at any given moment of the moving flux of relations. It is convenient to call " brown " the general collection of individuals who come within the sphere of the relation " more or less brown ". But correct reasoning always assumes under the classes the existence of a substructure of relations.

This being so, we have claimed that it is only when a child can handle the logic of relations, only, that is, when he can find the reciprocal counterpart of a relation, when he can pass from a relation to its " domain ", and vice versa, that he is capable of finding laws, of generalising, and consequently of handling the logic of classes and propositions in all its strictness. The results we have set forth above seem to us to give full confirmation to this interpretation.

But if things are to be seen in their true perspective, we must be mindful of a principle to which we have often drawn attention (*J.R.*, Chap. V, § 2) : it is that the order of conscious realisation is the reverse of the order of real construction.

For, from the point of view of conscious realisation, laws would seem to appear before the relations which explain them. In other words the child would seem to arrive by means of extra-logical inductive methods at a correct generalisation, at logical multiplication and addition, and hence at the creation of rigorous classes, before he is able to establish the actual relations which underlie this generalisation and explain the law that has been obtained. At any rate, we have often observed that the law appears before the explanation, and that at times there is even conflict between the law and the explanation. Thus in the case of the rise in the level of the water (Chap. VII), the child can predict the phenomenon as a function of the volume of the immersed body, but he still gives explanations which are based solely on the idea of weight. Something analogous to this can be observed in connection with floating bodies, the formation of shadows, etc. It would seem, therefore, that even when the general structure of a phenomenon is known, this structure has not necessarily been built up by means of the relations which explain it.

In point of fact, however, we do not believe that this can yield an argument in favour of the priority of the logic of classes over that of relations. If we turn from the order of conscious realisation to that of intellectual construction itself, we shall find that the establishment of laws presupposes the mastery of relations, and that to explain a law is simply to bring to the surface, by conscious realisation, those relations which were already implied in it. For when a law is, as in the earliest stages, simply the result of an empirical observation that has been repeated, when, that is to say, it is the outcome of extra-logical inductive processes, this law remains, child logic being what it is, subject to exceptions and contradictions. In short, it is not general, and gives rise only to pseudo-concepts devoid of any rigour. But if a law is the result of induction combined with logical multiplication and addition, if, in short, it is the fruit of strict and directed generalisation, it implies the presence of the logic of relations, and consequently the transformation of primitive concepts into relations properly so called. Thus the child only discovers the law and predicts the phenomenon of floating bodies when he implicitly substitutes the notion of relative weight in the place of the notion of absolute weight. He can only foresee the phenomenon of the rise of the water-level with certainty when he gets rid of the primitive idea of weight (*i.e.* weight as necessarily proportional to size) and distinguishes bodies that are light though big, and heavy though small. Now this dissociation of an idea again presupposes the relations of weight to volume, to condensation, etc. Similarly, the child cannot foresee the orientation of shadows until he can adopt a point of view which takes account of perspective. In short, before law can be discovered and consequently correct generalisations be made, action must have woven a network of relations between the objects of knowledge. If the explanation of the law does not come till later, this is simply because the order of conscious realisation is the opposite of the order of construction. We begin by becoming conscious of the work accomplished by the mind, and only afterwards do we come to grasp the processes which have enabled this result to be established. Let us conclude by saying that the progress from childish transduction to adult deduction presupposes three complementary processes : 1° a progressive relativity of ideas, arising from the fact that the self gradually becomes conscious of the personal character of its own point of view and of the reciprocity between this point of view and other possible ones ; 2° a progressive transformation of primitive mental experiments into constructions carried out by means of the logic of relations ; 3° a progressive generalisation, resulting from the fact that classes become rigid and well defined in the measure that they are conditioned by a substructure of relations.

§ 6. LOGIC AND REALITY.—Experience fashions reason, and reason fashions experience. Thus between the real and the rational there is a mutual dependence joined to a relative independence, and the problem is a singularly arduous one to know how much of the growth and elaboration of knowledge is due to the pressure of external things, and how much to the exigencies of the mind. This question belongs primarily to the Theory of Knowledge, but there exists from the genetic point of view a problem that is a very near neighbour to it, and concerning which we must add a few words. At each stage of intellectual development we can distinguish roughly two groups of operations: on the one hand, the operations of formal logic which condition the very structure of reasoning, and on the other hand, what Höffding calls the " real categories " (as opposed to formal categories), that is to say such notions as causality, reality, etc. We can now seek to find in what relation the logical structure characterising each stage stands to the corresponding real categories. Do the logical relations condition the real categories, or is the converse the truth ? In what measure are these two factors independent of each other ?

We have endeavoured in this volume to determine how the real categories evolved in the child's mind. In the preceding paragraph we were able to confirm the analysis we had made elsewhere of the formal development of thought in the child. We now hope to be able to show that there exists a parallelism between these two kinds of evolution.

In the first place, let us note the astonishing similarity of the general processes which condition the evolution of logic and that of the idea of reality. For the construction of the objective world and the elaboration of strict reasoning both consist in a gradual reduction of egocentricity in favour of the progressive socialisation of thought, in favour, that is to say, of objectivation and reciprocity of view-points. In both cases, the initial state is marked by the fact that the self is confused with the external world and with other people; the vision of the world is falsified by subjective adherences, and the vision of other people is falsified by the fact that the personal point of view predominates, almost to the exclusion of all others. Thus in both cases, truth—empirical truth or formal truth such as forms the subject-matter of argument—is obscured by the ego. Then, as the child discovers that others do not think as he does, he makes efforts to adapt himself to them, he bows to the exigencies of control and verification which are implied by discussion and argument, and thus comes to replace egocentric logic by the true logic created by social life. We saw that exactly the same process took place with regard to the idea of reality.

There is therefore an egocentric logic and an egocentric ontology, of which the consequences are parallel: they both falsify the perspective of logical relations and of things, because they both start from the assumption that other people understand us and agree with us from the first, and that things revolve around us with the sole purpose of serving us and resembling us.

Now, if we examine these parallel evolutions, logical and ontological, in greater detail, we shall distinguish three main stages in each. The first is that which precedes any clear consciousness of the self, and may be arbitrarily set down as lasting till the age of 2–3, that is, till the appearance of the first " whys ", which symbolise in a way the first awareness of resistance in the external world. As far as we can conjecture, two phenomena characterise this first stage. From the point of view of logic, it is pure *autism*, or thought akin to dreams or day-dreams, thought in which truth is confused with desire. To every desire corresponds immediately an image or illusion which transforms this desire into reality, thanks to a sort of pseudo-hallucination or play. No objective observation or reasoning is possible : there is only a perpetual play which transforms perceptions and creates situations in accordance with the subject's pleasure. From the ontological view-point, what corresponds to this manner of thinking is primitive *psychological causality*, probably in a form that implies *magic* proper : the belief that any desire whatsoever can influence objects, the belief in the obedience of external things. Magic and autism are therefore two different sides of one and the same phenomenon—that confusion between the self and the world which destroys both logical truth and objective existence.

The second stage lasts from the age of 2–3 to the age of 7–8, and is characterised, from the logical point of view, by egocentricity : on the one hand, there is an absence of the desire to find logical justification for one's statements, and on the other, syncretism combines with juxtaposition to produce an excess of subjective and affective relations at the expense of genuine logical implications. To this egocentricity corresponds, in the ontological domain, *pre-causality*, in the widest sense, meaning all the forms of causality based on a confusion between psychological activity and physical mechanism. For pre-causality is to physical causality what syncretism is to logical implication. Pre-causality confuses motive and cause, just as, in the sphere of logic, syncretism confuses subjective justification with verification.

Now among the various forms of pre-causality existing in this second period, two, of which one probably precedes the other, are particularly important : these are participation and dynamism. And each of these is dependent in its own way upon egocentric logic : participation is the ontological equivalent of transduction, and dynamism is closely connected with the predominance of conceptualism over the logic of relations, which predominance comes, as we saw, from the habits created by transduction.

With regard to transduction and participation, this is what we believe to be the truth : transduction passes from one singular or particular case to another, without bringing in any general laws or taking account of the reciprocity of relations. Thus to reason transductively about the formation of shadows is to dispense with laws

altogether. To do so deductively, *i.e.* by means of
generalisation or an appeal to already established laws,
would mean saying : " This copy-book makes a shadow
just like trees, houses, etc., etc. Now, what trees, houses,
etc., have in common is that they block out the daylight.
The shadow of the copy-book must therefore also come
from the fact that it shuts out the daylight." In this
way, we should bring in 1° analogy between individual
cases, and 2° a law stating what all these individual cases
had in common. The child, on the contrary, reasoning
transductively, brings in no general law. He begins,
indeed, as we do, by feeling the analogy of the shadow
cast by the book with the shadows of trees, houses, etc.
But this analogy does not lead him to abstract any
relation : it simply leads him to identify the particular
cases with one another. So that we have here, not
analogy proper, but syncretism. The child argues as
follows : " This copy-book makes a shadow ; trees,
houses, etc., make shadows. The copy-book's shadow
[therefore] comes from the trees and the houses." Thus,
from the point of view of the cause or of the structure of
the object, there is participation.

Another example. Roy (see *C.W.*, Chap. VIII, § 1)
tells us : " The moon gets bigger because we are growing
bigger." For us, such a sentence would have the following
meaning : 1° The moon is analogous to us and to all
living beings ; 2° all living beings grow bigger ; 3° the
moon therefore also grows bigger in virtue of the same
law. But for Roy the sentence means that we actually
make the moon grow bigger : Thus in this sense the moon
participates with us. Why ? Because, here again, the
analogy does not lead to the abstraction of relations
common to all the terms, relations which would constitute
a law. The analogy is felt as a cause, and is felt so to
the extent that the reasoning proceeds simply from
particular to particular.

Similar reflections can be made in connection with
dynamism. One of the outstanding features of trans-

duction is its conceptualism. Transduction is ignorant of the logic of relations, and therefore operates by means of concepts which have the appearance of being very general, such as " alive ", " strong ", etc., but are, in point of fact, merely syncretistic schemas resulting from the fusion of singular terms. Now from this to substantialism there is only a step. In *L'expérience humaine et la causalité physique* there is a remarkable chapter where M. Brunschvicg brings out the affinity existing between Aristotelian substantialism and the pseudo-ideal of traditional deduction. Something of the same kind happens on an appropriate scale, in the mind of the child. Just as with Aristotle the logic of subject and predicate leads to the substantialism of substance and attribute and to the dynamism of form and matter, so with the child conceptualism leads him to " reify " everything, and consequently to see active and living substances in all around him.

But as soon as logical thought breaks away from transduction and becomes deductive, the idea of reality also breaks away from all these forms of primitive realism. Thus during the third great stage of child development, a new parallelism grows up between logic and the real categories.

Having established the fact of this parallelism, the question remains as to the mechanism of the various factors involved. Is it the real content of thought that fashions the logical form, or is the converse the truth ? Put in this vague manner, it is obvious that the problem has no meaning. But if we are careful to distinguish logical form from what may be called psychological form (*i.e.* the factors of assimilation in the sense in which we defined the word), the problem may perhaps admit of a positive solution. For the moment, we must abstain from anticipating the answer. To establish its main features will be the task of a more searching study of the nature of assimilation.

INDEX OF NAMES

INDEX OF SUBJECTS